THE JEWISH FAMILY FUN BOOK

THE JEWISH FAMILY FUN BOOK

Holiday Projects, Everyday Activities, and Travel Ideas with Jewish Themes

by Danielle Dardashti and Roni Sarig

Illustrations by Avi Katz

JEWISH LIGHTS Publishing
Woodstock, Vermont

The Jewish Family Fun Book:
Holiday Projects, Everyday Activities, and Travel Ideas with Jewish Themes

© 2002 by Danielle Dardashti and Roni Sarig
Illustrations © 2002 by Jewish Lights Publishing

Library of Congress Cataloging-in-Publication Data

Dardashti, Danielle.
    The Jewish family fun book : holiday projects, home activities, and
  travel ideas with Jewish themes / Danielle Dardashti & Roni Sarig.
        p.   cm.
  Includes bibliographical references.
  ISBN 1-58023-171-3 (pbk.)
    1. Amusements. 2. Family recreation. 3. Fasts and feasts—Judaism.
    4. Travel—Religious aspects—Judaism. I. Sarig, Roni. II. Title.
GV1203.D27 2002
793'.01'91—dc21

                                      99-044914

10 9 8 7 6 5 4 3 2 1

Manufactured in the United States of America

Published by Jewish Lights Publishing
A Division of LongHill Partners, Inc.
Sunset Farm Offices, Route 4, P.O. Box 237
Woodstock, VT 05091
Tel: (802) 457-4000   Fax: (802) 457-4004
www.jewishlights.com

A book for Uri

CONTENTS

Holiday Fun

Fun at Home

Fun on the Road

ACKNOWLEDGMENTS

This book would not exist if it weren't for our families who raised us on "Jewish family fun." To our parents, grandparents, siblings, and extended family: We love all of you deeply and thank you for all that you've given us throughout our lives.

Many of our family members were directly involved with various aspects of this project: Danielle's father, Hazzan Farid Dardashti, whose patient guidance, vast knowledge, interesting ideas—even his photography skills and recipes—added so much to this book. A big *todah rabah* also goes out to Sheila Dardashti, Aliza and Michael Friedman, Danny Sarig, Galeet Dardashti, Michelle Dardashti, Hazzan Hamid Dardashti, Yadid Dardashti, and Schelly Dardashti, who all made specific contributions to the book.

To the outstanding team at Jewish Lights—it has been a pleasure! Stuart Matlins, Amanda Dupuis, Jon Sweeney, David Stein, the brilliant Emily Wichland, and our amazing editor, Bryna Fischer.

We'd like to thank our agents, Sheree Bykofsky and Janet Rosen; our attorney, Matthew Lifflander; and his assistant, Helen. Also, we would like to express special gratitude to Ted Robinson, Joel Silverman, and Eryn March for their help and creativity.

There have been countless other individuals who have played a part in the research and development of this book. We thank each and every one of them for the part they played in helping this project come together. Here are just some of them: Rabbi Avi Friedman; Rabbi Andy Vogel; Rabbi E. Noach Shapiro; librarians Hazel Carp, Diane Braun, and Penny Eisenstein from Greenfield Hebrew Academy in Atlanta; Randee Friedman from Sounds Write Productions in San Diego; dance instructor Steven Weintraub in Atlanta; Janice Alper, Adelle Salmenson, and Rebecca Gordon from Jewish Educational Services in Atlanta; Dawne Bear at the Jewish Federation in San Francisco; Vicki Compter at UJA in New York; Rebecca Hoelting for her Atlanta contacts; Simon Amiel with Hillel in D.C.; Rachelle Bradt at the Yeshiva University Museum in New York; Israeli dance expert Judy Brown in Jerusalem; Rachel Glazer and Elaine Gitlin from Beth Tfiloh day school in Baltimore; Liz Wolf in Raleigh; Lauren Roman at craigNco in California; Harold Messinger in Austin; Ruth Goodman Burger from the Israeli Dance Institute in New York; Cantor Sharon Walloch in Baltimore; Vivian Ellison and Fran Cook from the Home Depot greenhouse in Atlanta; David Firooz from JewishStore.Com; Shlomo Lehavi at Hataklit in Los Angeles; The Judaica Corner in Atlanta; Westside Judaica in New York; Haim Scheininger at Sisu; Judye Groner and Madeline Wikler at Kar-Ben Copies; Susan Schwartz at Davka; Jeff Astor, Debbie, and Emanuel at T.E.S.; Joe Buchwald Gelles with JeMM; Debbie at Behrman House; Esther Netter and Sherri Kadovitz at the Zimmer Children's Museum in Los Angeles; Suzanne Hurwitz, Michelle Chepenik, Barbara Kreissman, Harry Stern, Kim Goodfriend, and Deborah Goldstein from the MJCC in Atlanta; Mark Greenberg at the Museum of the Southern Jewish Experience; Shari Rosenstein-Werb and Lynn Williams at the Holocaust Museum in D.C.; Cantor Tali Katz at the Jewish Museum of Maryland; Cantor Bob Fisher in Las Vegas; Lorin Sklamberg from Living Traditions; Shmuel Batzri from Dance Washington; Heather

Johnson at the Jewish Museum San Francisco; Amy Berkowitz at Camp Tawonga; Ellen Barocas at NJY Camps; Ruth Shapira at Ramah in the Poconos; Laurie Kovens from the National Havurah Committee; Ellie Sandler at Spertus in Chicago; Aaron Katler with Endangered Spirit; Irene Bennett with OSRUI; Miriam Rinn and Jason Black with the JCC Association of North America; Matt Schuman from Maccabi USA; Michelle Spivak with the Jewish War Veterans of USA; and Bill Maurer from the Gomez Mill House.

INTRODUCTION

The idea behind *The Jewish Family Fun Book* is simple: You can find something fun in everything that's Jewish, and something Jewish in everything that's fun! It's all in your attitude. Even everyday things such as playing games, singing songs, or watering plants are Jewish activities if they're approached from a Jewish perspective. The goal of this book is to guide you toward a variety of terrific activities for kids and adults and to inspire your family to come up with your own ideas for Jewish fun.

Regardless of our level of observance, we all hope to connect our children with their Jewish heritage in a way that's both engaging and meaningful to them and that will strengthen our bond as a Jewish family. And while synagogue and Hebrew school are important, those elements alone do not complete the picture of Jewish life.

More than any outside influence (school, friends, media) as we grow up, our level of Jewish identity is determined by what we see going on inside our house. For example, having a Passover seder can either be a real drag or a dynamic, positive experience, depending on families' attitudes. And the way it's conveyed will determine the way children view it for the rest of their lives.

We're not saying parents should fake it for their kids' sake. We're saying lighten up and have a little fun, because it's just so easy to do. Families that understand this will not feel a need to seek out Jewish culture and observe customs only "because we have to" but will also find it natural and desirable to have a strong Jewish element in their lives.

As much as possible, we attempted to let the activities in this book speak for themselves; that is, we've provided a wide variety of accessible projects and materials with just enough background information to explain the relevance of each activity. In other words, less talk, more action. This way, families are able to use these activities or adapt them any way they see fit.

With this in mind, it's important to note (however obvious) that this is not the only source you'll ever need as a practicing Jew. Plenty of other important Jewish practices are not necessarily fun yet nevertheless valuable; and there is a lot more to learn about each subject we touch on. *The Jewish Family Fun Book* is a supplement to enhance your observance.

The book is divided into three sections:

- ▶ "Holiday Fun" includes crafts, recipes, activities, and unusual customs related to each holiday.
- ▶ "Fun at Home" has outdoor activities, games, and dances that are good for any time as well as ideas for "mitzvah" work and volunteerism; and extensive information on the best music, books, videos, computer software, and websites for Jewish families.
- ▶ "Fun on the Road" points you to Jewish places around the country that are fun for the whole family, such as kid-friendly Jewish museums, historical sites, and kosher restaurants as well as Jewish family camps.

You've read this far, so you're on the right track. But, as we said, this book is not just about *reading*—it's about *doing!* So roll up your sleeves, put on your dancin' shoes, and get out your thinking caps. We hope you have as much fun using this book as we've had writing it.

Holiday Fun

Shabbat

Shabbat is the ultimate Jewish family fun day. And the best part is—it comes every week! Shabbat is a break from the hassles and stresses of the rest of the week, so take the day to relax with the family. You'll be rejuvenated and more productive the other six days of the week. Wherever you find yourself—at home or elsewhere—for the next twenty-five hours from Friday evening to Saturday evening, try to do something special to set this day apart and make it a quality time for everyone.

One great idea for Friday night dinner is to go around the table and have everyone share something nice that happened to them that week or something nice they did for someone else.

Shabbat is not about things; rather, it's about time. Take time to talk to your kids…sing songs…take a walk…play games…give each other backrubs. Or make up your own family traditions for this day, doing whatever you enjoy. But above all, be sure you're relaxing together!

Hospitality: Mi Casa es "Jew" Casa

Hospitality is an old and important Jewish tradition. According to rabbinic teachings, it goes all the way back to Abraham and Sarah. He sat at the open flap of his tent waiting to welcome guests inside. She stood ready to fix a hot meal at a moment's notice. And neither of them would sit down to eat until they had tended to all of their guests.

This important Jewish principle applies all the time, not just on Shabbat and holidays. But since Shabbat comes every week and we're in less of a hurry, it gives us a regular opportunity to invite relatives, friends, neighbors, acquaintances, co-workers, and newcomers over to visit. Try to think especially of people who may not have anyone with whom to share Shabbat. And get the kids involved in determining whom to invite over and what to serve. They'll often come up with some great ideas.

By having guests, we share our traditions and open ourselves up to learn the customs of others. It makes Shabbat all the more special to have new faces, new voices, and new opinions at the dinner table. We benefit from it ourselves, and we're also bringing happiness to someone else. Everyone's a winner in the deal.

Can-Do Candlesticks

On Friday night, as Shabbat begins, traditionally a prayer is said as two candles are lit (see Appendix of Prayers, p. 235). The idea is to have more light than usual—one flame for weeknights, two flames for Shabbat. However, some families light an extra candle for each child in the family. So it's up to you how many candlesticks you need. Here's an easy way to make them out of clay.

WHAT YOU NEED:

Materials

▶ self-hardening clay
▶ Shabbat candle (for sizing)
▶ beads (optional)
▶ acrylic paint

Equipment

▶ forks (or other pointy utensils that aren't dangerous)
▶ paintbrushes (suitable for coating and for decorating)

HOW IT'S DONE:

1. Roll the clay into two balls the size of two small oranges—one for each candle- stick.
2. Press each ball down into the news- paper to flatten the bottom while keeping the top part rounded.
3. Use your thumb to press a hole in the top center of each clay ball, about one inch deep. Put a Shabbat candle into the holes to make sure they are the right size. Remove candle before decorating.
4. Carve designs in the clay using the forks or other utensils. Write words like "Shabbat Shalom" in English or Hebrew (see Appendix of Stencils, p. 246), or your family's names, or any type of designs you'd like.
5. If you choose to use beads, push them into the clay for extra dec- oration.
6. Allow the clay to harden overnight.
7. Paint the clay candlesticks. You may want to paint them one solid lighter color first, allow that to dry, then paint designs with darker colors on top of the first coat.

"Kid-ish" Kiddush Cup

It's nice for everyone at the table to have his or her own Kiddush cup for the Shabbat blessing over the wine or grape juice (see Appendix of Prayers, p. 236). So go ahead and make a whole bunch of these. Kids can make these "stained glass" Kiddush cups all by themselves!

WHAT YOU NEED:

Materials

▶ white glue
▶ water
▶ clear plastic cups (plastic gob- lets are best)

▶ colored tissue paper, cut in dif- ferent small shapes
▶ shellac

Equipment

▶ old or disposable bowl
▶ paintbrushes (for spreading glue and for shellac)

HOW IT'S DONE:

1. Using a paintbrush, mix together equal parts glue and water in the bowl.
2. Paint the glue/water mixture on the entire outside of the cup.
3. With your fingers, stick the pieces of tissue paper onto the cup, overlapping them and smoothing them down until you cover the entire cup. (The glue will soften the tissue paper.)
4. Brush the glue onto the entire cup again, over the layer of tissue paper.
5. Allow the cup to dry overnight. It will dry clear, and the tissue paper will let the light shine through the cup like stained glass.
6. Put a coat of shellac over the whole cup to seal your creation. (This should be done by an adult.)
7. After it dries, you can drink wine or grape juice out of it. Then rinse it out by hand; don't put it in a dishwasher.

Danielle's Dough-licious Shabbat Challah

The braided egg bread known as "challah" is something special. Yes, you can eat challah anytime, and you can eat any kind of bread on Shabbat. But come on, what would Shabbat be without challah? And if it's homemade—even better!

Don't forget to cover the challah when it's on the dinner table. It's as if we are protecting the challah's feelings, since the blessing over the bread comes last, after the prayers for the candles, wine, and washing of the hands (see Appendix of Prayers, p. 237).

WHAT YOU NEED:

Ingredients

▶ I egg at room temperature
▶ ¾ cup warm water
▶ 2 tbsp oil
▶ I tsp lemon juice
▶ 2 cups bread flour
▶ I tsp salt
▶ 2½ tbsp sugar
▶ I tbsp gluten (found in most health food stores)
▶ I tsp active dry yeast
▶ ¼ cup raisins (optional)
▶ wash: I egg yolk, beaten, and I tbsp water
▶ sesame or poppy seeds for topping (optional)

Utensils

▶ bread machine or large bowl
▶ measuring cup
▶ measuring spoons
▶ bread board or smooth surface

HOW IT'S DONE USING A BREAD MACHINE:

1. In the order listed, place the first nine ingredients in the machine's bread pan. Make sure the yeast does not touch the water. (Let the flour serve as a buffer between them.)
2. Set the machine on the dough cycle and press START.
3. After the cycle ends (which usually takes about 90 minutes), remove the dough from bread pan and place it on a lightly floured surface.
4. With lightly floured hands, punch down the dough and then divide it into three equal parts.
5. Roll the three parts into ropes of equal length, and lay them parallel to each other.
6. Pinch the top ends together to join them. Braid the ropes. Then pinch the bottom ends together.
7. Place the braided dough on the shallow baking pan, cover it with a damp paper towel, and let it rise.
8. After the dough has risen for a half hour, preheat oven to 375°F.

9. About 15 minutes later, when the dough has doubled in size, combine "wash" ingredients and brush onto braid. If desired, sprinkle it with poppy or sesame seeds.

10. Place loaf in oven and bake for about 30 minutes or until golden brown.

HOW IT'S DONE USING HAND MIXING:

1. Mix all the ingredients in a large bowl (except for toppings and "wash" ingredients). With lightly floured hands, knead the dough until it is completely blended.

2. Cover the bowl with a towel and set in a warm place for one hour to allow the dough to rise.

3. Knead a little bit more, and divide the dough into three equal parts.

4. Follow steps 5–10 above.

The "Super-Appealing, Spill-Concealing" Tablecloth

Creating your own tablecloth is not only a fun craft but your family can also use your creations for years to come. If you use fabric paint or permanent markers on the cloth you'll be able to throw it into the washing machine and it should come out just fine.

(If you want to do a smaller version of this project it makes a great challah cover. Since they won't have to be washed as often, feel free to get fancy and sew on all sorts of beads and gold trim. *Special tip:* Colorful tablecloths and challah covers are good for hiding wine and grape juice spills. They also make nice gifts for grandparents.)

WHAT YOU NEED:

▶ white sheet (or handkerchief, for a challah cover)
▶ fabric markers or fabric paint

HOW IT'S DONE:

1. With the fabric paint or markers, draw a simple design around the borders of the cloth. It can be Jewish stars, flowers, or anything you'd like to draw.
2. In the middle of the cloth, write "Shabbat Shalom" in English or Hebrew (see Appendix of Stencils, p. 246), and draw Shabbat-related symbols: candles, a Kiddush cup, challah, and Jewish stars. You can also use stencils if you want the designs to be just right.
3. Allow the paint or ink from the markers to completely dry before using.

Out with a Bang! Havdalah Fun

On Saturday evenings, the Havdalah ceremony marks the end of Shabbat and the beginning of the regular week. We wish one another a good week ahead and reflect on the one gone by. During this beautiful ceremony, we use a braided candle, wine, and great-smelling spices (called *besamim* in Hebrew) like cinnamon and cloves. There are prayers for each one of these items. We do not include them here, but you can find them in any standard prayer book; or you could ask a rabbi or cantor to help you learn more about the *Havdalah* prayers.

Making Your Own *Besamim* Box

The spice box, or *besamim* box, can be made out of any kind of fairly airtight container. The lid should lift or open to allow everyone to smell what's inside.

A fun and simple way to make a *besamim* box is to use a large sliding match box (or you can use a small match box for a teeny-tiny *besamim* holder). Once you've found the perfect box, all you need to do is decorate it.

One idea for decorating your *besamim* box is to paste on bits of colored construction paper and then cover it with clear contact paper (or just clear tape) to laminate it. Or you can paint your matchbox, or cover it with cloth or just about anything else you choose. However you do it, make sure to cover up the striker part of the box so it doesn't pose a threat.

When you're done decorating it, one final piece will make it a little easier to slide the box open and closed: Glue a bead onto the end of the inner, sliding box to create a knob on the little drawer. Then you can put your spices inside and slide out the drawer for *Havdalah*—or whenever you want—to take a whiff.

SOME EASY-TO-GROW HERBS FOR YOUR *BESAMIM* BOX

Both mint and rosemary have a fragrant, strong smell. English lavender also smells great, and it has pretty little purple flowers. They are easy to grow, either inside or outside. (But be sure you're dealing with *English* lavender. Other kinds are more fussy.)

The great thing about all three plants is that once they have been planted, they'll stay around a while. Depending upon your local climate, you may not see them during the winter if you plant them outside. Yet rest assured they're still there. Because they're perennials they will come back once the weather warms up.

You can buy the plants at a garden center (for a dollar or two) and plant them either in your garden or in a pot. Make sure they get plenty of light and stay moist, and they will soon take root and flourish.

Rosh Hashanah & Yom Kippur

Happy New Year! Rosh Hashanah, which usually falls in September, marks the beginning of the Jewish year. It's a time of joy and celebration—of blowing the shofar to alert everyone to this important holiday—and of eating sweets like apples and honey in hopes of a sweet year. It's also a great chance to spend quality time with your family.

The ten-day period between Rosh Hashanah and Yom Kippur (the Day of Atonement) is the climax of a month-long introspective period, when we think about changes we'd like to make for the year to come. The idea is that by the end of Yom Kippur, we should feel completely rejuvenated and ready to embrace the possibilities of a new year. That takes some work, though: We must apologize to those we've wronged, admit to ourselves the mistakes we've made, and decide to make some necessary changes—effective immediately. Unlike the secular new year—when the tradition is to party hard and worry about new year's resolutions the next day—Jewish tradition recognizes that change doesn't come so easily and therefore needs to be the focal point of the celebration.

Rosh Hashanah is a great time for your family to reflect together and make new year's resolutions. Talk about things you've each done wrong and decide to whom you each owe apologies. Between Rosh Hashanah and Yom Kippur, make those apologies. Then on Yom Kippur, talk again with your family about how you will all plan to avoid making the same mistakes in the new year. As the holiday liturgy puts it: "On Rosh Hashanah it is written, and on Yom Kippur it is sealed...."

While Rosh Hashanah and Yom Kippur observance is clearly a time for reflection and discussion, let's not become so obsessed with the importance of the holidays that we lose sight of the joy involved in welcoming the new year. If we do, we miss the point entirely—to brighten our own lives and the lives of the people around us.

Tooting Your Own Shofar

The shofar is blown at synagogue each morning for the entire month before Rosh Hashanah. Kids absolutely love to hear the sound of the shofar, so it's a great time to be there. If you're not at synagogue during those days, however, it's also nice to have a shofar of your own to blow at home. Even more than hearing it, kids are thrilled to get the chance to blow it themselves.

Unless you know how to play the trumpet, getting a shofar to make noise is not so easy to do. So children and parents tend to be delightfully surprised when they actually hear a sound come out. It's then that the shofar best fulfills its role as a "Jewish alarm clock": jolting us, waking us up, and reminding us to think about the past year and how we can make the next one better for everyone.

In biblical times, the shofar—made then, as now, from a ram's horn—was used to announce important arrivals or warn of enemies approaching. At over four thousand years old and counting, it's one of the oldest and most enduring musical instruments.

In case you can't get a real shofar—or it's too difficult for your kids to blow—here's a great toy substitute you can make with your kids that'll get everyone in the house to "wake up and smell the new year!"

WHAT YOU NEED:

Materials

▶ plastic party horn
(mouthpiece only)
▶ paper plate
▶ crayons or markers
▶ glitter glue (optional)

Equipment

▶ scissors
▶ clear plastic tape

HOW IT'S DONE:

1. Fold a paper plate in half.
2. Cut out the shape of a shofar as shown. (You'll have two shofar-shaped pieces.)
3. Color and decorate the two shofar pieces with crayons and markers. You can write *"Shanah Tovah"* (good year) in English or Hebrew with crayons, markers, or glitter glue (see Appendix of Stencils, p. 247). Allow the shofar pieces to dry if necessary.
4. Tape the top and bottom edges of the two pieces together to create a horn-shaped paper shofar.
5. Insert the plastic party horn into the small opening of the shofar, so that the mouthpiece is sticking out slightly, and tape it in place.
6. Toot your horn!

Have someone call out the name of the four different sounds made with the shofar before you make that sound:

▶ *Tekiah*—one long blast
▶ *Teruah*—three medium blasts
▶ *Shevarim*—nine short (staccato) blasts
▶ *Tekiah Gedolah*—a final very long blast (as long as you can hold your breath!)

Tashlich: Tossing Your Cookies for the New Year

Tashlich (which means "you shall cast [away]" in Hebrew) is a brief ceremony that's usually done on the afternoon of the first day of Rosh

Hashanah. The custom involves standing beside a body of water (for example, the local lake or stream) and throwing whatever bread crumbs we have in our pockets into the water. (Given that most of us don't already have pockets filled with bread crumbs, we bring bread or cookie crumbs with us.) The idea is symbolic: to purge ourselves of our sins, clean ourselves out, and make a fresh start. *Tashlich* is a physical way for us all to convey what we're trying to accomplish spiritually at this time of year. It's meaningful not only for adults but also for kids (especially if they can use their "sins" to feed the ducks).

Synagogues will sometimes plan a group trip to a nearby body of water to do *Tashlich,* which includes a few Bible quotations, readings, and songs. However, the custom is also valuable if you do it alone with your family and without liturgy. And if you don't live near a body of water, you can simply stand beside your swimming pool or at the kitchen sink. Before you throw your crumbs into the water, visualize which specific acts they represent. Picture yourself throwing that act into the water so you won't do it again.

Inside-Out Candied Apple

A very common Rosh Hashanah tradition is to eat apples dipped in honey in order to get a sweet start to the new year. (For a new year's blessing, see Appendix of Prayers, p. 240)
Here's a fun way to make a dipping bowl for the honey by using an apple:

WHAT YOU NEED

Ingredients
▶ apples
▶ lemon juice
▶ honey (or caramel!)

Utensils
▶ paring knife
▶ pretty plate

HOW IT'S DONE

1. After washing an apple, core it like a Halloween pumpkin by cutting from the top and hollowing out the insides. (An adult should be

the one to do this.) Do not cut or pierce the sides or bottom of the apple. (You're turning it into a cup to hold the honey.)

2. Rinse the inside of the apple with lemon juice to help prevent it from turning brown.

3. Fill the center of the apple with honey.

4. Place the apple cup in the center of the plate. Slice up another apple or two, and lay the pieces around the apple cup on the plate.

5. Pass the plate around—and enjoy.

Old Country Nut 'n' Honey Treats

Another traditional honey-related Rosh Hashanah treat is *taiglach*, honey candies that originated in Eastern Europe. The name is Yiddish for "many pieces of dough." Here's how to make them.

WHAT YOU NEED:

Ingredients

▶ 2 eggs (lightly beaten)
▶ 2 tbsp vegetable oil, plus enough to grease the pan
▶ 1½ cups flour
▶ ½ tsp salt
▶ ¾ tsp baking powder
▶ 1 cup honey
▶ ½ cup sugar
▶ ½ tsp ground ginger
▶ 1 cup nuts (coarsely chopped)

Utensils

▶ shallow baking pan
▶ mixing bowls
▶ whisk or fork
▶ stirring spoons
▶ board (or other smooth surface for rolling dough)
▶ saucepan
▶ large platter
▶ waxed paper
▶ measuring cup

HOW IT'S DONE:

1. Pre-heat oven to 375°F. Grease the pan well; set it aside.

2. Mix the eggs and oil in a bowl. In a separate bowl, sift together the flour, salt, and baking powder. Combine the two mixtures, and stir to make dough that is soft but not sticky. Add more flour if necessary.

3. Lightly sprinkle a board with flour. Place the dough on it. With lightly

floured hands, twist the dough into a rope about ½ inch thick. Dip a knife in flour, and cut the rope of dough into small pieces about ½ inch long.

4. Place the pieces into the baking pan, and bake for about 10 minutes or until slightly browned. Shake the pan a few times to keep the pieces separated and evenly browned.

5. To prepare the honey syrup, put the honey, sugar, and ginger in a saucepan. Stir until the sugar is completely melted. Cook it over a low flame for 5 minutes, stirring constantly so the honey doesn't burn.

6. Add the baked pieces of dough and the nuts into the pan. Stir gently over a low heat until the mixture is a deep golden brown.

7. Using cold water, wet a large platter or board. Pour the coated pieces onto it. When the candy is cool, wrap the pieces individually in waxed paper. (Makes about 40 pieces of candy.)

Sephardic and Persian Hors d'Oeuvres

Sephardic and Persian Jews have a great Rosh Hashanah tradition involving a bunch of different foods, each symbolizing a certain good omen for the New Year. This Rosh Hashanah seder is a terrific activity the whole family can take part in, at the dinner table before the meal. A special Hebrew prayer goes along with each item. Unlike other prayers for food, during this seder we're not thanking God for the food specifically; we're using these symbolic foods to ask God for a good year ahead. Below we've included passages from the prayers that explain the connections made. (For a complete list of these prayers, see p. 240–244). Say the prayer for each item, or simply discuss the item's significance. Then pass around the foods, and enjoy.

1. Apples dipped in honey: "May it be a sweet year."
2. Steamed leeks: "May all evil in the world be cut off." (Leeks grow like grass, and they're cut when harvested.)
3. Steamed or boiled beets: "May all evil in the world be wiped out." (The beet, which grows in the ground, is uprooted and must be cleaned off before we eat it.)

4. Dates: "I am God's servant." (Dates are among the biblical fruits from the Land of Israel; they represent the sweetness of the relationship between God and the Jewish people.)

5. Zucchini or squash: "Tear up the evil decree against us." (This prayer talks about starting over and planting the seeds of goodness for a new year. Zucchini and squash, which are full of seeds, must be replanted every year.)

6. Beans: "May our merits and our inspirations multiply" (like the number of beans produced from just one plant).

7. Pomegranate: "May we be as full of *mitzvot* (good deeds) as the pomegranate is full of seeds."

8. Fish: "May our merits multiply like fish in the sea."

9. Something from the head of an animal: "May we be in the forefront like the head, and not in the background like the tail." (This prayer is reminding us that we should be leaders and not followers.) Sephardim have used a fish head, perhaps because they lived near the water. But the prayer really calls for something from a ram's head "in remembrance of the ram that replaced Isaac.") Tongue may be the easiest for you to use.

A Persian twist: Iranian Jews do this same ceremony with slight modifications:

2. The leeks are eaten raw for this ceremony. Persians hold a bunch of the grass-like leek strands with both hands (one hand at each end) and say the prayer. Then they take a bite out of the middle and throw the remaining ends over their shoulders; what's in the left hand goes over the right shoulder, and what's in the right hand goes over the left shoulder. This furthers the theme of "May all evil in the world be cut off" with a symbolic gesture of "divide and conquer."

8b. Lung: The Persians substitute lung for the fish. The prayer says, "May our sins be light like the lung." (The meat from lung is very light meat.) You can special order it from some kosher butchers.

9. While the Sephardim have used a fish head, Persians usually use the tongue of a lamb or cow. (Fish wasn't as readily available in

Persia as it was in Spain. This might be the reason for both these changes in steps 8 and 9.)

Sending the Very Best New Year's Cards

Everyone loves getting cards for Rosh Hashanah, and homemade cards are the best kind. Wish a good new year (*Shanah Tovah,* in Hebrew) to your grandparents, aunts and uncles, cousins, teachers, and friends—and you'll make them all very happy. (To go along with your cards, make your own envelopes too. See the instructions in the section on "Arts & Crafts," p. 112)

WHAT YOU NEED:

Materials

▶ colored construction paper

▶ white paper

▶ glue

▶ sponges or potatoes (for paint stamps)

▶ paper towels, stamp pad, ink, or tempera paint (for stamps)

▶ reprints of a nice family photo

▶ collage items: pictures from other cards or magazines

Equipment

▶ markers and crayons

▶ scissors and/or knife (for parents' use only)

HOW IT'S DONE:

1. Fold a piece of colored construction paper in half.
2. Your piece of white paper should be slightly smaller than your construction paper. Fold it in half as well. (It will eventually be glued to the inside of the folded construction paper.)
3. Write your message on the white paper. Be sure to include a *Shanah Tovah* wish in either English or Hebrew (see Appendix of Stencils, p. 247), as well as your name and some decorations if you'd like.

4. Decorate the paper with drawings, using markers or crayons. In addition to (or instead of) drawings, you can make your own paint-stamp to use for decoration: Parents can either cut shapes (such as a Jewish star) out of a sponge or carve shapes from one end of a halved potato—using the rest of the potato as a handle. If you don't have an ink pad, then make your own by soaking some paper towels in paint. Press your stamp onto the pad and then onto the white paper.

5. After the decorations dry, glue the white paper with your message onto the inside of your card.

6. On the outside of the card, you can glue a current picture of your family or make a collage using pieces of other *Shanah Tovah* cards or pictures from magazines.

History in the Making: Designing Your Own Jewish Calendar

Since Rosh Hashanah is the start of the new year, it's also the time to start a new calendar. These do-it-yourself calendars also make great gifts.

WHAT YOU NEED:

Materials
▶ white paper (which you'll photocopy at least 12 times)
▶ colored construction paper (at least 12 sheets)
▶ glue
▶ yarn

Equipment
▶ ruler
▶ pencil
▶ hole puncher
▶ markers or paint
▶ calendar that includes Jewish holidays to use as a model

HOW IT'S DONE:

1. Make a grid for your calendar pages. To do this, take a blank piece of paper and, with a pencil, draw six equally spaced vertical lines down the page and four equally spaced horizontal lines across the page. You'll end up with a grid of 7 boxes across and 5 down, for a total of 35 boxes on the page.

2. Photocopy this sheet 12 times (plus a few extra in case you make mistakes while filling them in).

3. Glue each grid onto a larger sheet of colored construction paper, leaving enough room at the top for you to write the days of the week—above that, the name of the month—in both English and Hebrew. (Remember that Jewish months do not begin and end on the same days as secular months, so it's likely you will have parts of two Hebrew months within one secular month.)

4. Write the names of the days at the top of each of the seven columns going down, from Sunday *(Yom Rishon)* to Saturday (Shabbat).

5. Refer to a store-bought calendar for the same year to see on which day the secular and Jewish month begins, how many days are in the month, and on which days Jewish and secular holidays fall. (Start your calendar with whichever secular month Rosh Hashanah falls in this year—usually September.) Fill out the grid by writing the date in each box where a date should go. (Remember that each month probably starts on a different day of the week than the month before it.) Wherever a holiday occurs, draw a picture that corresponds to that holiday. Also mark any birthdays and anniversaries of family members and close friends that occur in that month.

6. Repeat the process in steps four and five with each of the remaining months.

7. Punch 5 holes along the top of the 12 sheets of paper, making sure the holes line up when the pages are stacked. Thread yarn through the holes to fasten the sheets together. Also, punch a hole at the bottom of the calendar (lining up on every page) so that you can hang the calendar open on the wall.

8. When the fastened calendar lies open to a particular month, the bottom page will contain the calendar while the top will be blank (it's the back of the previous month). To further decorate your calendar, you can draw pictures or paste photos on this page.

Sukkot

The holiday of Sukkot, which begins four days after Yom Kippur, is one of the most active holidays around—an excellent chance for shared family experiences. Best of all, it's the time to build a sukkah, a homemade Jewish hut where families eat and even sleep (weather permitting) for the seven days of this holiday.

The festival of Sukkot has two origins. Historically, it commemorates the Israelites' forty years of wandering in the wilderness, when they built temporary shelters to live in. Agriculturally, Sukkot celebrates the end of the harvest season and recalls the type of temporary dwellings our ancestors built out in the fields, where they'd stay while harvesting.

Once your family has worked together to construct your sukkah, spend as much valuable family time in it as is practical. This is a great way to emphasize a number of valuable lessons: First, it's not the kind of house we live in that's important but what takes place inside the home. We can take this hut and turn it into a magical place. For a week, the sukkah becomes our home.

Second, the sukkah represents the unpredictability of life. It can be blown away in an instant if a big, unexpected wind comes along. This is a perfect time to discuss the issue of homelessness with the family: what it would be like to live all year round with so little shelter (or none at all).

Sukkah-Building Basics

Sukkahs come in all shapes and sizes, but there are a few rules about how to construct them. The two main rules are these:

1. A sukkah has to have at least three walls (one of which can be an existing wall, like the side of the house).
2. The roof needs to provide mostly shade yet leave enough openings so you can see stars through it at night. Most commonly the roof is made out of *skhach,* tree branches or twigs, which suits both needs perfectly. However, it can be made out of any organic material as long as it's not something permanent, such as bricks or wood boards.

For an even simpler solution, many synagogues and Jewish gift shops sell sukkah-making kits with all the necessary materials (except tools) and directions for building the frame. They're usually pretty easy to put together.

TIPS FOR THE SUKKAH "INTERIOR DECORATOR"

Unlike the guidelines for constructing the sukkah, there aren't any rules for decorating inside; it's pretty much anything goes! But because the sukkah is exposed to the elements, fragile decorations won't keep well—particularly those that fall apart or run when they get wet. Here are a few sukkah decoration tips:

Sturdy vegetables and fruit Dried gourds, Indian corn, and pumpkins are available at this time of year and make great sukkah decorations. You can hang small ones from the roof with string and lay bigger ones in the corner. (You can also use artificial fruit. Fresh fruit isn't the greatest, since it can rot and attract bugs.)

Paper chains Take strips of construction paper and glue them into loops that are linked together to make paper chains. Similarly, you can make decorative chains by stringing together old plastic foam packing pieces (peanuts). For a fancier touch, pre-treat the pieces with gold and silver paint. You can also hang colorful strands of beads, like old necklaces (or Mardi Gras beads).

Artwork All kinds of paintings or drawings make nice sukkah decorations. You can hang ones that the kids make at school or have them create ones especially for the sukkah. Paintings of different types of fruit are especially good. Protect them from getting wet with plastic wrap or clear contact paper.

Ushpizin This term, which means "visitors," refers to the mystical custom of inviting a different aspect of God into the sukkah each night. Some contemporary Jews have extended this practice to include inviting people important to us who are no longer living yet are with us in spirit. We decorate the sukkah with pictures of our loved ones, role models, and heroes—anyone from biblical patriarchs and matriarchs, to family members who have passed away, to those people we admire like Martin Luther King, Jr., or Anne Frank. With these photos or drawings hanging in our sukkah, we invite them all to be with us as we celebrate. (You may want to bring these pictures inside overnight.)

Table decorations Every sukkah should have a table and chairs so that families and friends can eat meals inside. Specially decorated tablecloths, challah covers, and Kiddush cups add a special "homey" feel to the sukkah (see the "Shabbat" section).

Sukkah-in-a-Sukkah Centerpiece

Since eating meals is an important sukkah activity, table centerpieces offer another opportunity for decoration. (Or, if you aren't able to build a sukkah big enough to hold your family, this can be a symbolic way of "building" a sukkah to put on the dinner table inside your home.)

WHAT YOU NEED:

Materials

- shoebox (without lid)
- twigs with leaves (preferably evergreen)
- old magazines with pictures of fruit

Equipment

- tempera paints
- scissors
- paintbrushes
- glue

HOW IT'S DONE:

1. Draw a door on one side of the box, and cut it out. Or you can completely cut off one side of the box, because a sukkah only has to have three walls.
2. Paint the sides of the box with pictures of fruit, or glue on pictures of fruit that you cut out of magazines.
3. Place twigs with leaves across the open top of the box to complete the mini-sukkah centerpiece.
4. If you want to get really creative, make a mini-table to put inside your mini-sukkah (and put a mini-mini-sukkah table centerpiece on it).

All Shook Up! The *Lulav* and *Etrog*

In addition to the sukkah, another fun Sukkot custom is the shaking of the *lulav* and *etrog*. *Lulav* means "palm branch," but the *lulav* we traditionally use is actually made up of two smaller willow branches plus three small myrtle branches, all bound together. The *etrog* is a citron fruit; it has a great smell and looks like a big bumpy lemon. We hold these together and shake them firmly in a set pattern as a way of commemorating the holiday.

The *lulav* and *etrog* have symbolic significance relating to parts of the human body: The *etrog* represents the heart (being true); the *lulav* represents the spine (being straight with ourselves and others); the willow represents the lips (being careful what we say); and the myrtle represents the eyes (noticing what's important). Most synagogues have one or more *lulav* and *etrog* sets at this time of year that you can use in their communal sukkah. Or you can buy your own *lulav* and *etrog* (ask your synagogue or nearby Judaica shop at least a week before Sukkot begins).

The Real-Deal *Lulav* Shake

By shaking the *lulav* and *etrog* around us, we symbolically surround ourselves with Sukkot on all sides and bring it toward us. Hold the *lulav* in your right hand and the *etrog* in your left, with both hands touching each other. Stand facing the east as you say the special prayer (see Appendix of Prayers, p. 239), and then follow these steps:

1. Hold the assembled *lulav*-and-*etrog* directly out in front of you, then shake it (deliberately, so that it rattles) toward your body three times.
2. Hold the *lulav*-and-*etrog* to your right, and shake it toward your body three times.
3. Hold the *lulav*-and-*etrog* over your shoulder so it is behind you, and shake it back toward you three times.
4. Hold the *lulav*-and-*etrog* to your left, and shake it toward your body three times.

The Wacky 'n' Tasty *Lulav* "Shake"

After you shake the assembled *lulav*-and-*etrog*, a fun nontraditional Sukkot treat is to create a different, delicious kind of shake: an ice-cream shake. Just mix your favorite kind of ice cream with some milk in a blender. To symbolize the *lulav* and *etrog* (since we wouldn't actually want to eat these things!), green and/or yellow flavors of ice cream are best (lime, lemon, or mint flavors), or you can add food coloring to a vanilla shake. After you pour the shake into a glass, decorate it with a few small branches that you've washed clean (to represent the *lulav*) and some yellow candy-coated chocolates or lemon drops sprinkled on top (to represent the *etrog*). Add a straw and spoon, then start slurping!

Simchat Torah

Right after Sukkot is the holiday of Simchat Torah. After a whole year of reading a section of the Torah each week in synagogue, on Simchat Torah we celebrate because the cycle is finished. And now that it's done, what's next? Naturally, we start again! But not before we have a little fun first.

While the adults are the ones who read from the Torah, Simchat Torah is also a children's holiday. At synagogue, there's singing and dancing for all ages, and candy is given out. Plus, this is the only holiday when kids come up to the Torah to make a blessing (an *aliyah*), an honor usually reserved for people older than bar and bat mitzvah age.

During services for Simchat Torah, everyone parades around the synagogue and even out into the street. Adults carry Torahs while kids carry mini-Torah replicas or wave flags. Second only to Purim in its wild celebrating, Simchat Torah is a rare opportunity when having a party during services is not only acceptable, it's entirely appropriate!

Tiny Totin' Torahs

Here's a way for you and your family to make your very own mini-Torah that a kid can carry when parading and dancing on Simchat Torah.

WHAT YOU NEED:

Materials

▶ 2 empty paper towel rolls
▶ 2 or 3 sheets of white paper
▶ I strip of cloth (about the length of a shoelace)

Equipment

▶ paint (including gold or silver)
▶ clear tape
▶ markers
▶ paintbrushes

HOW IT'S DONE:

1. Paint the paper towel rolls, using at least a touch of gold or silver paint on the ends.
2. Using clear tape at the bottom and top of each piece of paper, attach two or three pieces of white paper together, end to end, to make one long sheet.
3. Glue or tape one end of the long paper sheet to each of the paper towel rolls. (If it doesn't hold well enough, you can staple it by sliding the stapler's bottom piece into the tube.)
4. Decorate the paper with words, stories, or pictures related to Simchat Torah or being Jewish.
5. When the decorations are finished, roll up the scroll.
6. Tie the strip of cloth around the scroll to hold the paper towel rolls together.

Fun Flags for the Simchah Strut

Besides mini-Torahs, kids often wave flags as they dance and parade around the synagogue on Simchat Torah. There's even a tradition of sticking an apple (or a candied apple) on the top of a (relatively thick) flagstick. Here's how to make a flag.

WHAT YOU NEED:

Materials
- ▶ poster board
- ▶ wooden dowel rod or stick

Equipment
- ▶ glue
- ▶ decorations: glitter, markers, tempera or poster paint

HOW IT'S DONE:

1. You can make your flag in the shape of a rectangle or a triangle. Cut whichever shape you choose out of the poster board.
2. Decorate the shape by drawing and coloring designs such as Torah scrolls and Jewish stars. Leave an inch or two of one side undecorated—this is where you'll glue the poster board to the stick.
3. Once the decorations dry, an adult should run a line of glue down the side of the flag. Lay the dowel flat on the glue, and leave it until it dries.
4. Start waving!

Hanukkah

Hanukkah is not a major festival in the Jewish religious calendar, but it's well known as a holiday that is a lot of fun. Plus, there are important messages to be learned in the Hanukkah story.

This eight-day holiday celebrates the miracles in the story of the military victory of the Hasmonean Jews, led by Judah Maccabee, over Syrian government forces in 164 B.C.E. It's the perfect winter holiday—a festival of light at the darkest time of year.

Because Hanukkah falls close to Christmas, during the past century the holiday has become largely associated with gift-giving in countries where most people are Christian. Gift-giving, however, isn't what this holiday is traditionally about. Since a big part of being Jewish is understanding how we are different, Hanukkah actually provides a great chance to talk with your family about that aspect of Judaism. It's important to recognize that being different is not a bad thing if we understand, enjoy, and take pride in our own holidays and customs—and respect the traditions of others as well.

Have a fun activity planned for each night of Hanukkah: Read Hanukkah-related books such as the story of the Maccabees; spend an evening creating gifts for one another (a poem, song, or craft); and play the dreidel game; design a menorah; cook up some latkes (potato pancakes) or *soofganiyot* (jelly donuts). Or have a Hanukkah party and do them all!

Miraculous Menorah Making

The menorah (or *hanukiyah,* in modern Hebrew) is the eight-cupped oil lamp or eight-branch candelabra that we light each night of Hanukkah. It actually has nine candles if you count the *shamash*, the helper candle usually set apart from the rest of the menorah and used to light all the other candles.

The story goes that after the Maccabees' victory, the Temple needed to be rededicated because it had been wrecked by the Greeks. There was only enough ritually pure olive oil left in the Temple's menorah to burn for one day, but the priest went ahead and lit its lamps anyway. The lamps miraculously burned for eight days, during which time they were able to purify more oil.

The Hanukkah menorah remembers this miracle. We light one candle the first night of Hanukkah, two the next night, and so on. Each person in the household can have her or his own menorah.

Today, menorahs come in all shapes and sizes. Here's an idea of how to create a whole variety.

WHAT YOU NEED:

Materials

▶ ceramic tile, or wood, or metal (for the base)
▶ 10 metal lug nuts; or 10 sea shells (all similarly saucer-shaped); or 10 walnut shell halves (carefully broken); or 10 bottle caps

Equipment

▶ glue
▶ inflammable decorations: paint, permanent markers, glitter glue, beads, small dreidels

HOW IT'S DONE:

1. Find something solid for the base of your menorah. This can be anything from ceramic tile to a nice piece of wood or a piece of metal, as long as it's big enough to fit all your candleholders on it. (They should be spaced far enough apart that the flames appear distinct when viewed from outside your window.)

2. Decide what you are going to use to hold each of the candles on the menorah: lug nuts, shells, bottle caps, or any other idea you come up with. You'll need 10 of whatever you choose: 1 for each of the 8 candles, plus the *shamash* needs 2, stacked on top of each other (to make it taller than the rest so that it stands out).

3. Glue the candleholders to the base in whatever pattern you choose. Traditionally, all the candles are in a straight line—it's easier to light the menorah that way—but it can also look interesting to use a squiggly or circular pattern. Usually the *shamash* is placed in the middle or at one end.

4. Decorate the menorah any way that you want: with paints, markers, glitter glue, beads, or all of the above. You can paint your name on it, glue dreidels to it, or make pictures of just about anything you'd like.

Spinning and Winning: Dreidels and Gelt

Legend has it that at one point when the Syrian king Antiochus had control of the Land of Israel, he forbade prayer and the study of Torah. Some Jews responded by sneaking out to remote caves to study and pray, and whenever they saw soldiers coming they would quickly put away their books, pull out spinning tops, and pretend they were gambling. This way, the soldiers would think the Jews had simply sneaked away to gamble, which was not a serious crime like praying.

Today, we continue to play with those spinning tops—*dreidel* in English (from the Yiddish word for "turn"), *s'vivon* in Hebrew—to remember what our ancestors had to go through to practice their religion. Plus, we play because it's fun!

Dreidel-Playing Basics: How to Be a Gelt-Shark

Dreidel is best when it's played for "high stakes"; that is, for pieces of chocolate Hanukkah gelt. Let's explain:

Gelt is the Yiddish word for money. But when people talk about Hanukkah gelt these days, often they're referring to pieces of chocolate that are wrapped in gold foil, made to look like ancient coins. The tradition of Hanukkah gelt is said to go back to the Maccabees. After they defeated the enemy and became the rulers of Israel, they minted coins so the Jews could have their own currency. Perhaps that's why in later centuries, before gift-giving was customary, kids would sometimes get real coins as part of the Hanukkah celebration.

To play dreidel, you must pay attention to the letter written on each of its four sides. The letters on the dreidel refer to the miracle of Hanukkah: The letter *nun* stands for *nes* (miracle), the letter *gimmel* stands for *gadol* (big), the letter *hay* stands for *hayah* (happened), and the letter *shin* stands for *sham* (there, meaning in the Land of Israel). (And in Israel, the fourth letter on the dreidel is the letter *pay,* which stands for *po,* which means "here"—"A great miracle happened *here.*")

However, when it comes to the dreidel game, the letters mean something else entirely. Players sit in a circle. Each person puts one or two pieces of Hanukkah gelt into the center. Then the dreidel is passed around the circle, and each player takes a turn spinning it. When the dreidel stops spinning, whichever letter is facing up determines what the player who spun it should do:

- ▶ If it stops on *nun,* then "nothing" happens; the next player goes.
- ▶ If it stops on *gimmel,* the player who spun "gets everything" in the center; and everyone has to put in their entry amount again to continue.
- ▶ If it stops on *hay,* the player who spun takes "half" of what's in the center.
- ▶ If it stops on *shin,* the player who spun has to "shell out" one piece of gelt to the center.

Hanukkah Delectables

All your typical Hanukkah foods are cooked in oil. Fried treats like latkes and donuts have become a tradition because of the miracle in the Hanukkah story, where the one-day supply of oil in the Temple lasted for eight days.

Lip-Licking Latkes

Potato pancakes, commonly called by their Yiddish name, latkes (they're called *levivot* in Hebrew), are the most popular Hanukkah food. Here's a latke recipe that'll make enough for at least six people. (But you may want to do just half a batch at a time, so that the raw mixture doesn't get discolored while you're frying the rest.)

WHAT YOU NEED:

Ingredients

▶ 6 large potatoes
▶ 2 eggs
▶ I tsp salt
▶ ¼ tsp pepper
▶ I large onion
▶ 3 tbsp flour
▶ oil
▶ topping: applesauce and/or sour cream

Utensils

▶ mixing bowl
▶ grater, knife, and cutting board (or food processor)
▶ measuring spoons
▶ slotted spatula
▶ plates
▶ paper towels

HOW IT'S DONE:

1. Mix the flour, eggs, salt, and pepper in a bowl or food processor.
2. Peel and grate the potatoes, and cut the onions, or shred them separately in the food processor.
3. Mix all ingredients except the oil and toppings (in the food processor: shred for a few seconds more) until fully mixed.

4. Pour oil into a frying pan, and heat on the stove.
5. Drop large spoonfuls of the potato mixture into the frying pan to form the pancakes. Fry the latkes on both sides until they are golden brown, adding more oil as needed.
6. Drain the latkes on paper towels to absorb the oil.
7. Serve hot with toppings.

Appetizing Applesauce

Applesauce adds a sweet and refreshing taste to steaming latkes. Here's how to make homemade applesauce.

WHAT YOU NEED:

Ingredients
▶ 2½ pounds apples
▶ ⅓ cup apple juice or cider
▶ I tbsp lemon juice
▶ ground cinnamon
▶ ground nutmeg (optional)
▶ honey or brown sugar to taste

Utensils
▶ paring knife
▶ cutting board
▶ heavy saucepan with lid
▶ measuring cup
▶ measuring spoons
▶ wooden spoon or potato masher

HOW IT'S DONE:

1. Peel, core, and quarter the apples, then place them in a heavy saucepan.
2. Add in the apple juice. Cover the pot, and bring the liquid to a boil, stirring frequently.
3. Lower the heat to simmer, and cook for another 20 minutes or until the apples are soft. Stir occasionally to be sure the apples don't stick to the bottom. You may need to add more liquid, depending on the type of apples used.
4. Add the lemon juice and ground spices.
5. Mash the apples with a wooden spoon or masher. If desired, add honey or sugar (start with a teaspoon, and add more to taste).
6. Allow the applesauce to cool, and serve it chilled.
7. Spread it on top of your latkes for a great tasting combination!

Fry 'em and Try 'em: *Soofganiyot*

Like latkes, *soofganiyot* (donuts or jelly donuts) are another greasy treat traditionally made on Hanukkah, especially in modern-day Israel. Here's a non-jelly recipe, which is a bit easier:

WHAT YOU NEED:

Ingredients
- ½ cup butter or margarine
- ¾ cup orange juice
- 6 tbsp sugar
- 2 packages dry yeast
- 4 cups flour
- 2 eggs (beaten)
- I tbsp pure extract vanilla
- 2 tsp lemon juice
- oil for frying
- sugar (powder or regular) or cinnamon for coating
- resealable clear plastic bag

Utensils
- measuring cup
- measuring spoons
- small saucepan
- wooden stirring spoon
- large bowl
- bread board or smooth surface
- bread bowl (greased)
- rolling pin
- butter knife
- frying pan
- slotted spoon

HOW IT'S DONE:

1. Heat the butter (or margarine), orange juice, lemon juice, and sugar in a small saucepan until the butter is melted. Mix well, and transfer the liquid to a large bowl, then allow it to cool for about 5 minutes.
2. Add the yeast, and mix well.
3. Add flour, eggs, and vanilla. Mix with a wooden spoon.
4. On a floured surface and with floured hands, knead the dough for about 10 minutes. Add more flour if the dough is too sticky.
5. Place the dough in a greased bowl, and allow it to rise for about 30 minutes.
6. Punch down the dough, and knead it for about 5 minutes, then cover and let it rise for another 30 minutes.
7. On a floured surface, roll the dough about one inch thick.

8. Cut off small round pieces from the roll, about the size of donut holes.
9. Heat about one inch of oil in a pan until it is hot.
10. Drop in the dough pieces and cook until they are golden, then lift the *soofganiyot* with a spoon and put them on paper towels to drain the oil.
11. Put sugar or cinnamon (or both) in the sealable plastic bag. Once the *soofganiyot* have cooled a little, add several to the bag, seal it, and gently shake until the *soofganiyot* are coated.
12. Serve them up!

Tu B'Shvat

Tu B'Shvat is the Jewish Arbor Day or Earth Day. The holiday comes on the fifteenth day of the Hebrew month of Shvat—thus the name Tu (the alphabetic equivalent of the number fifteen) B'Shvat (meaning "in Shvat"). While the holiday falls in January or February—when it's still cold in many parts of the Northern Hemisphere—at that time in Israel the rainy season is ending and the trees have begun to bud.

In the sixteenth century, the kabbalists (followers of Kabbalah, or Jewish mysticism) in the town of Sfat (in the Galilee) started a special tradition for Tu B'Shvat: a communal meal with a set order, similar in format to the Passover seder—complete with four cups of wine. But instead of celebrating freedom from slavery, the Tu B'Shvat seder celebrates the renewal of the trees. While this seder had fallen out of wide practice for many years, it has recently begun to make a comeback with the growing popularity of both Kabbalah and environmentalism.

Today, on Tu B'Shvat, many Jews direct their attention toward the produce in the Land of Israel and reflect on the way they treat nature. In preparation for Tu B'Shvat, we can review our recycling habits and look for ways to improve them. We can invite people over to celebrate with us, eat fruits associated with Israel, have a Tu B'Shvat seder, and maybe even plant a tree that will endure for many years to come.

"Fruits of Israel"

The foods that we especially try to eat on Tu B'Shvat are tree fruits traditionally associated with the Land of Israel: grapes, figs, pomegranates, olives, dates, almonds, and carob. The first five of these fruits are featured in the Book of Deuteronomy (8:8). Almonds are the first fruit trees to blossom at this time of year in Israel. And carob is a nonperishable fruit that grows wild in Israel.

The "Nature Nosh" Tu B'Shvat Seder

Because there are no set rules for the Tu B'Shvat seder, customs will vary, but all Tu B'Shvat practices involve sharing delicious natural foods and drinks with family and friends. This can come before dinner, after dinner, or instead of dinner.

To set up the seder, it's nice to decorate the table with flowers and plants, and provide each person with a clear drinking glass. In addition to the "fruits of Israel," try to serve some fruits that you have not yet eaten this season, and consider whipping up fruit smoothies or a fruit salad.

The following is an example of a simple seder. (For information about a family-friendly Tu B'Shvat Haggadah, see p. 154.) It involves drinking four cups of grape juice (or wine), each one representing a different season, and eating four types of fruit, each symbolizing a season as well as one of the four elements in nature: earth, water, air, and fire. Traditionally, Jews say a prayer of gratitude for each cup of wine and for each type of fruit consumed. For these prayers, see Appendix of Prayers, pp. 236–239.

WHAT YOU NEED:

Ingredients

▶ 2 bottles of grape juice (1 white, 1 red)

▶ 4 different types of tree fruit or nuts, arranged on serving plates:

- ◆ fruit with an outer layer that cannot be eaten (such as almond, kiwi, pomegranate)
- ◆ fruit with an inner core that cannot be eaten (such as date, peach, or plum)
- ◆ fruit that is completely edible (fig, carob, grape)
- ◆ edible seeds (such as sunflower seeds and pumpkin seeds)

Utensils

▶ clear (plastic) wine goblets for everyone

▶ plates for everyone

▶ nutcrackers (optional)

HOW IT'S DONE:

1. Fill the cups with white grape juice. This symbolizes winter. Drink approximately one quarter of the juice.

2. Eat the foods with a peel or shell that can't be eaten. The peels and shells represent the earth; we eat these nuts and hard-skinned fruits to remind us of the protection the earth provides, in the form of shelter and food.

3. For the second drink of juice, refill your cups to the top, using a small amount of red grape juice. This symbolizes spring, when white becomes pink as the new growth appears. Drink about half of the juice in the cup.

4. Eat the fruit that has a tough inner core and a soft outer part. With this fruit we remember that our "inner selves"—our hearts and minds—have to remain strong even when our "outer cores"—our bodies—are not. This fruit also symbolizes water, the second element of nature. Water seems weak but has great power.

5. For the third drink of juice, refill your cups to the top once more with red juice to make the juice even darker in color. This symbolizes summer, when we see bright-colored flowers and the sun shining bright. Again, drink about half of the juice.

6. Eat the fruit that is completely edible. This represents the third element, air, which has no barriers.

7. Refill your cups for a fourth time, again with red grape juice, to turn the color of the juice completely red. It reminds us of the rich colors found at the beginning of autumn.

8. Eat the fourth food, seeds, which represent the final element of nature: fire. This reminds us that fire can be created by a particle as small as a seed.

9. End the seder by enjoying any of the "fruits of Israel" that you have not yet eaten during the seder, as well as any other natural treats you have prepared.

10. While you are noshing (an English word taken from the Yiddish for "snack"), it's nice for each member of the group to promise to do something that is "nature positive," such as recycling more, saving water by turning off the tap while brushing your teeth, or conserving electricity by remembering to turn off the lights when you leave a room.

Hebrew Horticulture

Home Gardening

Planting is a great way to celebrate Tu B'Shvat. And kids love gardening: getting dirty, digging, planting something, and watching it grow. What could be more fun?

If, where you live, winter is warm enough to plant outside—well, you're very lucky! You can get a jump-start on spring by doing some outdoor gardening for Tu B'Shvat. But even if it's too cold during January or February for outdoor gardening, that shouldn't stop you from doing a little planting indoors. Here are some simple ideas:

▶ *Plant a window garden* Start a window flower garden with seeds or bulbs purchased at a garden center. Some of the best bulbs for an indoor pot are tulips, hyacinths, and narcissus. If you want, you can take these flowers out of their pots and plant them outside in the garden once spring comes. But they'll do well inside with plenty of water and light.

▶ *Grow baby fruit trees* Collect seeds from apples, oranges, lemons, or other fruit. Rinse them off, and let them soak in water overnight. Then, using good potting soil, plant the seeds in indoor pots. Keep the soil moist, and make sure the plants are getting plenty of light. Within six weeks you should see plants sprouting. If you want to try to get these plants to produce fruit and you live in an appropriate climate, you can transfer them outside once it gets warm out. But they'll make nice simple houseplants, too.

▶ *Make an avocado sprout* Fill a jar with water. Then take an avocado pit, and stick three toothpicks into it so that you can prop the pit at the mouth of the jar, with half of the pit dipping into the water (and the toothpicks holding the other half out of the water). In about a month, the avocado pit will crack open and a little tree will sprout out of it. Once this little tree gets going a bit, you can plant it into a pot of soil or outside. The avocado plant is very pretty and has nice big leaves.

Gardening by Phone or Keyboard

For Jews, tree planting and farming have traditionally been a big deal in the Land of Israel. The process of cultivating our ancient homeland symbolizes our deep roots there. If you'd like to plant a tree in Israel for Tu B'Shvat but you're not there to do it yourself, you can contact the Jewish National Fund at 800-542-8733, or www.jnf.org, and pay them to plant a tree for you. They'll send you a certificate with your name on it.

Turning Paper Back into a Tree

This craft makes a great table centerpiece for your Tu B'Shvat seder.

WHAT YOU NEED:

Materials

▶ paper towel tube
▶ shoebox lid

▶ 3 pieces construction paper (pick colors appropriate for tree leaves)

Equipment

► pencil
► sharp-edged scissors (for adult)
► paints (and brushes) or markers
► clear plastic tape
► scissors (for child)

HOW IT'S DONE:

1. Lay the box lid on your work surface so that its underside faces up. Stand the paper towel tube atop the middle of the box lid, and trace with a pencil the round bottom of the tube onto the lid.
2. Cut out the circle you traced, to create a hole in the box top, but don't cut any other part of the box lid. (Parents should do this step with sharp-edged scissors.)
3. Paint or color the tube and the box lid as you like. (The top of the lid will become the "ground"; its underside will not be visible.)
4. Stick the tube through the hole you cut in the lid.
5. Roll two or three pieces of colored paper together into a tubular shape (small enough to fit it later inside the paper towel tube). Tape one end of the paper in place so it will stay in that shape.
6. At one end of the colored paper tube, cut with your scissors 5 inches deep. Repeat that cut every half-inch (going around the tube) to create frayed strips at that end.
7. Slide the colored paper tube inside the cardboard tube, leaving the strips sticking out of the cardboard. Bend the strips over the edge of the cardboard tube so they look like tree branches.

Purim

As you may know, the "funnest" of all Jewish holidays is Purim, celebrated in early spring. The story of Purim, which is told in the Book of Esther (*Megillat Esther,* or "the *Megillah*"), is set in ancient Persia (modern-day Iran). Its two heroes are Esther—a beautiful young Jewish woman—and her uncle Mordecai. Esther marries the king, Ahasuerus, and becomes queen without disclosing that she is Jewish. The villain of the story, Haman, is the king's right-hand man. He gets permission to kill all the Jews in the land until Esther asks the king to spare her people—revealing that she is a Jew. When the king realizes the full import of Haman's evil plans he arranges for the Jews to be saved and orders that Haman be put to death.

While we traditionally dress up in costumes on this holiday, the real lesson of Purim, in fact, is that we don't need to disguise ourselves. Although it's easy to blend in, it's also important to remember who we are as Jews.

On Purim, few of the regular "synagogue rules" apply. There are carnival-like celebrations, funny skits, and people (including the leaders) acting generally silly. When you come to synagogue for the *Megillah* reading, you can bring your camera to take pictures of all the people in costume—especially the kids. Everyone listens carefully to the story until the reader comes to the word "Haman," at which point everyone in the synagogue makes a lot of noise, in order to drown out his name. We can boo, hiss, stamp our feet, and twirl or shake a noise-maker—called a *grogger* in Yiddish, *ra'ashan* in Hebrew.

The "Shake-Rattle-and-Roll" Grogger

WHAT YOU NEED:

Materials

▶ metal or plastic container with a lid or cap, such as a tennis ball can or small milk or juice carton
▶ colored paper, contact paper, stickers, etc.
▶ dried beans, seeds, or popcorn kernels

Equipment

▶ glue
▶ packing tape

HOW IT'S DONE:

1. Decorate the container's exterior with contact paper, colored paper, or stickers—and allow it to dry if necessary.
2. Fill the container with dried beans, seeds, or popcorn kernels. (These items are choking hazards, so young children should be supervised carefully.)
3. Put the lid or cap on. Tape or glue it shut around the rim or mouth (to prevent accidents). Get ready to shake, rattle, and roll!

The Costume Department

Kids can wear any type of costume on Purim, but it's especially fun to dress up like the characters in the Purim story itself. There are the good guys: Queen Esther and Mordecai. And of course, there's the ultimate bad guy, Haman.

"Purim Punim" Face Paints

Here's a quick and easy way to create a set of six different-colored paints. They're safe for use on cute little faces, for Purim or whenever!

WHAT YOU NEED:

Ingredients
▶ 6 tsp cornstarch
▶ 3 tsp water
▶ 3 tsp cold cream
▶ food coloring

Utensils
▶ muffin tin with 6 cups
▶ measuring spoons
▶ paintbrushes (the smaller the better)

HOW IT'S DONE:

1. In each cup of the muffin tin, put 1 tsp of cornstarch, ½ tsp of cold cream and ½ tsp of water.
2. Add different colors of food coloring to each cup, mixing some colors to create more options.
3. Mix well.
4. Now, get a friend or family member, and decorate each other's face! Have them do a small design on your forehead or cheek, or paint your entire face.

Crowns Fit for a King or Queen

The following is one possibility for making a homemade crown. Kids can also decorate their crowns with markers, sequins, or rhinestones.

WHAT YOU NEED:

Materials
▶ large paper or posterboard
▶ glitter glue or markers, rhinestones, sequins
▶ white glue

Equipment
▶ pencil
▶ scissors
▶ stapler

HOW IT'S DONE:

1. Take a large piece of paper or posterboard and wrap it around your head or your child's head. Figure out how much paper you need (allowing a little extra room so it can overlap), and mark the length.
2. Cut the paper or posterboard to size.
3. Decide how tall you want your crown to be, and then trim the paper or posterboard, using a zig-zag pattern to form the points of your crown. (Draw guidelines on the paper first if that helps.)
4. Lay the cut paper or posterboard out flat on your workstation.
5. Decorate the outside of the crown, using glitter glue or markers, rhinestones, and sequins. (Young children might do better with markers than with glitter glue.) Let your crown dry completely.
6. Wrap the paper around your head again to confirm the exact size the crown should be. Hold that size in place as you remove the crown from your head.
7. Staple the crown so that it remains circular and fits on your head.
8. Wear it like you're a king or queen!

An even easier method for making crowns is to take pre-made ones (like the ones you can get from Burger King) and then paint or decorate them as you please.

Three Points: A Haman Hat Trick

The villain Haman is said to have worn a triangular black hat. No Haman costume is complete without one. Here's how to make your own:

WHAT YOU NEED:

Materials
▶ black construction paper

Equipment
▶ ruler
▶ scissors
▶ pencil
▶ measuring tape
▶ clear plastic tape

HOW IT'S DONE:

1. From thick construction paper, cut out a circle that's 12 inches in diameter.
2. In the center of that circle, cut a smaller circle that's as big as the head of whoever will wear this hat (Measure first, to ensure that it will be just snug enough to stay above the person's ears.)
3. With a pencil and ruler, lightly draw a triangle on the paper, around the cut-out circle, out to the edges of the paper.
4. Fold the edges up along the triangle's lines, to form the 3-cornered hat.
5. Tape the edges in place at the inside corners, and there you have it: one "mean" Haman hat!

The *Purim-Shpiel* Must Go On!

Now that you're all dressed up, let's give you some place to go! The costumes you make will come in handy, since it's traditional on Purim to put on a play that tells the story of this holiday. In Yiddish it's called a *Purim-shpiel*.

Kids often know the story well enough from Hebrew school that they can put on the play themselves, but it's nice for parents to be involved as well. The whole family, as well as friends, can take roles in the *shpiel*, but be sure to invite some people who aren't in the play to be your audience!

If you don't want to be the actors yourselves, or if there aren't enough of you to play all the roles, you can put on a puppet show to tell the Purim story. And if you need some help telling the story, ready-made *Purim-shpiel* scripts are available in books or on the Web (see *The Whole Megillah* from Kar-Ben Copies, in the books section on p. 155; or go to www.akhlah.com/holidays/purim/purim_play.asp).

What a "Cast" of Characters: Papier-Mâché Puppets

Using puppets, you can perform a whole *Purim-shpiel* with only one or two people. Puppets made from papier-mâché—a soft material that can be molded but then hardens like a plaster cast—are fun and easy to make. But the process takes a few days, so plan ahead. Here's how to do it.

WHAT YOU NEED:

Materials
▶ dry laundry starch, or glue
▶ cold water
▶ newspaper
▶ balloons
▶ cardboard toilet-paper rolls (empty)
▶ acrylic paints
▶ cloth, yarn, glue (optional)

Equipment
▶ mixing bowl
▶ whisk
▶ paintbrushes

HOW IT'S DONE:

1. Mix the starch (or glue) and water in equal amounts. Stir completely, then allow it to stand and thicken.
2. Tear newspaper into strips. (Newspaper tears easily from top to bottom.) Dip these strips into the mixture so they become saturated with the white concoction to make the papier-mâché.
3. Blow up a balloon to roughly the size you would like your puppet's head to be. Let the balloon rest on top of a cardboard toilet-paper roll. This cardboard tube will become the handle for the puppet.
4. Wrap the papier-mâché around the balloon and the cardboard handle, shaping it to create the head of the character. Shape ears, nose, eyes, mouth, and hair (or you can paint these on later, after the head has dried).
5. Let it dry for about three days, depending on the thickness, until the head becomes completely hard.
6. Once it is dry, use acrylic paints to add color to the faces of the

Purim characters. You can also glue on hair or clothes using cloth or yarn. Or you can make one of the hats described above for your puppet to wear.

7. It's show time!

The "So-Good-You'll-Eat-Your-Hat" Hamantaschen

Hamantaschen are the traditional Purim treat. They are triangular-shaped cookies, said to look like Haman's hat. Use whatever kind of filling you like (we've made a few suggestions in this recipe). We guarantee they'll be delicious, or we'll eat our hat—as long as it's Haman's!

WHAT YOU NEED:

Ingredients

► 2 cups flour (plus extra for flouring the surfaces)
► ½ cup sugar
► 1½ tsp baking powder
► ½ tsp salt
► 2 eggs
► ½ cup margarine or butter
► 1 tsp vanilla
► suggested fillings:
  ♦ preserves or jams (apricot or raspberry are best)
  ♦ poppy seed filling (store bought)
  ♦ chocolate chips
► oil (for greasing the cookie sheet)

Utensils

► large mixing bowl
► measuring cup
► measuring spoons
► stirring spoon or food processor
► bread board
► rolling pin
► cookie cutter (or drinking glass)
► finger bowl with water
► spoon
► cookie sheet

HOW IT'S DONE:

1. Mix first seven ingredients in a large bowl. Blend well by hand or in a food processor until a stiff ball of dough is formed (add a little more flour if it is very soft).

2. Wrap the dough in plastic, put in the refrigerator, and allow to chill overnight.
3. Divide the dough in half.
4. Roll out one half of the dough until it is about ¼ inch thick. Then, using a cookie cutter (or the rim of a drinking glass), cut circles about 3 inches in diameter, in the dough. (Lift away the excess dough, and roll it out again until there is not enough to cut out circles.)
5. Dip your finger in water and run it around the edge of the dough circles you cut.
6. Preheat oven to 325°F.
7. Spoon the filling of your choice into the center of the circle—about one scant teaspoon per circle.
8. Fold the sides of the circle up, on top of the filling, three times, to turn the circle into a triangle. Pinch together the folds of dough where they overlap, starting at the three points of the triangle, to ensure that the pocket doesn't spread open.
9. Place the triangles on a greased cookie sheet and bake at 325°F for 12–15 minutes or until they start to brown on the bottom and edges.

Special Delivery: *Mishloach Manot*

While there's a lot of fun to be had during Purim, our good fortune is meant to be shared with others. That's why, in addition to the everyday Jewish value of *tzedakah* (providing for everyone's basic needs), Purim specifically involves giving money to the needy. Another part of Purim's celebration is delivering "care packages" to our friends and family. This is called *mishloach manot*.

These "care packages" can be filled with all sorts of ready-to-eat goodies and little gifts—including hamantaschen—and they're fun to assemble with your family. They can be carried in baskets, paper bags, or even containers that you've made and decorated yourself. Use stickers, ribbons, and markers to make the *mishloach manot* package as beautiful as you can. Then you can go and drop off the packages in person.

Backwards Day

Purim is the Jewish "Backwards Day." In the Book of Esther, there are many reversals of fortune: Instead of the Jews being massacred, they are honored, and their enemies are destroyed. Haman is killed on the same contraption he had built to kill Mordecai, and Mordecai is honored in the same way that Haman had planned for himself to be honored. The story also involves the reversal of roles. For example, the king takes orders from his servants when they give him the idea to put Haman to death.

With that in mind, why not celebrate this holiday as a "Backwards Day" in your house? Expand on your traditional observances, in the wild spirit of Purim. Have the parents and kids switch roles for a while. Wear your clothes backwards. Switch seats at the dinner table. Or eat breakfast for dinner.

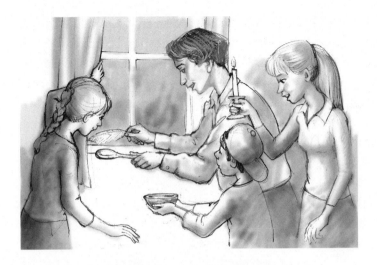

Passover

Passover, or *Pesach* in Hebrew, is a springtime holiday that celebrates freedom. We remember that our ancestors were slaves in Egypt and retell the story of the Exodus—how they were set free.

What are we all "enslaved" by today? Pressure to succeed at school or at work? Perhaps something else? Striving for excellence is important, but are we putting too much pressure on ourselves to "do it all"? Are we making time to take care of ourselves and to do the things that make us truly happy? Passover is a time to concentrate on freeing ourselves from that which enslaves us and to appreciate the freedom we have. A great way to do this is to focus on spending time with our families.

Passover Prep Work

Operation Feather-and-Candle

Among the many customs associated with Passover, one of the best known is the practice of eating only unleavened bread (made from dough that has not risen). All the food that is made from leavened bread is considered *chametz*, not kosher for Passover. We clean our houses of all the *chametz* on the days before the holiday starts.

After we've done a thorough "spring cleaning" in preparation for Passover, we do one final search for any *chametz* we may have missed the first time around. It's easy to make this tradition a fun activity for the whole family and make the kids feel like they're part of an important—and highly delicate—mission.

The custom (going back to the days before the Dustbuster and flashlight) is to carry a candle, a feather, and a wooden spoon on this hunt for *chametz*. You use the feather to sweep the food into the wooden spoon. The candle is used for light, since the search is done at night, traditionally one night before Passover begins. It's more meaningful and exciting to do this search with the lights off.

Parents can carry the candle (or use a flashlight to be safe); kids can carry the feather and wooden spoon. Have a paper bag handy so you can put all the *chametz* in it and dispose of it properly.

Note to parents: To make sure the search is successful, it's customary to hide a few wrapped pieces of bread or crackers (classic *chametz* culprits) around the house beforehand. Or, stuff a wrapped candy bar under the cushion of the couch; when the kids find it, they'll have a final *chametz* snack before Passover begins.

Undercover Matzah

Matzah is the flat—that is, unleavened—bread that the Israelites brought with them when they were rushing out of Egypt, when they had no time to wait for the bread to rise. By eating matzah on Passover, we celebrate freedom.

On the Passover seder table, we stack three pieces of matzah to use for display and for ceremonial eating. (Also, the middle matzah in the stack will be broken in two and half of it set aside as the *afikomen*—see p. 62). And of course, there's plenty more matzah that's just for regular eating with dinner.

Here's an easy way to make a cover with three pockets to use for your special stack of three pieces of matzah.

WHAT YOU NEED:

Materials

▶ 4 square pieces of felt or fabric, bigger than a piece of matzah (you can buy pre-cut squares at a craft store)
▶ sewing thread (or safety pins)
▶ bottles of fabric paint
▶ glue
▶ decorations: sequins, buttons, rhinestones

Equipment

▶ sewing needle and thimble, or sewing machine

HOW IT'S DONE:

1. Stack the four pieces of felt on top of one another.
2. Around three sides of the stack, sew the pieces together (or just pin them with safety pins) to create a pouch with three pockets— one for each of the three pieces of matzah.
3. Decorate the top piece of felt (you can do this before or after you've attached the pieces) using fabric paint. Write "Matzah," in English or Hebrew, in the center of the cover (see Appendix of Stencils, p. 246).
4. Glue on sequins, buttons, and rhinestones for a finishing touch.

The Wide World of *Charoset*

The most delicious item found on the seder plate is called *charoset*. It's a fruit-and-nut mixture that looks like cement or mud. It represents the mortar that the Israelite slaves used when building the Egyptian cities for Pharoah.

Here are two different recipes for *charoset*, taken from two different parts of the world.

A Traditional Ashkenazi *Charoset*

WHAT YOU NEED:

Ingredients

- ▶ 6 large apples, peeled and cored
- ▶ 2 cups crushed walnuts
- ▶ 2½ tsp cinnamon
- ▶ 3½ ounces honey
- ▶ I cup sweet red wine

Utensils

- ▶ food processor
- ▶ measuring cup
- ▶ measuring spoons

HOW IT'S DONE:

Blend all the ingredients in a food processor until it's almost smooth. Refrigerate. Serves 20.

Farid's Persian Version *Charoset*

WHAT YOU NEED:

Ingredients

- ▶ 2 cups shelled pistachio nuts
- ▶ I cup shelled pecans
- ▶ I cup shelled walnuts
- ▶ 2 cups shelled filbert nuts
- ▶ 2 medium-size apples, peeled and sliced
- ▶ 2 medium-size pears, peeled and sliced
- ▶ 2 cups raisins
- ▶ I cup pitted dates
- ▶ 2 tsp cinnamon
- ▶ ½ tsp ginger
- ▶ ½ cup sweet red wine

Utensils

- ▶ food processor
- ▶ measuring cup
- ▶ measuring spoons
- ▶ mixing bowl
- ▶ mixing spoon

HOW IT'S DONE:

1. Chop all the nuts in the food processor, and place them in a large bowl.
2. Chop the apples and pears together in the food processor.
3. Add the raisins and dates to the apple and pear mixture, and process again.
4. Combine all the ingredients in the bowl.
5. Add cinnamon and ginger, and mix thoroughly, kneading by hand. Refrigerate. Serves 25.

Note: Leftover *charoset* stays good in the refrigerator for several weeks. Both at the seder and later, always add a bit of wine, and mix just before serving.

The Family Fun Seder

We have seders in our homes each year to pass down from generation to generation the story of the Exodus.

The Haggadah is the guidebook that takes us through the seder. There are many *Haggadot* (plural of Haggadah) out there, with a variety of different styles to choose from. Quite a few are specially designed for family participation. Take the time to look at a few and pick out the one that feels most comfortable for your family. Familiarize yourself with the Haggadah before the seder; decide ahead of time which parts you're going to do, which parts you'll skip, and what discussions and activities you'll add to personalize the seder for your family. Here are some ideas to make the seder fun and meaningful.

Charting the Seder Course

With a Haggadah as a guide, your family can make a chart that lists all the parts of the Passover seder. Placing this simple prop on your seder table is a great way to keep young kids tuned in and involved with what's happening. During the seder, they can follow along and keep track of how far you've gotten in the seder and how much is left. They'll like putting stickers next to all the parts that have been completed, and they'll look forward to all the parts coming up.

WHAT YOU NEED:

Materials
▶ construction paper
▶ clear contact paper
▶ stickers

Equipment
▶ markers
▶ scissors

HOW IT'S DONE:

1. On the construction paper, make a chart with the order of the seder, listing the Hebrew or English words for each part of the seder (see Appendix of Stencils, p. 246). Use the fourteen-item list in your Haggadah, or alter it according to your family's own traditions.

2. Draw pictures for the different parts, such as a Kiddush cup for the Kiddush, and matzah for the ceremonial eating of the matzah.

3. Laminate the paper with clear contact paper to make it a placemat for the seder. Trim with scissors.

4. Give out stickers to the kids. As you finish each part of the seder, they can use a sticker to mark the part you've just completed.

Enough Food to Go Around

During the seder, we say, "Let all who are hungry come eat, let all who are needy come to our Passover feast." Since we don't really expect those who are hungry to just walk in, try this to give real meaning to those words: When guests ask what they can bring to your seder, tell them to bring cans of food that you'll donate to a local soup kitchen. Also, make an effort to invite some guests who don't otherwise have a place to go for Passover.

Dress Up and Lie Down

Instead of doing the seder at the dining room table, sit on the floor around your coffee table, or on pillows and cushions in your living room. At our family's seder, we've found this to be a great way to take away any "stuffy atmosphere" that may come with a formal dining room setting and to make the whole event more fun and cozy. Also, it allows us to have our seder in a truly "reclining" position, as the Haggadah says we should, in order to show that we are free—and to make "this night different from all other nights."

Dress up in comfortable Israelite/Egyptian garb for the evening. Have participants take off their shoes. String up sheets or tapestries around your living room so your seder looks as if it's being held in a tent. Kids and adults really get into this, and it sets the right kind of mood for a "Family Fun Seder." It lets everyone know, right off the bat, that this is not going to be "seder-as-usual." And since we are supposed to retell the Passover story as if it happened to us personally, dressing up helps fuel our imagination.

Encourage your guests to "feel comfortable"—to feel free to ask for another pillow or to sit in a chair if they'd like that better than the floor. Also encourage them to ask questions throughout the seder. Questions are an important part of this holiday, because questions push us all to think, share ideas, and come up with answers. With new questions and new discussions every year, no two seders are ever exactly alike. Strive to retell the story of the Exodus in a way that is fresh and relevant to your life today.

Let All Who Are Hungry Eat Already!

People sometimes start to get impatient during the seder, when everyone should be enjoying the discussion and traditions. That's often simply because they're so *hungry*! But they don't need to stay hungry. Near the beginning of the seder, once you've said the prayer over the *karpas* (the green vegetable), then it's okay to serve any vegetables from the earth. This includes carrots, celery sticks (and vegetable dips), or other veggie recipes. Pass them around so people can snack on these during the seder. That way, instead of focusing on how hungry they are, everyone can focus on the seder activities.

Middle Matzah Mania

Once the *afikomen* is broken off from the middle matzah and wrapped in a cloth napkin, some families follow an old custom where the leader of the seder takes the *afikomen* and puts it on his or her shoulder, as if it were a sack of food being carried out of Egypt by the Israelites. The leader takes a few steps and says, "This is in memory of our ancestors, who left Egypt carrying the bread of affliction on their shoulders." Visual images like this make it easier for kids to follow the story.

Sometimes the leader of the seder asks a child to march with the *afikomen* on his or her shoulder (several kids can take turns). The leader asks the child, "Where are you going?" And the child responds, "Out of Egypt." Then the leader says, "And what are you carrying on your shoulder?" And the child answers, "The matzah, the bread that didn't have a chance to rise before our journey."

Of course, there's more fun in store with the *afikomen*. Perhaps the seder tradition most popular with kids is hiding this piece of matzah. After dinner, the seder cannot resume (and conclude) until the *afikomen* has been found. But who hides it? And then who finds it? Well, there are many variations on this tradition. But for the most part, they fall into two categories:

1. The leader of the seder slips away at some point during dinner and hides the *afikomen*. The children search for it, and there's usually a reward for the child who finds it.
2. In other families, the kids sneak off with the *afikomen* and hide it from the leader of the seder, who has to pay a "ransom" to get it back.

Interactive Israelites

The seder is all about teaching the Passover story to the next generation. It's much easier for kids to learn and understand what it's about when you make the seder interactive and fun for them. Rather than simply sitting and reading, act out as much of the Haggadah as possible, and include skits and songs in the seder. This will surely make it more memorable.

It's not easy to make up skits or songs right on the spot, so ask your guests to prepare something ahead of time. Assign a different part of the seder to each family or individual who's coming (and leave some ideas open for last-minute guests).

Parts of the seder to assign include the Four Questions (how about thinking up "Four More Questions"), the Four Sons (do a skit with them), or the Ten Plagues (make a list of the "Top Ten Rejected Plagues"). It's okay if some parts are done by more than one group, because everyone will approach it in a different way. Make sure your guests understand that their assignment doesn't need to be too elaborate. Tell them to simply have fun with it!

A "Dayenu" You Won't Be Able to Get Enough Of!

The song "Dayenu" (meaning in Hebrew "enough for us") has a fun traditional melody and repetition to it, but there's a way to make it even more exciting. Persian Jews have a custom of hitting each other with scallions during the chorus of this song. Some say we are remembering the whips of the taskmasters, which the scallions resemble, when we do this. Others say we're being playful with the meaning of the song, since people are hitting us with scallions while we're singing, "Enough! Enough!" Either way, it's fun to get a chance to give our siblings a good playful smack or two with one of those long green onions!

Open Up! It's Elijah!

At the right point during the seder, you can ask an unsuspecting kid to go open the door to let in the prophet Elijah, as is the custom. The trick is: Without the kids knowing, an adult should dress up as Elijah and be waiting outside the door when it's opened. As "Elijah" dramatically enters, it's always funny to see the look of surprise on everyone's faces—adults as well as kids!

For a fun competition, to keep track of the forty-nine days between the start of Passover and the holiday of Shavuot (these forty-nine days are called the *omer* period) see the Lag B'Omer section, on p. 72.

Yom Ha'Atzmaut
(with Yom Ha'Shoah and Yom Ha'Zikaron)

Yom Ha'Atzmaut is Israeli Independence Day, similar to the American Fourth of July. This holiday celebrates the day—May 14, 1948—when Israel became its own country and the Jewish people gained their national independence for the first time in nearly two thousand years. Because the holiday is celebrated according to the Jewish calendar, it rarely coincides exactly with May 14, but rather with a different date each year in late April or early May.

Yom Ha'Atzmaut is a national holiday for Israelis, rather than a religious holiday. It is also observed by some Jews around the world. It has developed into a festival like Purim or Hanukkah, celebrating an against-the-odds victory for the Jewish people.

As is Jewish custom, though, we do not enjoy our victory without acknowledging loss; there can be no good without bad. Therefore, on the day before Yom Ha'Atzmaut we remember all the soldiers who have lost their lives in the struggle to create and protect Israel. This day is called Yom Ha'Zikaron, or "Remembrance Day." At the end of this sad day, a siren sounds all over Israel so that the entire nation remembers the fallen soldiers one more time. When the sirens end, Yom Ha'Zikaron ends and Yom Ha'Atzmaut begins. Celebrations erupt all over the country, with fireworks, music, and dancing in the streets.

One week before Yom Ha'Zikaron and Yom Ha'Atzmaut is another sad day, called Yom Ha'Shoah, Holocaust Remembrance Day. On this day, a siren also sounds across Israel, and the entire country comes to a halt. Everyone stops whatever they are doing for a couple of minutes to remember the victims of the Holocaust. People even stop their cars and get out. In America and other countries, people also commemorate those lost in the Holocaust with special services and programs at synagogues, Jewish community centers, and Holocaust memorials.

These three important days offer a good time to take pride in the existence of Israel and also to discuss the events that led to the creation of Israel and the difficulties the country still faces. To celebrate Yom Ha'Atzmaut we can eat Israeli foods, listen to Israeli music, do Israeli dancing (see music and dance section, pp. 134–138), and make crafts. It's also fun on this day for the whole family to dress up in blue and white, the colors of the Israeli flag. And you can also make your own Israeli flag (see p. 29 for the flag-making directions in the Simchat Torah section, but paint your flag to look like Israel's flag, with two horizontal blue stripes and a solid blue Star of David in the center).

Israeli Food Is-really Good

Many of the foods that we commonly recognize as Israeli are actually Israeli versions of generic Middle Eastern foods. These treats are also enjoyed by people in Israel's neighboring Arab countries. By eating these foods in celebration of Israeli independence, we also recognize that Jews and Arabs are ancient cousins with many things in common culturally.

The "Stuff-It-'Til-It-Stuffs-You" Falafel

Having falafel for lunch in Israel is as common as having a burger in America. Falafel are balls of deep-fried ground chickpeas mixed with yummy spices. They're usually served in a pita pocket with hummus and Israeli salad (see recipes below), tahini (sesame) sauce, and other goodies—even french fries. It's a vegetarian delight, though with all this deep-frying, you can be sure it's not health food!

WHAT YOU NEED:

Ingredients

- ▶ 1 16-ounce can chickpeas (drained)
- ▶ 1 large onion, chopped
- ▶ 7 tbsp finely chopped parsley
- ▶ 1 egg, lightly beaten
- ▶ 1 tsp salt
- ▶ ½ tsp ground hot red pepper (for spicy, 1 tsp)
- ▶ 1 tsp garlic powder
- ▶ ½ tsp ground cumin (for spicy, 1 tsp)
- ▶ ½ to 1 cup bread crumbs
- ▶ vegetable oil

Utensils

- ▶ can opener
- ▶ knife and cutting board
- ▶ small bowl or cup
- ▶ fork (to beat the egg)
- ▶ mixing bowl
- ▶ mixing spoon
- ▶ measuring spoons
- ▶ blender
- ▶ frying pan
- ▶ slotted spoon
- ▶ paper towels or brown paper bags

HOW IT'S DONE:

1. Mix the chickpeas and the onion. Add the parsley, egg, salt, and spices.
2. Whirl the ingredients in a blender, adding bread crumbs until the chickpea mixture is firm enough to form small balls that won't stick to your hands.
3. Form the mix into balls about the size of a quarter (or larger), and flatten them slightly.

4. Fry them in one-inch-deep hot oil until they are golden brown on each side.
5. Remove the falafel from the oil with a slotted spoon, and drain the balls on a paper towel or brown paper bags.
6. Allow them to cool off slightly before making your falafel pita.

Aliza's Spreadable Edible Incredible Hummus

Like falafel, hummus is made from chickpeas. But instead of their being fried, the chickpeas are mashed into a delicious smooth spread that is then either added to a falafel pita or eaten as a dip. Here's how to make it.

WHAT YOU NEED:

Ingredients

▶ 2 cups canned chickpeas
▶ I cup tahini (sesame) paste (found in most health food stores and kosher markets)
▶ ¾ cup lemon juice
▶ 4 garlic cloves, minced
▶ ½ tsp salt
▶ ½ tsp cumin
▶ olive oil, chopped parsley, paprika (optional)

Utensils

▶ measuring cup
▶ measuring spoons
▶ food processor or blender

HOW IT'S DONE:

I. Place all the ingredients (except parsley and paprika) in a food processor or blender. Mix until the chickpeas are smooth.
2. Store the hummus in a covered container in the refrigerator.
3. Serve cold or at room temperature. Just before serving, pour on I tbsp of olive oil and sprinkle chopped parsley and/or paprika on top.
4. If desired, reserve ¼ cup of unmashed chickpeas to sprinkle on top or mix in with the spread to make "chunky" hummus.

Slice 'n' Dice Israeli Salad

The vegetables in Israeli salad are cut small so they fit easily into a falafel pita. But this salad is also delicious when eaten alone. Here's how to make it.

WHAT YOU NEED:

Ingredients
- ▶ 2 big tomatoes
- ▶ 2 cucumbers
- ▶ ¼ onion (or 2 scallions)
- ▶ 2 tbsp chopped parsley
- ▶ olive oil, to taste
- ▶ lemon juice, to taste
- ▶ salt and pepper

Utensils
- ▶ measuring spoons
- ▶ mixing bowl
- ▶ stirring spoon

HOW IT'S DONE:

1. Dice the tomatoes, cucumbers, and onions in small pieces.
2. Mix the vegetables in a medium-size bowl.
3. Add the chopped parsley, olive oil, lemon juice, salt, and pepper. (Start with a small amount of each, and season to taste.) Mix it all up.
4. Refrigerate the salad until ready to eat.

"Jew"elry

The Star of David is not only a symbol for the Jewish people as a whole, it is also a national symbol of Israel found on the Israeli flag. Here's a "sharp" fashion accessory that can be worn by a girl or a boy on Yom Ha'Atzmaut, whether marching in an official Independence Day celebration or simply showing Israeli pride.

WHAT YOU NEED:

Materials

▶ 6 Popsicle sticks per necklace
▶ string
▶ glitter glue, beads, sequins
   (optional)

Equipment

▶ glue
▶ tempera
   or acrylic
   paint

HOW IT'S DONE:

1. Make a triangle out of three of the Popsicle sticks, with the ends overlapping, and glue them together.
2. Form a second triangle with the other three sticks.
3. Glue one triangle on top of the other to form a Jewish star.
4. Decorate the star with paint, glitter glue, beads, or sequins.
5. Allow the star to dry, then put a string through the top point to make a necklace.

Lag B'Omer

Lag B'Omer is not among the best-known or most important Jewish holidays, but it's a holiday with plenty of opportunities for fun. The name Lag B'Omer means "the thirty-third day of the *omer*": *Lag* is a combination of the Hebrew letters *lamed* and *gimmel*, whose numerical values are thirty and three; and the *omer* is the period of forty-nine days between the start of Passover and Shavuot.

The *omer* is considered a sort of mourning period for the twenty-four thousand students of Rabbi Akiba said to have been wiped out in a plague nearly two thousand years ago. Traditionally, Jews don't have weddings, get haircuts, or throw large celebrations during the *omer*. But on the thirty-third day of the *omer*, these restrictions are lifted.

Why the reprieve on Lag B'Omer? According to the Talmud, the plague left students dying in droves on each day of the *omer*. But on the thirty-third day, the plague somehow stopped for just one day.

Burning Bright and Shining Light

One favorite way that Jews around the world celebrate Lag B'Omer is by building bonfires and gathering around to roast marshmallows, sing songs, and tell stories. The bonfires relate to a second historical event connected with Lag B'Omer. It is said that on this day, the great Jewish mystic Rabbi Shimon Bar Yochai (the kabbalistic work the *Zohar* is often attributed to him) revealed the secrets of the Torah while an "intense light" emanated from his body.

Since having a bonfire means being outdoors, Lag B'Omer is also associated with fun activities such as grilling on the barbecue, having a picnic, or going on a hike with family and friends.

If you spend Lag B'Omer at a park or campground and plan to have a bonfire, be sure to follow all the necessary safety precautions. For some basic guidelines on campfire safety, see www.smokeybearstore.com/smokey_bear_campfire_safety.htm.

Don't Lag B'hind

The *omer* begins on the second day of Passover and goes for forty-nine days until the start of Shavuot. There's a prayer we say on each of those forty-nine days, and in that prayer we mark what day we're up to in the counting of the *omer*. Remembering to count each and every day is the key, because if you forget to do it even just one day, you're technically not allowed to count any of the remaining days of the *omer*. You can turn this daily counting into a competition among your family members.

HERE'S HOW:

Everyone in the family has to remember to count each day of the *omer*. Every day, each person writes the number of the day (for example, "Day 1") and his or her name on a small piece of paper and puts it in a designated jar on the kitchen counter. At the end of each day, you check the jar. Everyone who remembered to count the day gets one point, and anyone who forgot loses a point (or they're out completely, if you want to play hardball). At the end of the forty-nine days, the person with the most points is dubbed "Count *Omer!*"

Viva *Lag* difference!

The plague that killed Rabbi Akiba's students was said to have been brought on by their own hateful behavior toward one another: intolerance, jealousy, gossiping, and general lack of respect. So one of the holiday's themes is the importance of respecting fellow Jews. Make this holiday an opportunity to concentrate on what you have in common with other Jews who you might otherwise consider to be very different from you.

You could help organize a Lag B'Omer celebration that brings families together from a variety of different congregations in your community. Or you could help arrange a joint activity or project, like a clean-up day or visiting the sick or elderly.

Shavuot

The holiday of Shavuot occurs seven weeks after Passover, usually in late May. It celebrates two things: the giving of the Ten Commandments (and many believe the whole Torah) at Mount Sinai after the Israelites left Egypt, and also the first fruits of the harvest in ancient Israel.

Pick-'Em-Yourself Fruits and Vegetables

Shavuot is a great time to take your kids to an apple orchard, strawberry field, or vegetable farm to really get into the feel of this harvest holiday. In many parts of the U.S., late spring—when Shavuot occurs—is prime season for picking certain kinds of fruit. If you call your state agriculture department or your local farmer's market, or look in the local telephone directory or on the Internet, you can usually find "pick-your-own" farms in your area that are open to the public at this time of year. Call ahead; sometimes the picking season is longer or shorter, depending on the weather.

In the Book of Ruth (which takes place at harvest-time and is therefore linked to Shavuot), we learn that when you harvest you're supposed to leave part of your crop for the poor. With that in mind, it's a nice idea to donate a portion of what you pick to a homeless shelter. If this is not practical for you to do (or if the shelter will not accept unsealed or perishable foods) then you can donate canned goods.

Midnight Read and Feed

According to Jewish lore, the Torah was given on Mount Sinai at daybreak, but the Israelites over-slept and were not prepared for it, so God had to wake them up! To make up for this, it has become a tradition to stay up the entire night on Shavuot, reading the Torah or other Jewish books.

This can be one night when bedtimes don't count, when you let the kids stay up as late as they want as long as they're reading something that has to do with Judaism. They'll be thrilled by the idea. It's also a tradition in some communities to have light, refreshing snacks sometime in the middle of the night. For many, watermelon is the all-time favorite. Some synagogues arrange a late-night learning group that you can take part in, too.

The Land of Cheese Blintzes

On Shavuot, it's customary to eat both dairy and sweet foods, since we are celebrating the harvest of the "land of milk and honey." The most popular holiday food has become cheese blintzes with sweet toppings. That lets you cover all your bases in one great treat.

WHAT YOU NEED:

For the pancakes:
▶ 2 eggs
▶ ½ tsp salt
▶ I cup milk
▶ I cup flour
▶ butter

For the filling:
▶ I pound dry cottage cheese or farmer cheese
▶ I egg
▶ salt and pepper, or sugar (to taste)
▶ measuring cup

HOW IT'S DONE:

1. Beat 2 eggs with salt until they're fluffy.
2. Stir in the milk and flour to make a smooth batter.
3. Melt a very small amount of butter in a six-inch frying pan.
4. Pour into the pan just enough batter (about 2 tbsp) to make a thin coat that covers the whole bottom of the pan.
5. Tilt the pan from side to side to distribute the batter while cooking for a minute or two, until the edges dry and pull away from pan.
6. Remove pancake from pan, and place on a paper towel to cool. Stack the pancakes after they cool.
7. Repeat until no more batter remains.
8. Blend the cottage cheese, egg, salt, and pepper (or sugar) in a blender or with a hand mixer until smooth.
9. Place a heaping teaspoon of filling on the fried (bottom) side of each pancake, and fold the sides of the pancake over the filling. Tuck in the ends to keep the cheese inside.
10. Fry the blintzes in butter or oil until golden brown, or bake them at 350°F in an oven until crisp and brown.
11. Serve with jelly or fresh fruit. Makes 15 blintzes.

A House Blooming with Flowers

There is a Shavuot custom of decorating the home with flowers and plants. We do this not only because the first fruits of the harvest were brought on this holiday but also because of the teaching that when the Torah was given to the Jewish people at Mount Sinai, the desert around it bloomed and sprouted flowers.

Prize-Winning Paper Cutting

Another customary Shavuot decoration is the paper-cut design. The folk art of paper cutting was practiced in nineteenth-century Poland by people of many different backgrounds and religions, including the many Jews who lived there.

Particularly on Shavuot, paper-cut designs decorated the windows in the Jewish shtetls, perhaps because they were an inexpensive way to beautify a home. Floral decorations and ancient symbols were used: menorahs, crowns, vines, and flowers. These cutouts were generally made from white paper and mounted on a contrasting color backing, with a short text included.

Below are some basic instructions to get you started on some Shavuot paper cutting. Start with really simple designs. You'll learn with experience and become a pro in no time.

WHAT YOU NEED:

- ▶ white paper
- ▶ colored construction paper (larger than the white paper)
- ▶ glue
- ▶ scissors (and graphic arts knives for parents only)
- ▶ pencils
- ▶ picture frame (to fit)

HOW IT'S DONE:

1. Fold the white paper in half or in fourths, depending on whether you want the designs to appear two times or four times.
2. Lightly sketch in pencil, on the outside of the folded paper, the designs you want to create. (For more elaborate designs, stencils can be used.) If you are creating a design such as vines, don't let the shapes you make run into one another or it will mess up your design.
3. Carefully cut out the design.
4. Unfold the paper to reveal the entire cutout. On the back of your cutout, put a small amount of glue at the corners and a few other spots.
5. Paste the cutout onto the construction paper, and line it up so that it lays flat against the background. If you want to include some writing, leave space for it at the bottom or top.
6. If you choose to include words, write them in the space you left for it. Write "Happy Shavuot" or "Happy Holiday" *(Chag Sameach)* in English or Hebrew (see Appendix of Stencils, p. 247), or anything else you'd like to include.
7. Frame your creation, and hang it up to show everyone.

Tu B'Av

It's the Jewish holiday of love. Tu B'Av celebrates romance and marriage, so some view it as a sort of "Jewish Valentine's Day." These days, the observance of this minor secular holiday includes matchmaking and sending roses.

Tu B'Av is the fifteenth day of the midsummer month of Av (*Tu* combines the Hebrew letters *tet* and *vav*, which have the numeric value of fifteen.) It falls six days after Tisha B'Av (ninth of Av), a far more widely observed day of Jewish mourning and fasting. On Tisha B'Av, we remember the many tragedies in Jewish history that occurred on that date, including the destruction of both the First and Second Temples in Jerusalem.

In contrast, Tu B'Av commemorates historic events that helped to unify the Jewish people, including some that deal specifically with marriage and courtship. For example, a law had been enacted during the time of Moses requiring women who inherited property to marry someone from their own tribe. Once the Jewish people settled in the Land of Israel, it was on Tu B'Av that this law was declared obsolete and annulled. Not only was this a victory for women's rights, but it also helped to unify Israel as a single nation, once intermarriage between tribes became more common.

It Takes Tu B'Av to Tango

On this "holiday of love," it was a custom in ancient Israel for young, single women to dress in white clothes and go out dancing in the vineyards. Unmarried men would watch, hoping to find a wife. The women wore clothes they had borrowed from each other so they couldn't be judged according to the quality of their dress (that is, how rich they were).

For a fun Tu B'Av celebration, you can stage your own little dress-up-and-dance party, with your family or friends. Have everyone collect a few pieces of white clothing of their own, then put all the clothes into a pile and have everyone pick something out of the pile to wear.

When everyone's dressed in each other's white clothes—underlying how we're all equal as Jews, and that it's what's inside that matters more than the kind of clothes we wear—it's time to start dancing! (For some tips on where to begin, see the dance section of this book, pp. 134–138.) If you really want to go all-out, pack up the boom box and take the kids out to an orchard or forest meadow for some "dancing in the vineyards."

Invent a Yente: Tu B'Av Matchmaking

Does your family know a nice Jewish single man and a nice Jewish single woman who might be good together? In honor of this holiday of romance, get the whole family involved in matchmaking, setting up the pair on a blind date.

The kids should play an active role in this "project" by helping to think up good matches. Or, if they know the people well enough (and feel comfortable doing this) they can actually make the matchmaker phone calls themselves—to fill in the prospective couple on the Tu B'Av "tradition," tell each of them about the other, and pass along each other's phone numbers. Remember, as the old bit of Jewish lore holds: Make three successful matches and you get an automatic ticket to heaven!

To My Love on Tu B'Av

One nice way to celebrate this holiday is to write notes (similar to Valentine's Day cards) expressing your feelings to the people you care about. Use generic cards that are blank inside so you'll have room to write a nice message. Or better yet, create your own simple heart-shaped cards.

WHAT YOU NEED:
▶ construction paper
▶ pencil
▶ scissors
▶ markers, glitter glue, crayons, etc.

HOW IT'S DONE:
1. Fold a piece of construction paper in half.
2. Using the folded edge of the paper as one side of your heart, lightly draw in pencil a heart shape on the paper.
3. Cut out the heart shape with the scissors to create your heart-shaped card.
4. On the front of the card, write "Happy Tu B'Av: The Jewish Holiday of Love" (since people who don't know about this holiday might be wondering why you're sending them a Valentine in the middle of the summer).
5. Draw designs around the words as you like.
6. Write a message on the inside of the card, telling the recipient how much they mean to you.
7. Deliver your cards—by hand, if they're going to people who live in your house, or by mail if they're going to someone who lives far away (for directions on how to make your own envelopes, see p. 112).

Celebrating Secular Holidays in a Jewish Way

Many of the holidays we celebrate as Americans contain ideas and messages that work just fine within a Jewish context or that can have Jewish values tacked onto them. When the kids have the day off from school, or your family is enjoying a three-day weekend courtesy of one of these national holidays, talk about the significance of these days, and try to draw a Jewish connection. Make the holiday relevant to our lives not only as Americans but also as Jews.

At the most basic level, it's easy to bring Judaism into our secular holiday celebrations with everyday customs such as saying a blessing to mark a particular day or custom. You don't need challah to say the *ha'motzi* blessing on bread. If you're having a cookout for Memorial Day or the Fourth of July, hot dog buns work just as well!

Martin Luther King, Jr., Day (January)

There is a significant historic connection between the histories of African-Americans and Jews. We share memories of being subjected to slavery, prejudice, and persecution. But African-Americans and Jewish Americans also have a lot of positive things in common, such as rich cultural heritages and spiritual religious music.

Celebrate this holiday alongside the African-Americans in your community by honoring Dr. Martin Luther King, Jr.'s call for justice, peace, and equality. These values are very much in line with Jewish values of social justice. Take your family to march in a parade, listen to a gospel choir sing, hear a speech, or simply talk with your kids about Dr. King's importance and what Jewish tradition teaches about freedom and prejudice.

Like Passover, this holiday celebrates freedom. But instead of telling our own story, this is the time to let others tell their story—and our turn to listen.

Memorial Day (May)

As we kick off summer with Memorial Day barbecues or trips to the beach it's nice to take a moment to remember what this holiday is all about. Similar to the Israeli Yom Ha'Zikaron, this day honors United States war veterans, both living and dead.

The Jewish War Veterans (JWV) of the U.S.A. is the oldest active veterans' service organization in America. It was organized in 1896 by Jewish veterans of the Civil War. The group has a program called "The Care Package Campaign," which sends both useful and thoughtful materials and supplies to American Jewish troops serving around the world, on the holidays or any time. The packages contain cards, gifts, treats, reading material, Judaica, and long-distance calling cards.

FOR MORE INFORMATION ▶ Jewish War Veterans of the United States of America: 1811 R Street, NW, Washington, DC 20009. Phone: 202-265-6280; website: www.jwv.org.

Independence Day (July)

Fireworks, barbecues, and picnics—these are all ways we celebrate the Fourth of July. But what we're really celebrating is freedom and independence. The birth of the United States of America on July 4, 1776, established a nation that has for more than two hundred years held freedom and democracy among its primary values and acted as a beacon for those values around the world.

At the time of the Declaration of Independence, about two thousand Jews were living in the thirteen colonies. Some of them fought and died in the Revolutionary War, while others helped the war effort in other ways. They include:

- ▶ Francis Salvador—sometimes referred to as the "Paul Revere of the South"—was the first Jew to die in the Revolutionary War, soon after it began, on July 31, 1776. A year before he died, he was elected to the South Carolina state legislature, becoming the first Jew elected to a legislature in the United States (see p. 198 for information about the Salvador Memorial in Charleston, S.C.).
- ▶ Haym Solomon, a Jewish businessman, is largely credited with financing the American Revolution. He raised money to pay for soldiers' clothes, housing, and food.

These individuals fought to create a country where people would be free regardless of religion or class. Today, the United States is truly a dynamic nation made up of diverse people, thanks in part to their efforts. Use this day to explore with your family the topics of freedom, diversity, and the values that are both Jewish and American.

Labor Day (September)

It has become a "last fling of summer" celebration, but Labor Day started as a celebration of workers by the labor unions. In 1884, on the first Monday in September, the Knights of Labor organization held a

big parade in New York City to honor the working class. They decid-
ed to make it an annual event and named it "Labor Day." The Socialist Party held a similar celebration on May 1, known as May Day,
which has since become an international holiday for workers.

In 1894 the U.S. Congress passed a law recognizing Labor Day
as an official national holiday. Today, Labor Day is observed not only
in the United States but also in Canada and other countries.

Many Jewish immigrants were active in the workers rights and
socialist (worker-oriented) movements in New York City from the
time they arrived as immigrants through the 1940s. They were in
groups like the Arbeiter Ring (which means "Workman's Circle" in
Yiddish) and took leading roles in important unions such as the
ILGWU (International Ladies' Garment Workers' Union). Groups like
these worked to ensure that the needs, rights, and safety of working
people would be respected by large companies.

Even if you are not part of the workers movement, were your
parents or grandparents involved in it? Find out, and talk to them
about why labor unions were so important at that time. If you're
lucky, maybe they'll even teach you some folk songs about unions
and workers. Talk with your family about the fairness of labor practices and working conditions today, both in the United States and
abroad. Where unfairness exists, discuss how you each can make a
difference.

Columbus Day (October)

Columbus Day is celebrated on the second Monday in October to
commemorate Christopher Columbus' first
landing in North America, on October
12, 1492. He had set sail a few months
earlier on an expedition sponsored by
Spain.

At that very same time in Spain,
Jews were having an extremely difficult
time. For hundreds of years previously, Spanish Christians, Mus-

lims, and Jews had coexisted in relative harmony. But in the late 1400s, the Spanish monarchs began an Inquisition, overseen by the pope, to enforce Christianity. The year of Columbus' first voyage, 1492, all the Jews who refused to convert to Christianity were expelled from the country.

Because of what was going on in Spain at the time, there are theories that suggest Columbus himself was Jewish and the expedition was partially supported by Jews in search of a refuge. It is almost certainly true that secret Jews were among Columbus' crew members, including Luis de Torres, a close aide and translator to Columbus who was well versed in Hebrew.

Columbus Day offers a wide range of issues for Jewish families to discuss. You can talk about the value of discovery, and perhaps even go for a hike or trip to a place you've never been before (pretend to be explorers!). When thinking about Columbus' interactions with the Native Americans, you can discuss the importance of respecting the property and cultures of others and learn about the connections between Jews and American Indians. (See the book *Jewish Heroes of the Wild West*, listed in our book section on p. 140.) With older kids, it's a good time to discuss the Inquisition and the importance of sticking to your beliefs.

Thanksgiving (November)

Thanksgiving is very compatible with Jewish values. As you spend the day feasting with family, remember to give thanks for all that you have. You can go around the table at Thanksgiving dinner and say one thing for which you're thankful or have the children draw pictures beforehand of those things.

Since the holiday commemorates the feast that newly arrived English settlers shared with Native Americans, ask people at the table who were themselves immigrants to discuss their early experiences in this country and how they adjusted to their new land.

Note that by coincidence, a form of the Hebrew word for "thanks" is also used as the Hebrew word for "turkey," both pronounced "ho-doo."

A great way to show thanks is to give back some of what you have to help others. Donate food and money to a soup kitchen, or spend part of the day helping out there. (Many soup kitchens have Thanksgiving dinners for the needy.)

Fun at Home

Volunteerism:
Mitzvot & Tzedakah

If you've ever done volunteer work you know that it not only makes others feel good but makes you feel good, too. Volunteerism can be a fun and fulfilling experience for everyone involved. Not only that, the act of doing good deeds—sometimes called *tikkun olam* (repairing the world) or *gemilut chasadim* (acts of loving-kindness)—is a cornerstone of Jewish life.

Another Hebrew term used for good deed is *mitzvah*. The more basic meaning of the word though is "commandment." Among the 613 commandments for Jews in the Torah are many good deeds. For instance, there's a commandment to "feed the hungry and clothe the naked," which you can do by volunteering at a soup kitchen or by donating clothes to the needy. And there's a commandment to "honor the elderly," which you can do by visiting a retirement home.

Another commandment is *tzedakah*. We often use this word to mean "charity," but it actually means "righteousness." *Tzedakah* is not just about giving; it's also about recognizing what others actually need. Some may need money, while others may need your time and attention. *Tzedakah* should be well thought out. According to the medieval Jewish scholar Maimonides, the best kind of *tzedakah* helps others to help themselves. As the saying goes: "Give people a fish; they eat for a day. Teach them how to fish; they eat for a lifetime."

There are countless ways for you and your family to perform *mitzvot* (the plural of mitzvah) in your community. In the coming pages, we'll give you some ideas for projects that are helpful, rewarding, and potentially a lot of fun.

Tzedakah in the House

It's often said that "charity begins at home." Not only does that mean helping the people who are closest to you, it also means you can begin communitywide activism right in your own house. Here are some ways to go about doing that.

Make Your Own *Tzedakah* Box

A *tzedakah* box is a container that holds the money you set aside for charity. Any container will do just fine—even the most dilapidated box can hold funds that will be extremely helpful and valuable to someone else. Still, it's nice to decorate your *tzedakah* box. And if having a fun-looking *tzedakah* box helps draw people's eyes to it, donations may come in even quicker!

WHAT YOU NEED:

Materials

▶ old magazines, with lots of pictures
▶ container with removable plastic lid (tennis ball can, coffee tin, etc.)
▶ clear contact paper (optional)

Equipment

▶ glue stick
▶ scissors (and graphic arts knife for parents only)

HOW IT'S DONE:

1. Cut out magazine pictures of *tzedakah*-related items: food, clothing, people, or words that seem to fit with this theme.
2. Glue the pieces of paper onto the container until it is completely covered.
3. Once the glue has dried, cut a slit in the plastic lid that is large enough to allow a quarter to drop in.
4. If you want, you can protect your creation by covering it with clear contact paper.
5. Display your *tzedakah* box somewhere in the house where you will see it and remember to fill it regularly with coins.

Grassroots *Tzedakah*

The possibilities for at-home *tzedakah* are as unlimited as your imagination. Here are a few general ideas, though you and your family can think up any number of others. Some of the activities below are described elsewhere in the book but can be applied to help others:

- ▶ Make get-well cards for the sick. (For instructions on making cards, see p. 18.)
- ▶ Make a meal or bake challah (see p. 6) and donate it to a homeless shelter.
- ▶ Make "care packages" for the elderly. Include fun things like a deck of cards, a joke book, slippers, lipstick, or lip balm.
- ▶ Have a function at your house as a fund raiser for a worthy cause. It could be a party, performance, haunted house, carnival, yard sale, arts and crafts sale, lemonade stand, or anything else that will attract people to come.
- ▶ Organize a basketball or softball game in your neighborhood, and invite the elderly to watch or underprivileged kids to play.
- ▶ Hold a two-on-two basketball tournament in your neighborhood and donate the entry fees to charity.

Mitzvot in the Community

Going beyond the home in family *tzedakah* activities is a great way to show kids how each of them is responsible for the welfare of the community around them. Plus, it offers a terrific opportunity for fun and meaningful family outings.

Showtime at the Retirement Home!

Kids (and parents) who are born performers will always have a captive audience at retirement homes and assisted-living communities. The residents love visitors, especially young ones. Many elderly people have children and grandchildren who live far away; having young people around is the next best thing to having their own family near them.

Activities that kids and parents can prepare and perform together (along with kids' friends) include

- ▸ singing songs
- ▸ storytelling
- ▸ folk dancing
- ▸ putting on a play (based on a familiar story or one you've made up)
- ▸ making a puppet show
- ▸ giving an oral presentation on something of interest (for example, a really neat science experiment done for a school project)

Call the retirement home as far in advance as you can to arrange a visit so the volunteer coordinator can put it in the newsletter or put up signs to announce your activity. That way you'll have a larger audience. Most places are quite enthusiastic about these types of programs; they may even provide punch and cookies or arrange a little party around the event.

If your family isn't the performing type, there are still ways to "perform" a mitzvah at a retirement home. Some possibilities include

- ▸ making paintings and giving them to residents
- ▸ baking cookies for the residents (be sure to check first with the volunteer coordinator about any dietary guidelines you need to follow)
- ▸ donating books for residents to read to the kids

For the elderly, interaction with children is usually so enjoyable that even if you haven't had time to bake cookies or prepare anything, a visit is still appreciated. Sometimes just talking to residents and holding their hands is enough to brighten their day. Maybe a resident would like to watch a sports game on TV with your family or sit around the piano and sing. Some retirement homes have "adopt-a-grandparent" programs, where children are matched up with residents. That way, kids get to bring artwork and cookies to specific people on each visit.

Doing these sorts of activities at hospitals is also nice—whether a children's hospital or otherwise—though many hospitals are not as "performance-friendly" as retirement homes. Some don't allow visitors under age eighteen, while others have strict requirements that all volunteers go through volunteer training. Be sure to find out what all the rules are before you plan a trip to a hospital.

Finally, when you've finished with your visit, talk with your kids about the rewards of doing these kinds of activities. Discuss how it feels to do something nice for someone and how it helps the people you meet.

Some kids like to receive a certificate of achievement for doing the mitzvah. Parents can buy the blank certificates at an office supply store (or download them from the Internet), fill them out, and even frame them. Or better yet, you can organize an arts and crafts activity around designing your own family's "mitzvah certificates," to be awarded whenever a family member performs a good deed.

Special Trips to Special Homes and Shelters

Giving to the needy is always a good lesson for children, but rather than having the Salvation Army or Goodwill pick up items from your home, taking kids to drop off the donation in person makes for an experience they'll never forget.

Most homeless shelters, group homes for kids, and homes for battered women and children will accept several kinds of donated items: furniture, clothing, toys, and household items are usually greatly needed. Call beforehand to find out if they need the item you want to donate, and then arrange a time for the family to deliver the donation.

While anonymous donations are a very special kind of *tzedakah,* it can also be rewarding for kids to visit the shelter where their donated toys are going so they can visualize and better understand this act of charity. Or your child can write a letter to leave with the donated toys, addressed to "Dear Friend" and including your address, so the child who receives the toy can write back. Besides donating items and money, you can give of your time as well. Shelters usually need volunteers, especially in the kitchen. There are lots of ways to include the kids, such as having them bake brownies at home and then serve the treats at lunch at the shelter, or encouraging them to design decorations for a holiday meal.

More Ways to Get Involved

Going out in the community to volunteer as a family—without an arranged group or organization sponsoring the event—is very important because it teaches children that they can make a difference on their own. In addition, there are agencies that have volunteer programs in which you and your kids can take part, and which offer good examples of how a larger community can come together to do a mitzvah.

Great sources for potential family volunteering opportunities are local Jewish community centers or synagogues. Call to find out about programs, which may include helping recent immigrants adjust to life in the U.S. or trips to homeless shelters. Be sure to explain specifically what you and your family would like to do as volunteers because some organizations may simply be looking for volunteers to work in an office or to make calls on the phone. While these are also worthy volunteering projects, they won't offer the same opportunities for hands-on "family fun" *tzedakah.*

One of the best sources for volunteer projects outside the Jewish community is your local branch of the United Way. It can direct you to groups like Habitat for Humanity, a national organization that helps to build suitable homes for low-income families. If you and your family have a specific area of interest (for example, the environment), the United Way can direct you to the organization that's right for you. Volunteering in that area of special interest will only add enthusiasm and enjoyment to the project.

Some other groups to know about:

▶ The Coalition on the Environment and Jewish Life (COEJL), a group providing a Jewish perspective on environmental concerns. Phone: 212-684-6950 x210; e-mail: info@coejl.org; website: www.coejl.org.

▶ Mazon: A Jewish Response to Hunger, a national organization that gives money to local groups that feed the hungry. Phone: 310-442-0020; e-mail: mazonmail@mazon.org; website: www.mazon.org.

Arts & Crafts— and Fun Things to Eat

Around-the-House Designs for Days Around the House

It doesn't have to be a holiday for your family to make Jewish crafts at home. There are plenty of opportunities for family fun projects that are good to do all year round, on a rainy day or just because. Here's a whole bunch.

Mezuzah Magic

While no Jewish home is complete without a mezuzah on the front doorpost, you can also hang *mezuzot* (the plural of mezuzah) in the doorway of almost any room in the house. Kids will love the chance to make a mezuzah for their own bedrooms. These *mezuzot* make great gifts as well.

Here's a way to make a mezuzah from homemade clay. The special prayer scroll that goes inside each mezuzah can be purchased at Judaica stores. Besides this project, your family can use this clay recipe for all sorts of other things as well.

WHAT YOU NEED:

Materials

▶ I cup salt
▶ I ½ cups warm water
▶ 4 cups all-purpose flour
▶ food coloring (optional)
▶ acrylic paints
▶ water-based sealer (nontoxic)

Equipment

▶ mixing bowl
▶ measuring cup
▶ toothpicks
▶ baking pan
▶ paintbrushes

HOW IT'S DONE:

1. Stir the salt into the warm water, and let it cool.
2. If you wish, add drops of food coloring to the water until it becomes the color you want. Otherwise, skip this step, and simply paint your mezuzah later.
3. Add flour to the water and knead it for 8–10 minutes until it has an even, clay-like consistency.
4. Mold the "clay" into the shape of a mezuzah. Make sure you leave the back or inside hollowed out so you can fit the prayer scroll inside. And don't forget to leave two small holes at the top and bottom so you can nail the mezuzah to the doorpost. Other than that, it's entirely up to you how to shape your mezuzah: It can be long and thin, or wide and fat; it can have smooth edges or decorative sides. If you want, use toothpicks to scratch designs—such as Jewish stars or anything else you'd like—into the "clay."
5. Bake the mezuzah in the oven at 325°F for 30–60 minutes until the clay is completely dry and hard. Allow it to cool completely after you remove it.
6. Paint it any colors or designs you choose, and allow the paint to dry completely.
7. Cover the entire mezuzah (including the back) with water-based sealer, and allow it to dry.
8. Insert the scroll, and your mezuzah is ready to be nailed to a doorpost.

Cosmic Judaica: Glow-in-the-Dark Stars of David

Who says you need to be outside to gaze up at the stars? These Jewish stars can shine above you in your bedroom. Kids will love having these glow-in-the-dark stars to decorate their ceiling. And they're all that much more fun when you make them yourself!

WHAT YOU NEED:

▶ white poster board
▶ scissors
▶ newspaper
▶ glow-in-the-dark paint (nontoxic)
▶ paintbrush
▶ double-sided adhesive tape

HOW IT'S DONE:

1. Draw Jewish stars on the poster board. They can be as large or small as you want.
2. Cut out the stars.
3. Paint the stars with the glow-in-the-dark paint. Allow the paint to dry completely.
4. Cover the back of the stars with pieces of double-sided adhesive tape.
5. Stick the stars to the ceiling. (Children should perhaps let their parents take care of this step.)
6. Turn off the bedroom lights, and watch the stars glow.

Playful Place Mats

Since so many Jewish family activities revolve around group meals and great food, personalized place mats are sure to get plenty of use. If you and your children are making placemats for yourselves, let each person design his or her own; if you are making them for others, think of what sort of designs they would like. You can also add the person's name in English or Hebrew.

If you'd like, design your placemats with specific holidays in mind; add symbols and pictures specific to that holiday (e.g., matzah for Passover, apples and honey for Rosh Hashanah). See the Appendix of Stencils on pp. 246–247 for ideas.

WHAT YOU NEED:

Materials
- ▶ white posterboard (11" x 17")
- ▶ clear contact paper

Equipment
- ▶ crayons and markers (various colors)
- ▶ scissors

HOW IT'S DONE:

1. Using the crayons and markers, decorate the piece of posterboard.
2. Cut two pieces of contact paper slightly larger than the posterboard.
3. Unpeel one sheet of contact paper, and carefully lay it down on your work surface with the sticky side up.
4. Carefully lay your posterboard on the contact paper.
5. Repeat steps 3 and 4, covering the other side of the posterboard with contact paper.
6. If necessary, trim the edges of the contact paper.
7. Use your place mat for your next meal!

How to Grow a Family Tree

Here's a project that combines the fun of drawing, coloring, cutting, and pasting with the fascinating subject of family connections. Making a family tree lets children chart their family and maybe even learn something about their ancestors.

WHAT YOU NEED:

Materials

▶ scrap paper
▶ green construction paper
▶ poster board

Equipment

▶ thin-tip black marker
▶ pencil and eraser
▶ crayons, markers, or paint (brown and green, plus other colors)
▶ glue stick

HOW IT'S DONE:

1. Choose a set of grandparents or great-grandparents to be the root of the tree (you can do separate trees for each set of grandparents).

2. On a piece of scrap paper, list all of the sons or daughters that came from your "root couple," along with the husbands or wives of those children. Then, next to each of the sons or daughters, list all of the children that each of the sons or daughters had. Continue this until you reach the youngest generation in your family.

3. With the green construction paper, cut out one small leaf-shaped piece (approximately 2 inches) for each name you have on your list. On each leaf, write the name of one person on your list, proceeding until you have made a leaf for everyone.

4. On your poster board, sketch a large tree (do it first in pencil, in case you mess up). Start with a wide trunk at the base, which then splits into a branch for each child that the grandparents ("root couple") had. Then each of those branches should then split into a smaller branch for each child they had, and so on until you have enough branches to account for the whole family.

5. Use crayons, markers, or paint to color the tree and the grass on the ground.

6. Paste the leaves with the names of the "root couple" on the trunk of the tree. Then on each branch that comes off the trunk, paste the names of their children, along with their children's husbands or wives. On each smaller branch, paste the names of the children's children, and so on until all the names have been pasted.

Tallit "Tie-Dye-enu"

When kids get to be bar/bat mitzvah age (thirteen years old), it's common for them to receive a *tallit*, the prayer shawl worn while in synagogue on Shabbat and holidays. There are many *tallitot* (the plural of *tallit*) available for purchase in Judaica stores and gift shops, but designing your own *tallit* allows you to personalize it in a way that makes wearing it more fun and special.

The only requirement for a *tallit* is that it have four sets of *tzitzit* (tassels—that is, eight strings tied in a particular pattern on the four corners of the shawl). But other than that, there are no limits on how the shawl can look. One relatively easy way to design your own *tallit* is to tie-dye the shawl, using whatever colors and patterns you choose.

Depending on how involved you want to get in putting the whole thing together, this can be a great long-term project for older kids and adults. It's a difficult challenge to go through the process of trimming the material, dyeing the fabric, and then tying on the *tzitzit*, but the thrill of having created a one-of-a-kind *tallit* makes the extra effort worthwhile.

Shawl-om

To make your *tallit*, you must start with a large piece of fabric to make into your shawl. Cotton is the least expensive and easiest to use, though silk also works well. The size of the fabric depends on the wearer. It should be about the length of the person's arm-span and anywhere from 12 inches to 36 inches in width, depending on your preference.

Fabric can be cut to size at a fabric store and comes in many patterns, though plain white is best if you're planning to tie-dye. You'll need to hem the material to create a smooth edge. Or you can buy border trims and sew them onto the edges of the shawl.

It's possible to find a large scarf in a department store or arts-and-crafts store that will already be hemmed and will be the right size for you. That will save you some time preparing the shawl for tie-dyeing.

The Hows-and-Whys of Ties-and-Dyes

Fabric dyes for tie-dye can be bought at arts-and-craft stores. If you buy a set of dyes, it will often come with complete instructions of on how to tie-dye safely and without making a mess of your house. If not, *make sure you get complete instructions* (more detailed than those here) *before you undertake dyeing.*

Basically, you'll need to mix the dyes with water, and depending on the type of dye you get, you may also need to add some other ingredients, such as soda ash and urea. (These may be included in a special tie-dye kit, or ask someone at the store where to get these ingredients.) In addition to the dyeing material, you'll need other supplies to keep the dyeing safe, tidy, and effective.

WHAT YOU NEED:
▶ Rubber bands (to tie around the fabric to create designs)
▶ Rubber or plastic gloves (to protect hands)
▶ Newspaper or plastic lining (to cover your work area and protect surfaces from drips)
▶ Buckets and bowls (to mix the dye in, and/or for dipping the fabric into the dye)
▶ Squeeze bottles or brushes (to apply the dye to the fabric if you don't want to dip the fabric)
▶ Plastic bags (to put the fabric in afterward)
▶ Plenty of paper towels or rags (to cleanup)

Part of the fun and excitement of tie-dyeing is that you never know exactly how it will come out. Experimenting can lead to some amazing designs, though there are also techniques to help you create the design you want. Try some of these basic tying ideas.

HOW IT'S DONE:
1. Use rubber bands to block the dye from reaching certain parts of the fabric.
2. To create a symmetrical design, fold the fabric in half before doing anything else to it with rubber bands or folds.
3. To create stripes, pleat the fabric either vertically or horizontally.

4. To create a bull's-eye design, grab a bit of fabric from the center of the shawl, and tie it off with a rubber band. Tie more rubber bands lower down on the fabric "rope" you are creating. When you apply the dye, put colors between each rubber band.

5. Fold the shawl into triangles (the way flags are folded), and dip the corners into dye to create another interesting design.

6. Follow the dye manufacturer's instructions for drying the fabric and setting the dye. After you've applied the dye, put the shawl into a plastic bag and let it set for at least 3 hours (or overnight). Remove the fabric from the bag, and rinse it to get rid of excess dye. Then remove the rubber bands, and lay the fabric flat to dry.

All-Important Finishing Touches: *Tzitzit* and *Atarah*

Once your shawl is dyed and ready, you need to attach the parts that make the shawl into an official *tallit*. The *atarah* (collar, or "crown"), although not required, is found on nearly all *tallitot*. It is a thin strip (approximately eighteen inches long and two or three inches wide) that goes at the center of one of the long edges. This is the part that wraps around your neck when you drape the *tallit* around you.

The *atarah* can be decorated in many ways; often, the prayer you say when you put on the *tallit* is embroidered or written there (see Appendix of Prayers, p. 240). Or you can simply put your name on the *atarah*, and decorate it with glitter and paint (or perhaps you'd like to tie-dye it as well). Sew the *atarah* on to the shawl, or iron it on using two-sided fabric adhesive.

The final step in creating the *tallit* is to attach and tie the *tzitzit* strings to the four corners of the shawl. Create reinforced loopholes in the corners, ironing on patches there and then punching holes through the patches so that you can string the *tzitzit* through. *Tzitzit* can be purchased from a Judaica store, and they will come with directions on how to tie them. There is a very precise and involved way they must be tied (coiled seven, then eight, then eleven, then thirteen times, separated by double knots). It helps to have a second person assisting when tying.

Then you're ready to go! Congratulations!

Incredible Edibles

The only thing more fun than making a project with the whole family is making a project with the whole family...and then eating it! Here are some fun and delicious activities.

All-Purpose Candy Clay

Make your kitchen into a candy factory with this recipe. With only a few simple ingredients you can design sweets for any occasion: Shape them like a dreidel for Hanukkah; candlesticks for Shabbat; Jewish stars for Yom Ha'Atzmaut; or any other shape for other times of the year (flowers, hearts, etc.). They make great gifts, dinner party desserts, or snacks for around the house.

WHAT YOU NEED:

Ingredients
▶ 10 ounces chocolate
▶ ⅓ cup corn syrup

Utensils (and supplies)
▶ saucepan
▶ nonstick pan or baking sheet
▶ wax paper
▶ stirring spoon
▶ measuring cup

HOW IT'S DONE:

1. Over medium heat on the stove (keep small children at a safe distance) melt the chocolate in a pan, stirring until smooth (or follow package directions for microwave).
2. Add the corn syrup, and blend evenly.
3. Remove the pan from heat, and pour the concoction into a shallow nonstick pan or onto wax paper.
4. Once it has cooled enough to touch, spread it with your fingers into a sheet about ½ inch thick.

5. Cover with a piece of wax paper, and leave it to stiffen for a few hours.
6. Once stiff, the candy clay can be molded into any shape you like.

"Me-shugga" Cookies

Sugar cookies are fun to make and eat any time of the year, but if you can make them into Jewish cookies, they're even more special. (Some say they taste better, too!) Many Judaica stores or general gift shops sell cookie cutters in the shape of Jewish stars and other symbols.

    If you're short on time, buy prepared cookie dough. It works well and tastes good. But if you want to make your cookies from scratch, here's a quick and easy recipe.

WHAT YOU NEED:

Ingredients

- ½ cup butter or margarine, softened
- 1 cup sugar
- 1 egg
- ¼ cup milk
- ½ tsp vanilla
- 2¼ cups flour
- ½ tsp salt
- 2 tsp baking powder
- colored sugar or cake gel

Utensils

- measuring cup
- measuring spoons
- 2 mixing bowls
- stirring spoon
- electric mixer
- bread board or smooth surface
- cookie cutters
- cookie sheet

HOW IT'S DONE:

1. In one bowl, stir the flour, baking powder, and salt.
2. In a second bowl, cream the butter and sugar together with an electric mixer; then add the egg, milk, and vanilla, and beat well.
3. Blend the contents of both bowls together thoroughly; then divide the dough in half and cover both halves with plastic wrap.

4. Chill the dough for 1 hour; then pre-heat the oven to 375°F.

5. On a nonstick (lightly floured) surface, roll the dough out flat so it is about ⅛ inch thick.

6. Using your cookie cutters (dip them into flour first to prevent sticking), cut the dough into the desired shapes.

7. Place the cut dough onto a cookie sheet, and decorate with colored sugar or cake gel.

8. Bake for about 10 minutes.

9. Allow them to cool down before gobbling them up! Makes about 36 or 48 cookies.

Adorable Adornments for Great Gifts

Whether it's for a *chag* (holiday), a *yom hooledet* (birthday), or any old reason, fun gifts and cards need fun wrapping paper and envelopes. And just as a gift is extra-special when it comes with a handmade card (for instructions on making cards, see p. 18), homemade wrapping paper and envelopes add an even more personal touch to the presents you give.

That's a Wrap!

For the most part, making homemade wrapping paper is quick and easy. The main trick is the decorations, for which we recommend you use paint stamps cut from sponges or potatoes. The shapes will depend on the occasion: Cut a dreidel shape for Hanukkah, or queen's crown shape for Purim, or simply a Star of David for general purposes. What other shapes can you and your family think up?

WHAT YOU NEED:

Equipment

▶ scissors and knife

▶ small dishes

Materials

▶ sheets of plain white paper (2' x 2' sheets are a good bet and can be found in art supply stores)

▶ sponges or potatoes

▶ tempera or poster paints (assorted colors as you like)

▶ paper towels

▶ metallic or other permanent markers (assorted colors)

HOW IT'S DONE:

1. Spread out 1 or more sheets of white paper.
2. Adults can cut the sponge or one end of a potato into various shapes to use as stamps.
3. Soak some paper towel swatches in paint. Press the potato stamp or sponge stamp onto the paper towels and then onto the paper. Switch colors, shapes, and patterns to design your own custom-made wrapping paper.
4. Create additional decorations using the markers (see the Appendix of Stencils on pp. 246–247 for ideas).
5. Let the paper dry, then use it to wrap up your gifts!

And the Envelopes, Please...

You'll never need to buy envelopes again! These homemade envelopes can be created in conjunction with your homemade cards and wrapping paper—you can impress friends and relatives with your coordinated designs. Or send these envelopes with holiday or birthday cards.

WHAT YOU NEED:

Materials

▶ paper envelope (card or letter size)

▶ sheet of lightweight cardboard

▶ brown paper grocery bags or construction paper

Equipment

▶ pencil, pen, or thin marker

▶ scissors

▶ glue stick

HOW IT'S DONE:

1. Taking care not to rip the paper, separate the folds of an envelope so that the paper becomes a single flat sheet.
2. Lay the unfolded envelope onto the cardboard, and trace around the edges of the envelope with a pen or marker to draw the shape on the cardboard.
3. Cut out the shape with scissors.
4. Use the cardboard shape as a stencil to trace additional shapes onto the grocery bags or construction paper.
5. Cut out the shapes.
6. Fold the shapes in the same way that the original paper envelope had been folded (before you flattened it) to create new envelopes.
7. Glue the bottom and side flaps of the new envelopes down to secure the envelopes' pockets.
8. Decorate the envelopes with the same stamps and markers you used to design your cards or wrapping paper (see pp. 111–112). Don't forget to leave some space on the front of the envelopes for the name (and address).

Sports, Games & Outdoor Fun

Like a Maccabi

The Maccabiah is the "Jewish Olympics." Held every four years in Israel, it features the top Jewish amateur athletes in all age groups, from all over the world. Events include everything from badminton to basketball, water polo to wrestling. Maccabiah athletes represent their country—but more, the games represent Jewish solidarity throughout the world.

Even if no one in your family qualifies as a "Jewish Olympian," there are still many ways to get involved with Maccabi programs. Maccabi USA/Sports for Israel, which sends the U.S. delegation to the World Maccabiah Games, also sponsors U.S. teams to smaller competitions around the world. And the group supports even smaller local and regional Maccabi events of the Jewish Community Center (JCC) Association of North America.

The JCC Maccabi Games are open to Jewish teenagers ages thirteen to seventeen, regardless of athletic ability. Many local Jewish community centers around the country organize teams to take part in the regional Maccabi Games that are held each summer. Most JCCs have open tryouts. If your local JCC is not participating, or you don't have a local JCC, contact the JCC Association to find out how you can get involved.

Parents can participate as coaches or chaperones. And if there are Maccabi Games planned in your area, you can be a host family for visiting athletes. There's plenty of fun for everyone who takes part.

For more information:

▶ Maccabi USA/Sports for Israel: 1926 Arch Street 4R, Philadelphia, PA 19103. Phone: 215-561-6900; e-mail: maccabi@maccabiusa.com; website: www.maccabiusa.com.

▶ JCC Maccabi Games: JCC Association of North America, 15 E. 26th St., New York, NY 10010. Phone: 212-532-4949; fax 212-481-4174; e-mail: info@jcca.org; website: www. jccmaccabi.org.

Jewish Scouting for Everyone

Like sports, scouting is a great way to get kids involved in outdoor recreation. Just as the Maccabi Games work to reinforce Jewish identity through sports, the National Jewish Committee on Scouting (NJCS) promotes Jewish identity through scouting. Joining the Boy Scouts can be fun and enriching for Jewish boys as they hike, camp, and learn important lessons about teamwork. Through the NJCS, many synagogues sponsor Boy Scout troops. These groups are oriented toward Jewish scouts and may add a Jewish slant to regular scouting activities.

Similarly, the National Jewish Girl Scout Committee, associated with the Girl Scouts of the USA, encourages Jewish girls to get involved in scouting. The organization sponsors programs and gives out awards for Jewish Girl Scouts. It also arranges cultural exchanges with groups like the Israel Boy and Girl Scouts Federation.

Moms and dads can get involved by becoming troop leaders. They can also show support by encouraging kids to use their scouting skills at home or on family camping trips.

For more information:

▶ National Jewish Committee on Scouting: Relationships Division, Boy Scouts of America, 1325 W. Walnut Hill Lane, P.O. Box 152079, Irving, TX 75015-2079. Website: www.jewishscouting.org.

▶ National Jewish Girl Scout Committee: 33 Central Drive, Bronxville, NY 10708. Phone: 914-738-4603; e-mail: NJGSC@aol.com; website: www.njgsc.org.

Go "Ga-Ga" for Ga-Ga

Ga-Ga is a popular kids' game in Israel and at Jewish camps. It's fun and easy but can also be an exciting, fast-paced game.

WHAT YOU NEED:

▶ At least two players, though it's most fun with a large group.

▶ A ball (more than one can be used for large groups). Make sure the ball bounces well; it should be about the size of a basketball but softer (plastic bouncy ones are best).

▶ A playing area. Ga-Ga can be played indoors or outdoors, though playing within a limited (walled or fenced) area makes the game more fun.

HOW TO PLAY:

To start: A referee or leader bounces the ball in the center, and with each bounce all the players say "ga." After three bounces ("ga-ga-ga"), the ball is in play and any player may run up and hit it.

The object of the game is for players to hit other players with the ball, below the knee. Any player hit by a ball below the knee is out.

Players cannot hit the ball with any other part of their body besides their hand and cannot pick up or throw the ball, or else they are out. If a player is hit by the ball, but not below the knee, the player who hit the ball last is out.

If the ball goes out of play, there is a time-out. The referee or one of the players can go get the ball and start the game again by bouncing the ball in the center while others say "ga-ga-ga."

The last person left after everyone else has been eliminated is the winner.

Shesh-besh

Shesh-besh is the Middle Eastern name for backgammon. This is the most common board game in Israel and all throughout the Middle

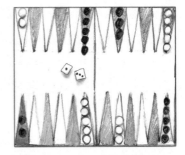

East. The game is too complicated for very young kids, but it's lots of fun for older kids and parents to play.

Shesh-besh involves two opponents who roll dice to move their playing pieces (called "stones") around a board while trying to block the other from doing the same. Basic addition skills are required, and the more you play, the more you'll develop a sense of the strategy required to win this often fast-paced, highly competitive game. And if you get really good, you might even get up the nerve to challenge an Israeli to a game of *Shesh-besh*.

Backgammon boards, complete with dice, stones, and directions how to play, are easy to find in stores where board games such as checkers and chess are sold.

"This Challah's-for-the-Birds" Feeder

Shabbat Shirah, the Sabbath on which the Song of Moses (Exodus 15) is recited, has traditionally been a time for Jews to reflect on and celebrate birds, who are said to sing the praises of God. *Shabbat Shirah* falls in the winter, and in some climates, birds (at least those that haven't flown south for the winter) are having trouble finding enough food to eat. What better way, then, to celebrate *Shabbat Shirah*—or to help out the birds any time of the year—than with an easy-to-make bird feeder?

Just like us, birds love challah (especially on Shabbat), so make the bird feeder out of leftover challah. Simply cover some pieces of challah completely with a thin coat of peanut butter. Then press the pieces into a dish of birdseed until they are completely covered with seeds. That's it!

Now all you have to do is find a place to put your challah bird feeder. Poke the pieces through a low branch on a tree (preferably one too thin for squirrels to get to), or simply place it in the tree securely. Then stand back and let the birds go to eat while you watch to see how many different kinds of birds come to visit your "this challah's-for-the-birds" feeder.

Jewish
Music & Dance

The Parent-and-Kid-Friendly
Jewish Music Guide

Of the many great artists writing and recording music for Jewish families, we've gone through and picked out twenty we think offer the best combination of fun (lyrics and music), accessibility, relevance, musical production quality, and educational value.

Though some of these artists have made other albums, the CDs we've noted are the best ones we know for parents and kids to listen to together. All of them include words and transliteration and are available in both CD and cassette unless noted otherwise.

In addition to Judaica shops, music stores and book stores, you can find many of these recordings online at www.amazon.com, www. jewishmusic.com, www.soundswrite.com, www.jewishstore.com, or other places. In some cases, you can also order the albums through the artists themselves, so we've listed contact information for some of them.

Debbie Friedman

Friedman is probably the most popular composer, performer, and recording artist in the arena of American Jewish music, and her reputation is well earned. She consistently writes terrific songs, plus she has a beautiful voice and great Hebrew pronunciation.

Her most recent children's album, *The Alef Bet*, is a real treat. It's an outstanding collection of Friedman's most popular kids' songs for every day (as opposed to holiday-themed). These original Friedman compositions ("Alef Bet Song," "B'ruchim Habaim," "Im Ein Ani Li") are used widely in camps, schools, and synagogues across the country for good reason—they're both educational and so much fun! The album comes with an activity kit and songbook. We highly recommend it.

Shanah Tovah is an album that takes us through the year with terrific kids' songs for the Jewish holidays and some tunes for anytime. Our favorites include the calypso "Mah Nishtanah" and the exciting ragtime-style "613 Commandments."

Shirim Al Galgalim is a lively holiday album, filled with songs that make you want to get up and dance. It's also quite prayer oriented, with Friedman reciting many of the holiday blessings during the songs. The action-packed, New Orleans marching band–styled "Plant a Tree for Tu B'Shvat" and the country and western "L'Shanah Tovah" (which includes a shofar blowing) offer great melodies and simple lyrics that make it easy for young kids to sing along.

Miracles and Wonders, an album of Hanukkah and Purim tunes, features the Friedman classic "The Latke Song" (recorded by many others) and the funny "Haman's Song," about the ultimate bad guy.

For Jewish family fun music, Debbie Friedman is the place to start.

Craig Taubman

My Newish Jewish Discovery features Craig Taubman, a fantastic musician, songwriter, vocalist, and performer, on what could be the coolest, hippest, and funniest Jewish kids' album you'll find anywhere! The album also manages to deal with important Jewish values such as being yourself, respecting parents, appreciating what you have, and playing fair. "My Mother Called Me a Name" and "A Candle in the Middle" are both funny and cute—and have surprise endings. Taubman's young daughter sings, and Ed Asner reads a poem on the album. You're sure to sing along with the exciting, insanely energetic "Shigaon," and you may even learn a few Hebrew words in the process. Parents and kids of all ages will love this album. Highly recommended.

My Jewish Discovery is also fun and full of great songs. "Holi-Daze," an exciting and hilarious rundown of all the Jewish holidays, sounds like a melody that would be in a Disney movie (not surprising, since Taubman has written music for Disney). "Hanukkah Rap," featuring hip-hop versions of Hanukkah classics (and lines like, "Go, Judah!… Judah's in the house!"), is great as well.

Taubman has also produced the delightful *Celebrate!* compilation boxed set, which includes three CDs (*Celebrate Shabbat, Celebrate Passover,* and *Celebrate Hanukkah*) with various Jewish recording artists taking part, adding their best songs to the collection. And a new children's album called *Celebrate Kids!* is also a great compilation CD. (Contact: 818-760-1077; www.craignco.com.)

Cindy Paley

Paley is a talented and well-known performer of Jewish music, with a beautiful voice and relaxed style that encourage the listener to sing along.

What a Happy Day is a lively collection of terrific everyday songs for young children. Many focus on teaching kids simple Hebrew words, and others are just for fun. Hebrew versions of "Old McDonald Had a Farm" and "If You're Happy and You Know It" are also included.

Zing Along With Cindy Paley collects Yiddish folk songs for children into an album that's well done, both vocally and instrumentally, with a terrific song selection. English narration and stories sprinkled throughout treat us to an entire performance of Yiddish culture. And kids are sure to get a kick out of the song "Oy Mayn Kepele," which includes the lyrics *"Oy mayn tushele* ("Oh my tush!") / Sing this little song / If you've been sitting down too long."

A Singing Seder offers a crash course in Passover melodies. It's a great way to brush up on old songs and learn some new ones, including some Israeli folk songs and the African-American spiritual "Go Down Moses." The album helps you through the whole seder.

Hanukkah: A Singing Celebration will put you in the mood for dreidels, menorahs, and latkes the moment you pop it into the CD player! This fun Hanukkah album includes the blessings as well as all the "Hanukkah classics." Paley introduces the Hebrew songs with a helpful one-line English explanation. (Contact: 818-907-6942; cindypaley@aol.com.)

Peter and Ellen Allard

We highly recommend the Allards' album *Sing Shalom: Songs for the Jewish Holidays*. Ellen Allard's lyrics are clever and catchy; her melodies are fun but also beautiful. Songs range in style from folksy sing-alongs ("Lotsa Lotsa Matzah") to rockin' ditties ("Judah Maccabee, the Hammer") to country and western square dance ballads ("The 15th of Shvat" and "There Are 10"). Then there's "Sukkat Shalom," a sweet, quiet song for Shabbat. Well-produced, with great-sounding voices and instruments, the album takes us through the entire Jewish year. Plus, it's good for all ages. (Contact: 888-746-4481; www.PeterandEllen.com.)

Rich Glauber

The Soul Parade is not a well-known album, but it should be. Glauber, a talented musician and singer, approaches a wide range of values—including family, love, and diversity—in a way that's both smart and funny. While Glauber includes Bible motifs, Jewish foods, and Yiddish expressions, this is not a "religious" album. It takes a humanistic approach to Jewish culture with no mention of holidays or God.

The song "Keep the Dream Alive" mentions Abraham and Sarah but also Martin Luther King and Rosa Parks. The song "Chicken Soup" is a hilarious Shel Silverstein–styled account of a boy's tenth birthday, when his grandmother made him eat every kind of Jewish food imaginable. This well-produced album may be too complex for preschoolers, but it is great for elementary age and up.

Sue Epstein

Nu!?!? From Sue: Fun Jewish Songs Little Kids Love to Sing is a well-produced CD with a real pop sound—very fun, happy, lively, and upbeat. In part, that's because Epstein has a fabulous voice; it's sweet and crisp even when she speaks! And the musicians are also great. Epstein includes a wide variety of songs, including some that are religious in theme (like her beautiful "Ki Eshmera Shabbat"). Except for a couple that are somewhat corny ("Kipah"), the songs (including "Hineh Rakevet" and "Mishpacha Song") are simply adorable.

I've Got That Shabbat Feeling is another feel-good album from Epstein. "I've been Polishing the Candlesticks" (to the tune of "I've been Working on the Railroad") is classic Epstein: she's just so darn cute that you and your kids can't help but love her!

Rabbi Joe Black

Black's *Aleph Bet Boogie* is a blast! It's filled with groovin' blues songs with Jewish themes and a sense of humor that your kids will really appreciate. The title song, "Aleph Bet Boogie," begins: "So you say you want to learn to be cool? That's easy. You go to Hebrew school." Other favorites include a rockin' "Build a Sukkah" and an energetic "Sufganiyot." Black is extremely likable and relaxed and ends the album by teaching us a few Israeli sing-alongs. He's having such a good time, it's impossible for listeners not to have fun as well!

Everybody's Got a Little Music is another a good album from Black, with standout tracks like the hilarious "Latke Hamentaschen Debate" and the country-style "Yodel Dreidel." The album combines fun songs with terrific instrumentation. (Contact: 505-344-6230.)

Rachel Buchman

On Buchman's Hanukkah CD *Shine Little Candles,* the liner notes say "Rachel Buchman is having a Hanukkah party and we're all invited!" That's exactly what this album feels like. Buchman is charming as she hosts this musical extravaganza. She does different character voices, tells stories, and sings a variety of Hanukkah songs in English, Hebrew, Yiddish, and Ladino. Buchman also chooses a nice group of guests for her party; on the album we hear from an older Yiddish-speaking couple, some Israeli parents, and a bunch of lively kids.

Guest kids and parents also show up on Buchman's *Jewish Holiday Songs for Children,* a twenty-three-song CD that is notable not only for its fine arrangements and performances but also for its unusual selection of mostly lesser-known holiday music, including songs for Lag B'Omer and Tu B'Shvat. Buchman also has CDs of secular children's music, including *Sing a Song of Seasons.*

Alan Eder and Friends

Reggae Passover is an enjoyably unique musical experience for the whole family. Alan Eder, an expert in the area of African music, has produced a refreshing album that takes traditional themes of Passover and presents them in a quite untraditional way, with West African and reggae instruments, rhythms, and melodies. Along with a large group of excellent musicians, Eder takes us on an exciting journey to a place where Passover's theme of freedom seems to fit right in. Eder also offers karaoke versions of six of the songs at the end of the CD, so that you and your family can sing the lead vocals the next time around.

Reggae Hanukkah is another really good album of Eder's that we like almost as much. Besides the reggae, ska, and drumming found on the first album, there are also Middle Eastern, Brazilian, and Latin influences. (Contact: 805-297-0374; e-mail: ReggaePass@aol.com.)

Tanja Solnik

Generation to Generation: A Legacy of Lullabies is a beautiful collection of quiet Yiddish, Ladino, and Hebrew songs. Solnick's gorgeous voice makes it the perfect album to relax to—or for putting baby to sleep. It includes Jewish lullaby classics like "Rozhinkes Mit Mandlen," "Durme, Durme," and "Numi, Numi." (Contact: 615-383-8141.)

Paul Zim

Cantor Paul Zim, the self-proclaimed "Jewish Music Man," has been performing and recording Jewish music for years. He has several albums aimed at younger Jewish listeners that are quite entertaining. He's an enjoyable old-school Jewish performer—think Borscht Belt meets Barney. Spoken narratives often introduce his songs, and the choruses feature children's voices.

Zimmy Zim's Zoo includes eighteen songs about animals. There are classic Hebrew kids' songs like "Shubi Dubi" (about a teddy bear) and some folk songs in English like "Goin' to the Zoo."

The Kooky Cookie Kids is a sing-along album for preschoolers. The songs are cute: "Wiggle Your Fingers" asks kids to do motions as they listen to the song; "Put a Chicken in the Pot" (to the tune of "London Bridge Is Falling Down") is about preparing chicken soup for Shabbat.

If you like these albums Zim has many more, including *It's Jewish Holiday Time*, which takes us on a train ride through the Jewish year, and other children's recordings devoted to Shabbat, Hanukkah, Passover, and Israeli folk songs. (Contact: Sameach Music 888-3-SAMEACH; www.paulzim.com.)

Sally and the Daffodils

Tap Your Feet to a Jewish Beat is adorable. Sally Heckelman enlists a group of fourteen kids from her street—Daffodil Lane in Silver Spring, Maryland—to form her backup singers, the Daffodils. Her own children are in the group, and some of the kids' parents make guest-singing appearances as well. The album features twenty songs for Shabbat, holidays, and anytime, including a mix of songs by other contemporary artists, original arrangements of traditional songs, and completely original material. While the vocals are for the most part just average, the instruments—such as on the energetic "Hey Artzenu/Tzena" medley—are excellent and lots of fun. (Contact: 301-649-7042.)

Serenade

This group's album *Best of Serenade* is not specifically for kids, but we're listing it here because side two of the album is fantastic for Israeli folk dancing! It has all the most basic Israeli dancing songs, including songs to accompany some of the dances we teach you how to do (see pp. 134–138). The album has been out for more than twenty years, but it's still the best one around that has all these songs ("Mayim," "Tsena Tsena," "Zemer Atik," "Tayish," etc.). There are no words or transliteration. (Contact: 707-823-3916.)

Fran Avni

Avni's *Latkes and Hamentashen* is presented like a storybook: Hanukkah on side one and Purim on side two, told with a combination of narration and original songs. The songs are all in English, with cute, simple lyrics that are perfect for young kids. The album has an activity book to go along with it (sold separately).

The Seventh Day is a nice Shabbat album, with a mix of familiar songs and great original ones. This cassette-only album has a jazzy feel that's lots of fun, though it doesn't come with written lyrics. (Contact: FAVNI@aol.com.)

Jill Moskowitz

Miracles: Hanukkah and Passover Songs for Kids features some of the very best and most singable songs for these two holidays. Moskowitz includes some traditional melodies, some originals, and some that other artists have made popular. The recording is simple but sweet, with just Moskowitz's voice, a few instruments, and a group of young children singing along. "Lots of Latkes," sung in a round with the sounds of latkes frying, dreidels spinning, and Maccabees marching, is particularly fun. (Contact: jillm@savion.huji.ac.il.)

Margie and Ilene

Just in Time for Hanukkah contains all the Hanukkah "classics" as well as the prayers. Margie Rosenthal and Ilene Safyan have beautiful voices and great Hebrew pronunciation, with simple acoustic guitar and flute accompaniment. This is a wonderful album the whole family will enjoy.

Around our Shabbat Table includes beautiful songs that'll set the Shabbat mood in your home. Many of the songs are somewhat formal, but there's also an exciting bluegrass "L'Cha Dodi" (set to the tune of "She'll be Comin Round the Mountain") that's sure to get the whole family jumping! (Contact: 503-221-1848; ILESAF@home. com; www.sheeramusic.com)

Peri Smilow

Songs of Peace starts with a terrific "Hineh Ma Tov" medley, ends with a very pretty "Sim Shalom," and contains lots of great songs in between. Smilow has a beautiful voice and is accompanied by lots of great musicians (drums, violin, clarinet, cello, horns, flute). She includes traditional Hebrew folk songs, some rearranged with original melodies and others set to familiar modern melodies (including a romping "Lo Yisa Goy" to the tune of "Down By the Riverside"). This is not specifically a children's album, but it's one the whole family will enjoy. (Contact: 617-868-1129; www.perismilow.com.)

Myrna Cohen

Lullabies & Quiet Time starts out upbeat and lively, and though it gradually winds down we recommend it more for quiet-time than for actual sleep-time. She has a gorgeous, warm voice (though her Hebrew pronunciation is not great). It's terrific for preschool and early elementary school kids. Singing along with Cohen as she teaches us some Hebrew words *("Slicha, Toda, B'Vakasha")* and Jewish values *("Mitzvah Goreret Mitzvah")* is a group of young children. You can buy this album on cassette by itself or on a double CD with another one of Cohen's recordings, *Special Days*. (Contact: 800-9-SOUND-9; www.soundswrite.com.)

Mark Bloom

Funky Punky Holidays, which features songs about the holidays and other Jewish themes, shows Bloom to be both a talented musician and a lyricist (though not particularly funky or punky). One particular favorite, "When You Speak a Little Yiddish," is a ballad about the Yiddish language; it's also nice when Bloom's children make guest appearances on the album. His songs offer plenty of fun but also have a lot of words, so they're better for families with kids over age ten. (Contact: 612-553-2679; www.markbloom.com.)

Robbo

A Part of a Chain: Fun Jewish Songs for Your Family is a well-produced album that tells stories from the Bible and deals with contemporary Jewish themes as well. "Tower of Babel" has funny lyrics, and Robbo (Robb Zelonky) provides theatrical performances throughout. Since he's a Hebrew school music teacher, he can get away with a song like "Hebrew School Blues," which is sung from a kid's perspective, whining about having to go to Hebrew school. (Contact: 888-999-SING.)

Kids' Favorites from Israel

Unlike the albums featured above, these popular kids-oriented recordings are made in Israel and feature mostly Hebrew songs. They're not as easy to find in regular music stores, but some Judaica stores have a nice selection of Israeli music.

Shlomo Gronich and the Sheba Choir

This Ethiopian children's choir sings beautiful Hebrew songs, often incorporating African-style melodies and rhythms. With a mix of popular Gronich originals and traditional tunes, this album is great for kids of all ages. Parents will love it too!

Ofra Haza

With a gorgeously sweet voice and exotic style all her own, this popular Yemenite-Israeli singer (who passed away in February 2001) performs classic Israeli children's songs on *Songs for Children.* It's a really fun album that the whole family will enjoy.

Ha Keves Ha Shisa Asar

This album, an Israeli version of *Free to Be You and Me*, is still popular more than twenty years after its release. Featuring songs written and sung by popular Israeli singers like Yoni Rechter, David Broza, Gidi Gov, Yehudit Ravitz, and Yonatan Geffen, it's a fun collection that's easy to sing along with and is geared especially toward young kids. Plus, sold separately, there's a picture book with the words to all the songs.

Festival Shirey Yeladim: Volumes 1, 2, 3

This is an outstanding collection of some of the most popular Israeli childrens' songs. These catchy tunes originated at the Children's Song Festivals in Israel, written and recorded in the 1960s and 1970s. They were recently re-released on this series of CDs, with new and old Israeli singers appearing.

Kool Klezmer and Alternative Jewish Music for Teens

While teens may feel like they've outgrown much of the children's and family-oriented music listed above, you'll be happy to know there are many great contemporary artists making Jewish-styled music that will surely appeal to older kids—and adults as well. Modern groups are combining traditional Jewish sounds with jazz, rock, reggae, and even hip-hop to create some of the most exciting and eclectic music around today. Here's just some of the most listener-friendly "new klezmer" and other left-of-center Jewish music choices that are available through Amazon.com (or other online record stores) or at your local CD store.

Klezmatics

Aside from the somewhat more traditional Klezmer Conservatory Band, this New York group is perhaps the best known of the contemporary klezmer bands, with members active in many areas (including KlezKamp [see p. 212], Living Traditions, and lots of sideline klezmer bands). Of the group's many albums, *Jews with Horns* and *Rhythm & Jews* are the most fun. Though more oriented toward secular Yiddish culture than religion, many of the Klezmatics' songs offer subtle messages of tolerance and social action as well as a terrific combination of traditional (Hasidic melodies), folk (Yiddish labor songs), and contemporary popular music.

New Orleans Klezmer Allstars

Fresh Out the Past and *The Big Kibosh*, the two widely available CDs by this talented young Louisiana instrumental group, are worth seeking out. There's not much that's overtly religious here (some of the band members are not even Jewish), but there are plenty of hip cultural references and great contemporary klezmer music that gets mixed with some wonderful New Orleans jazz.

Hasidic New Wave

A group headed by Klezmatics' trumpeter Frank London, Hasidic New Wave dedicates itself largely to creating brash and exciting (and sometimes noisy) modern jazz music with traditional Jewish melodies. Hasidic *niggunim,* as well as Ladino and *Mizrachi* (often translated as Middle Eastern and North African) elements, are combined with a healthy dose of irreverence (one song is called "Hebe Bop") on their albums, including *Jews and the Abstract Truth* and *Psycho-Semitic.* The group's latest CD, *From the Belly of Abraham,* is a collaboration with Senegalese drum ensemble Yakar Rhythms that's subtitled "Adventures of the Afro-Semitic Diaspora."

Don Byron

This eclectic African-American clarinetist has, since his days with the Klezmer Conservatory Band, been one of klezmer's most accomplished musicians. *Don Byron Plays the Music of Mickey Katz,* his tribute to the popular klezmer musician from the 1950s, captures both Katz's "shticky" side ("Frailach Jamboree") as well as some seriously terrific playing. What's more, Byron's ability to cross cultures sends an important message about respect for the traditions of others and about music's power to overcome ethnic differences. (Unfortunately, he no longer plays klezmer as part of his live or recording repertoire.)

King Django

King Django, a popular figure on the independent ska scene, investigates his Jewish heritage on the album *King Django's Roots & Culture*. With a combination of ska and reggae rhythms, klezmer touches, and Jewish themes, King Django offers a very cool take on some very old material (including a ska "Heveinu Shalom Aleichem").

Wally Brill

Brill's remarkable album *The Covenant* combines modern electronic "ethno-techno" music with samples from his collection of old 78-rpm records of famous early twentieth-century cantors. Cutting-edge even by the standards of popular music, tracks like "Kiddush Le-Shabbat" (featuring Cantor Ben Zion Kapov-Kagen and an exotic "trance" rhythm) works as a tool for learning the Shabbat prayers and wouldn't sound out of place in a dance club, either.

Zohar

Similar to Brill but even more sophisticated in its blending of cantorial music and dance beats with classical and Middle Eastern elements, the U.K. duo Zohar have released two terrific CDs, *Elokainu* and *One.Three.Seven*. Everything from the voice of famed cantor Moshe Koussevitzky and Israeli pop singer Zehava Ben to Arab and English vocalists combine with cutting-edge electronic music for cohesive, peaceful, and thoroughly contemporary music.

Knitting on the Roof

A wonderfully irreverent tribute to that most famous of Jewish musicals, this compilation comes courtesy of Knitting Factory Records, one of the best sources of weird and progressive Jewish music (also home to Hasidic New Wave). Underground favorites such as the Residents,

Magnetic Fields, Eugene Chadbourne, and Negativland have their way with "Matchmaker," "If I Were a Rich Man," and others. The interpretations are not always completely successful, but they're always interesting.

Festival of Light (Vols. 1 and 2)

These compilations were marketed by mainstream record labels as Hanukkah albums, though only some of the songs actually have holiday themes. Still, there's a wide variety of Jewish-related music, with styles including alternative pop (They Might Be Giants), rock (Marc Cohn, Peter Himmelman with David Broza), New Age (Rebbe Soul), jazz (Don Byron), folk (John McCutcheon), and electronic (Wally Brill).

Israeli Folk Dancing: *Motza'ei-Shabbat* Fever!

As the state of Israel was forming in the 1940s, Israeli folk music and dances were made up on the spot as part of the whole new culture that was developing. You can feel the energy and excitement in these songs and dances and even in the ones that are still being created today. They combine the traditions of Jews that were coming to Israel from all over the world: Europeans, Yemenites, and Jews from other Arab countries.

These days, in many communities around the world, families can take part in Israeli folk dancing sessions at synagogues, universities, Jewish community centers, camps, or other organizations.

Here are some simple Israeli folk dances and basic steps to get you going.

Dance 101: Basic Steps

Tcherkessia (pronounced "chur-ka-ZEE-ah")

This step is based on an old Russian dance from the Tcherkessian (Circassian) mountains. The step has four beats, but your left foot stays in the same place during all four beats. (Imagine you have some gum stuck on your left foot as you hold it to the floor.) Start with your feet next to each other, facing forward. To count the four beats, you can say "chur-ka-zee-ah."

HOW IT'S DONE:

▶ Beat 1: Step directly forward with your right foot.
▶ Beat 2: Rock your weight back on your left foot. (Remember, don't pick up that foot!)
▶ Beat 3: Step directly backwards with your right foot, behind your left foot.
▶ Beat 4: Rock your weight again back to your left foot.
▶ Repeat again and again.

Grapevine

This is the main step in many basic Israeli dances, including Mayim and Tzena. People also often do the Grapevine step in hora dances (or if you're not very coordinated, you can just run or jump around in a circle for the hora).

This step is like the Tcherkessia, with four beats, but instead of keeping one foot planted, we're constantly moving toward the left. Start with your feet together, toes pointed forward, then move "front, side, back, side." Let your hips swivel, following your right foot naturally, "front, side, back, side."

HOW IT'S DONE:

▶ Beat 1: With your right foot, step to the left, crossing in front of your left foot.
▶ Beat 2: With your left foot, step to the left.

▶ Beat 3: With your right foot, step to the left, crossing in back of your left foot.

▶ Beat 4: With your left foot, step to the left, to end up as you started.

"Front, side, back, side. Front, side, back, side." Repeat this over and over.

Stepping Forward: Some Easy Dances

Tzena

This dance goes along with the popular song "Tzena," which, if you don't know how it goes, is easy to find on Israeli music compilation albums (like the Serenade album, see p. 128). The different parts of the dance go along with parts of the song, so it's much easier to learn this dance if you can sing along or listen to the music.

HOW IT'S DONE:

▶ Section 1: Do eight sets of the Grapevine step, moving to the left (or clockwise in a circle).

▶ Section 2: When the high part of the song begins, start with the right foot and skip to the right (counter-clockwise around the circle) sixteen times.

▶ Section 3: During the four strong beats of "Tze-na, Tze-na," bounce in place four times, then immediately go into three repetitions of the four-beat Tcherkessia step. Clap on the first beat of each Tcherkessia as you step forward.

Repeat section 3, then start from the beginning again.

Mayim

This is probably the best-known Israeli folk dance. When you have the music to follow along to (or can sing it), it's also easy to do.

HOW IT'S DONE:

▶ Section 1: Do four Grapevine steps to the left.

▶ Section 2: When the song goes, "Mayim, Mayim, Mayim, Mayim," start with your right foot and, with each of the four beats, take a step (so it's four steps) into the center of the circle, lifting your arms up as you go in toward the center. Clap your hands on the fifth beat as you step in place with your right foot. Then take four steps backwards with each beat, starting with your left foot, bending down slightly and lowering your arms as you move away from the center of the circle. (Imagine you are drawing the water, or *mayim*, out of the well as you come in, and then spilling the water out as you move out.)

▶ Section 3: When the song goes, "Hey! Hey! Hey! Hey!," turn to your left and, starting with the right foot, jog forward four steps (clockwise around the circle).

▶ Section 4: On the next "Mayim, Mayim" section, bounce for eight beats on your left foot. Meanwhile with your right foot, step lightly forward, directly in front of your left foot on the odd beats (1, 3, 5, 7) and then lightly back to the right side on even beats (2, 4, 6, 8). After eight beats (step hard on the eighth beat), switch and do this with the opposite feet. Bounce on the right foot, stepping lightly with the left foot in front of the right, then back to the side, eight times. This time, clap on every odd beat.

Repeat the whole thing over again, for the duration of the song.

Bottle Dance (Flasch Tanz, *in Yiddish*)

This is a stunt that would be done at weddings in Eastern Europe to fulfill the mitzvah of entertaining the bride and groom. Kids pick up this dance very quickly and love it. When you do the bottle dance at a wedding, you're not just showing off, you're entertaining!

HOW IT'S DONE:

▶ Step 1: Take a plastic liter bottle with a little liquid in it (maybe a fifth of the way full). Wear a hat that will allow the bottle to balance on your head.

▶ Step 2: Place the bottle on your head and practice trying to stand still.

▶ Step 3: Now practice walking carefully.

Soon you'll be able to progress to more difficult things, like moving side to side, jumping up and down, or squatting. Now you're doing the bottle dance. (And if all else fails, you can cheat by attaching the bottle to your hat with Velcro!)

Kozatzke

This is based on the Ukrainian dance of the Cossacks but has become a traditional Jewish dance over the years. Grab a friend or sibling, get in the middle of the circle at any bar mitzvah or wedding, do the Kozatzke, and you'll be the hit of the party! The dance takes two people.

HOW IT'S DONE:

▶ Step 1: Grab a partner. Squat down and face each other.
▶ Step 2: Extend arms in front of you, cross them, and hold hands—right hand to right hand, and left hand to left hand.
▶ Step 3: Each of you put your right leg out while keeping your left leg bent. Then quickly change so that your left leg is out and right leg is bent.
▶ Step 4: Repeat this over and over as fast as you can, switching with each beat of the music if possible.

You can also do the Kozatzke by yourself, with your arms crossed over your chest. But it's more fun to do holding on to someone else, and it's easier to learn that way.

Books & Stories
for Jewish Families

Family Fun Books

Jews are not known as "the People of the Book" just because of our deep connection to the Torah. The Jewish love of books extends beyond religious texts to include books of just about every kind—including great children's and family books. There have been thousands of books published that would be great additions to a Jewish family library, and obviously we couldn't include them all here. The books listed below are our suggestions of just some of the great Jewish kids' books widely available for purchase through book stores and online book sites (including www.amazon.com and www.jewishstore.com) or by contacting the publishers directly (see listing at the end of this section).

▶ All-Around Fun and Adventure

The Best of K'Tonton: The Greatest Adventures in the Life of the Jewish Thumbling, K'Tonton Ben Baruch Reuben, by Sadie Rose Weilerstein, illus. By Marilyn Hirsh (Jewish Publication Society, 1988)

Great for ages six and up, the collection of sixteen stories about the beloved "Jewish Tom Thumb" follows K'Tonton's adventures through each of the Jewish holidays.

The Do-It-Yourself Jewish Adventure Series, by Kenneth Roseman (UAHC Press, 1993)

This terrific series of books, geared toward early teens, is designed so that the reader is the main character and must make choices that direct the course of the story. Depending on the choices, the story can have many possible outcomes, making for an exciting read that takes us on a first-hand tour through Jewish history. There are six volumes so far, including *The Melting Pot: An Adventure in New York, The Other Side of the Hudson: A Jewish Immigrant Adventure,* and *The Cardinal's Snuffbox.*

Great Jews in the Performing Arts, by Darryl Lyman (Jonathan David Publishers, 1999)

More a reference text than something you'd read with your child from cover to cover, this book has sections on one hundred different Jewish performing artists and small blurbs on two hundred others. Included are Jerry Seinfeld, Adam Sandler, Roseanne Barr, Tina Louise, Rosanna and Patricia Arquette, the Three Stooges, and Harrison Ford (who knew?!).

Jewish Heroes of the Wild West, adapted for young readers by Marian Maidens (Bloch/American Jewish Historical Society, 1997)

This is an adaptation for young readers of the book *Jews among the Indians* by M. L. Marks. It tells the story of four Jews from the nineteenth century who played important roles in exploring and settling the West and who had close interactions with the Native Americans who lived there (one even became an Indian chief!). Though the book is too complex for very young children, kids ages nine and up will find these stories very interesting.

Jews in Sports, by Joseph Hoffman, illus. by Janet Zwebner (Pitspopany Press, 1996)

A combination of factual histories on extraordinary Jewish athletes—from long ago as well as recently—and fun cartoon seek-and-find games, this book strikes a perfect balance to keep sports fans of all ages fascinated.

The Story of the Jews: A 4,000 Year Adventure, by Stan Mack (Jewish Lights Publishing, 2001)

For older kids, particularly those who love comics, this book is a must-have. Famed cartoonist Stan Mack presents a brief but authoritative history of the Jewish people in comic book form, from the time of Abraham up to the present day. With lively illustrations, an appropriate use of humor, and easy-to-follow explanations of some complex issues, the pages of Mack's history read quickly and stick with you afterward.

Wandering Stars: An Anthology of Jewish Fantasy & Science Fiction, edited by Jack Dann (Jewish Lights Publishing, 1998)

This unique book for teens and adults will thrill the science fiction fans in your house. Originally published in 1974, the collection of short stories features work by Isaac Asimov (who also writes the introduction), Bernard Malamud, Isaac Bashevis Singer, and more. With story titles like "On Venus, Have We Got a Rabbi," how can you go wrong? A second volume, *More Wandering Stars: An Anthology of Outstanding Stories of Jewish Fantasy & Science Fiction,* was published in 1999.

▶ Favorite Folk Tales

The Adventures of Hershel of Ostropol, by Eric A. Kimmel, illus. by Trina Schart Hyman (Holiday House, 1995)

This colorful collection of ten Yiddish folk tales centered on Hershel, a legendary Jewish trickster, is a delight for children (ages four and up) and parents alike.

The Boy Who Stuck Out His Tongue: A Yiddish Folk Tale, by Edith Tarbescu, illus. by Judith Christine Mills (Barefoot Books, 2000)

This is a funny story of a naughty boy who sticks his tongue out one too many times—and gets it stuck to a wrought-iron fence. The whole town comes together to help free him.

The Diamond Tree: Jewish Tales from Around the World, by Howard Schwartz and Barbara Rush, illus. by Uri Shulevitz (HarperCollins, 1991)

A collection of fifteen Jewish folk tales from all over the world, featuring fun illustrations. Great for parents and kids of all ages, particularly older kids.

God Said Amen, by Sandy Eisenberg Sasso, illus. Avi Katz (Jewish Lights Publishing, 2000)

A sweet, fanciful, and often funny story that everyone can identify with, about the importance of meeting people half way. Based on an old Hasidic tale, with delightful illustrations by our own Avi Katz, this book has a message for kids and grown ups about not letting personal ego get in the way of what's best for everyone.

Golem, by David Wisniewski (Clarion Books, 1996)

This new version of the famous Jewish "Frankenstein" story is extremely well done—it even won the prestigious Caldecott Medal. Older children will be thrilled by this monster tale, and adults will be surprised at how subtle and sophisticated it is. Younger children, however, will find it scary and perhaps even sad, so use discretion.

It Could Always Be Worse: A Yiddish Folk Tale, by Margot Zemach (Farrar Strauss & Giroux, 1990)

A favorite Jewish folk tale with a sly lesson of how everything—even misfortune—is relative. Well-illustrated and told for young readers.

Joseph Had a Little Overcoat, by Simms Taback (Viking, 1999)

A Caldecott Medal winner, this richly detailed, ingeniously designed book adapts the old Yiddish folk tale about how to make "something from nothing." It's essentially the same story as *Something from Nothing*, which we also recommend in this section, but the books vary in execution and are wonderful for different reasons. You probably don't need both, but you won't go wrong with either.

The Mysterious Visitor: Stories of the Prophet Elijah, by Nina Jaffe, illus. by Elivia Savadier (Scholastic, 1997)

This collection of eight stories, drawn from folk tales that span the entire Jewish world, deals with Elijah's mythic appearances. A rich theme in Jewish writing, these Elijah stories make fun and exciting reading for older children, and they're great for reading aloud to younger kids as well. This was given the Sydney Taylor Book Award, presented by the Association of Jewish Libraries for outstanding Jewish children's books.

Seven Animal Stories for Children, by Howard I. Bogot and Mary K. Bogot, illus. by Harry Araten (Pitspopany Press, 1997)

Each of these short stories teaches a different value such as respect, modesty, or honesty. "Thinking thoughts" at the end of each story encourage further discussion between parent and child. Recommended for children ages five and up.

Something From Nothing, by Phoebe Gilman (Scholastic, 1992)

A clever retelling of this touching Yiddish folk tale of how to make something from nothing, this will delight parents and children of any age. A wonderful side story involving mice (told in pictures) provides even more fun.

Ten Traditional Jewish Children's Stories, by Gloria Goldreich, illus. by Jeffrey Allon (Pitspopany Press, 1996)

This collection offers a great overview of some of the best and most famous Jewish stories, including tales of Chelm, Hershel of Ostropol, the Golem, and more. In addition, each story ends with questions for further thought and discussion. Recommended for readers ages eight and up.

While Standing on One Foot: Puzzle Stories and Wisdom Tales from the Jewish Tradition, by Nina Jaffe and Steve Zeitlin, illus. by John Segal (Henry Holt, 1996)

A great collection of eighteen stories that keep readers involved in the action by asking them to solve puzzles and come up with solutions to challenging and thought-provoking questions. Terrific for reading with kids ages eight and up.

The Wise Shoemaker of Studena, by Syd Lieberman, illus. by Martin Lemelman (Jewish Publication Society, 1994)

This folksy Jewish twist on the "don't judge a book by its cover" theme features lively illustrations and is likely to draw cackles of laughter from young children.

▶ Bible Stories and More

Benjy's Bible Trails, by Chaya M. Burstein (Kar-Ben Copies, 1991)

Though the book is centered on Benjy's travels to Israel, the real action comes through a wealth of fun activities that are suitable for young children, including word search, seek and find, and coloring pages.

The Book of Miracles: A Young Person's Guide to Jewish Spiritual Awareness, written and illustrated by Lawrence Kushner (Jewish Lights Publishing, 1997)

A great book for kids nearing bar and bat mitzvah age to share with their parents, this slim volume conveys the relevance and beauty of Jewish values and belief through parables, *midrashim*, and examples drawn directly from biblical texts. Written in a straightforward but sophisticated style (for kids ages 10 and up), the book manages to be simple and clear without talking down to smart kids.

But God Remembered: Stories of Women from Creation to the Promised Land, by Sandy Eisenberg Sasso, illus. Bethanne Andersen (Jewish Lights Publishing, 1995)

With four stories about women mentioned only briefly in the Bible or known through *midrashim,* this book relies on the author's imagination to flesh out the important roles female heroines played behind the scenes in biblical times. Each tale points to a greater lesson about Jewish values, suggesting why these women should be remembered.

Daughters of Eve: Strong Women of the Bible, by Lillian Hammer Ross, illus. by Kyra Teis (Barefoot Books, 2000)

Talk about Girl Power! This book tells the stories of eleven women whose names may not be very prominent in the Bible but are very strong role models for girls and women of today. We hear stories about Miriam, Zipporah, Ruth, and more. For ages ten and up.

Does God Have a Big Toe? Stories About Stories in the Bible, by Marc Gellman, illus. by Oscar de Mejo (HarperCollins Children's Books, 1993)

Not actually Bible tales, but rather modern *midrashim* (amplifications of Bible stories), older kids (ages eight and up) will love these funny, smart stories that provide fresh meanings and new understandings of age-old tales. Gellman did a sequel called *God's Mailbox.*

In Our Image: God's First Creatures, by Nancy Sohn Swartz, illus. Melanie Hall (Jewish Lights Publishing, 1998)

A beautifully told tale of how the animals and all that God had created took part in determining what humans would be like. Adapted from the biblical story of man's creation, it illustrates how all things are connected in nature.

King Solomon and the Queen of Sheba, by Blu Greenberg and Linda Tarry, illus. by Avi Katz (Pitspopany Press, 1997)

This is a story of interracial marriage in the Bible. King Solomon and the Queen of Sheba meet, fall in love, get married, and conceive a child, but then have to go their separate ways. With beautiful illustrations, this book imagines how the Jewish religion might have come to Ethiopia.

Noah and the Great Flood, by Mordicai Gerstein (Simon & Schuster, 1999)

Gerstein's retelling of the Bible's Noah tale is augmented with details drawn from folklore and the author's own imagination. The additions make the tale even more magical and entertaining (featuring giants and made-up creatures), and they add new layers of meaning. Gerstein also has a great version of the Jonah story called *Jonah and the Two Great Fish,* and both books are suitable for kids ages four and up.

Sefer Ha-Aggadah: The Book of Legends for Young Readers, by Seymour Rossel, illus. by Judy Dick (UAHC Press, 1998)

This is an English translation and adaptation for young readers of the classic work compiled by Hayim Nahman Bialik, which covers Bible legends and tales of the sages. A rich and important work of Jewish/Hebrew literature, this is a wonderful addition to any family's library. (An activity book supplement is also available.)

The Ten Commandments for Jewish Children, by Miriam Nerlove (Albert Whitman, 1999)

This lovely book begins with a summarized version of the story of Moses receiving the Ten Commandments. Then the book presents each of the commandments, one by one, in a manner easy for children to grasp and with beautiful, sensitive illustrations by the author.

▶ Israel Exploration

Chicken Man, by Michelle Edwards (Lothrop, Lee & Shepard, 1991)

A charming tale of Rody the "Chicken Man," who makes working with the chickens seem like so much fun that everyone else on the kibbutz wants to do it. A National Jewish Book Award winner, it's great for younger kids.

Imagine Exploring Israel, by Marji and Michael Gold-Vukson (Kar-Ben Copies, 1993)

Each page of this creative drawing book provides some ideas and instructions for pictures to draw, each designed around an Israeli theme. It's suitable for all ages.

Kids Love Israel, Israel Loves Kids: A Travel Guide for Families, by Barbara Sofer, photos by Karen Benzian (Kar-Ben Copies, 1996)

This guide to Israel's many sites and attractions is especially designed with kids in mind. It is a handy resource for parents and older kids on family trips. Given the fast pace of change in Israel, it is slightly out of date. But Kar-Ben Copies maintains a website with updates for the book at www.karben.com/kli.html.

Snow in Jerusalem, by Deborah daCosta, illus. by Cornelius Van Wright and Ying-Hwa Hu (Albert Whitman, 2001)

This is a wonderful and touching story of two boys, both living in Jerusalem's Old City but still worlds apart. Avi lives in the Jewish Quarter; Hamudi, in the Muslim Quarter. When the boys discover they're both caring for the same stray cat, will they be able to agree on how to share what they both love so much? The story is simple, but the implications are profound.

▶ Holiday Treats and Treasures

Chocolate Chip Challah: An Interactive Family Cookbook, by Lisa Rauchwerger (UAHC Press, 1999)

From the chocolate chip challah of the title to Rock-a-My Sole Fish, to Yentl (Lentl) Soup, this cookbook offers fun recipes for every holiday and Shabbat. In addition to the author's reminiscences about her grandmother and others who taught her to cook, space is left for you to write your own family recipes and thoughts. Plus, there are two accompanying activity books that are sold separately.

Drawing Your Way through the Jewish Holidays, by Eleanor Schick (UAHC Press, 1997)

A great source for the budding Jewish artist, this book takes you step-by-step though the process of making realistic drawings of many common holiday symbols, including candlesticks, Kiddush cups, seder plates, and more. It's appropriate for all ages but is best suited for kids over age seven.

The Family Treasury of Jewish Holidays, by Malka Drucker, illus. by Nancy Patz (Little, Brown, 1994)

This great book offers a taste of just about everything that's found in the other books in this holiday section. There are stories—new and traditional—recipes, songs, crafts, and information about all the major Jewish holidays and Shabbat. A terrific collection with lots for everyone to enjoy and something for all ages.

Fun with Jewish Holiday Rhymes, by Sylvia Rouss, illus. by Lisa Steinberg (UAHC Press, 1992)

The many holiday-related rhymes found in this attractively designed book will delight young kids and make everyone laugh.

Jewish Holiday Games for Little Hands, by Ruth Esrig Brinn, illus. by Sally Springer (Kar-Ben Copies, 1995)

This activity book offers pictures and instructions on how to play holiday-related games and provides game pieces and boards when necessary. Activities like "Put Mordecai on the King's Horse" (a variation of "Pin the Tail on the Donkey") offer simple fun with a basis in the story or traditions of the holiday. Kar-Ben Copies has an entire *For Little Hands* series, great for young children. Specific topics include Israel, High Holy Days, Hanukkah, and Passover, plus a special holiday crafts volume.

My Jewish Holiday Fun Book, by Ann D. Koffsky (UAHC Press, 2000)

This slim workbook features pictures to color, puzzles and mazes to complete, cut-out projects, and other activities relating to each holiday and Shabbat. If you use this book correctly, its pages will be ripped out, drawn on, and colored beyond all recognition by the time you're through.

The Uninvited Guest and Other Jewish Holiday Tales, by Nina Jaffe, illus. by Elivia Savadier (Scholastic, 1995)

This book contains seven stories, one for each major holiday and Shabbat, which include both original stories and folktales. Best for kids ages eight and up, though the beautiful illustrations make this great for kids of all ages.

▶ Shabbat Tales

Mrs. Moskowitz and the Sabbath Candlesticks, by Amy Schwartz (Jewish Publication Society, 1991)

Wonderful for all ages, this is the story of grandma's Shabbat candlesticks and how they inspire her to get a whole lot accomplished without even trying.

Once Upon a Shabbos, by Jacqueline Jules, illus. by Katherine Janus Kahn (Kar-Ben Copies, 1998)

A cute story of Shabbat and the virtue of compassion—even for mean and angry bears—this funny picture book is great for young children.

The Sabbath Lion: A Jewish Folktale from Algeria, retold by Howard Schwartz and Barbara Rush, illus. by Stephen Fieser (HarperTrophy, 1996)

The classic tale of a boy's travels through the desert and his adventures with a lion he meets. A magical story, beautifully told and illustrated, for ages four and up.

The Shabbat Box, by Lesley Simpson, illus. by Nicole in den Bosch (Kar-Ben Copies, 2001)

Ira is thrilled that it's his turn to take the fun-filled Shabbat Box home from school. But he loses it in the snow, so he makes a new one to bring back to school on Monday. This is a gorgeously illustrated book, with diverse faces and with a dad who's cooking Shabbat dinner. It also includes directions for making your own Shabbat Box.

▶ Rosh Hashanah and Yom Kippur

Days of Awe: Stories for Rosh Hashanah and Yom Kippur, by Eric Kimmel, illus. by Erika Weihs (Puffin Books, 1991)

A well-made collection featuring three stories that relate in some way to the High Holy Days. For kids ages four and up, as well as their parents, it's a great way to get into the spirit of the season.

Gershon's Monster, by Eric A. Kimmel, illus. by Jon J. Muth (Scholastic, 2000)

A chilling Rosh Hashanah tale, based in Jewish folklore, of Gershon the baker and how all the bad deeds he tried to sweep away grew to have serious repercussions. While younger children might be frightened by the book's monsters, older kids will be thrilled by this very exciting and very relevant moral tale.

The Hardest Word: A Yom Kippur Story, by Jacqueline Jules, illus. by Katherine Janus Kahn (Kar-Ben Copies, 2001)

This story about the Ziz—a mythical giant bird who's so clumsy he knocks the stars out of the sky—will delight school-age children. Sent on a quest to find the hardest word to say, he finds it isn't "good-night" or "spaghetti"—it's "sorry."

K'Tonton's Yom Kippur Kitten, by Sadie Rose Weilerstein, illus. by Joe Boddy (Jewish Publication Society, 1995)

In this adventure of K'Tonton, the favorite Jewish children's book character, the pint-sized boy learns a valuable lesson about repentance and forgiveness through his experiences with a stray kitten. Appropriate for all ages.

Rosh Hashanah: A Holiday Funtext, by Judy Bin-Nun and Franne Einhorn, illus. by Heidi Steinberger (UAHC Press, 1998)

This large and attractive book has a homemade feel to it, which is good because the activities inside will have you cutting out pages, drawing, and pasting all the way through it. The book is filled with simple activities for early school age children.

Sammy Spider's First Rosh Hashanah, by Sylvia A. Rouss, illus. by
Katherine Janus Kahn (Kar-Ben Copies, 1996)

Sammy Spider lives in the home of the Shapiro family and envious-
ly looks on as they prepare for Rosh Hashanah. Through Sammy,
children learn about different customs of the holiday. Plus, this book
teaches about sizes: big, middle-size, and small. This book is part of
the Sammy Spider series, which includes books for Hanukkah,
Passover, Purim, and Tu B'Shvat. All the books in this series are
geared for preschool children.

Sophie and the Shofar: A New Year's Story, by Fran Manushkin, illus.
by Rosalind Charney Kaye (UAHC Press, 2001)

Sophie's loud Russian cousin Sasha moves in next door. Ironically,
after Sophie mistakenly accuses him of stealing her father's prized
shofar, the two children end up forging a great friendship. Plus Papa
lets them both try out his shofar!

The World's Birthday: A Rosh Hashanah Story, by Barbara Diamond
Goldin, illus. by Jeanette Winter (Harcourt Brace, 1990)

In this book for all ages, Daniel decides to throw the world a birthday
party to celebrate Rosh Hashanah, and invites everyone over.

▶ Sukkot and Simchat Torah

Sukkot: A Family Seder, by Judith Z. Abrams, illus. by Katherine Janus
Kahn (Kar-Ben Copies, 1993)

With just the right amount of information (about fifteen text pages),
this is a simple and terrific guidebook to a Sukkot seder—down to
its own "four questions" about the holiday. The volume also includes
sukkah-building instructions and sheet music for some songs.

Tamar's Sukkah, by Ellie Gellman, illus. by Shauna Mooney Kawasaki
(Kar-Ben Copies, 1999)

This is an adorable book about a little girl named Tamar, who is decorating her sukkah and getting it ready for Sukkot. She enlists a group

of "big" kids in the neighborhood to give her a hand and then to celebrate with her. This book, geared for preschool age children, is available as both a paperback and a board book.

When Zaydeh Danced on Eldridge Street, by Elsa Okon Rael, illus. by Marjorie Priceman (Simon & Schuster, 1997)

A beautifully illustrated story of a girl who visits her Zaydeh during Simchat Torah and gets to see an entirely different side of him and his Jewish observance. Good for kids ages four and up.

▶ Hanukkah

Dreidel, Dreidel, Dreidel, by Stephen Carpenter (HarperCollins, 1998)

Push a button, and this musical board book plays the popular Hanukkah dreidel song. Along with beautiful illustrations of kids playing dreidel and other Hanukkah scenes, the pages feature the lyrics to the song so that you can sing along as you read.

A Hanukkah Treasury, edited by Eric A. Kimmel, illus. by Emily Lisker (Henry Holt, 1998)

A compendium of new and old stories, fun facts, songs, recipes, traditions, and games having to do with Hanukkah, all collected by one of the foremost Hanukkah authors. Great for families and kids of all ages. Kimmel has also written many terrific original Hanukkah stories, including *Zigazak, The Chanukah Guest, The Chanukah Tree*, and *Hershel and the Hanukkah Goblins*.

Jason's Miracle, by Beryl Lieff Benderly (Albert Whitman, 2000)

This could be considered the boy's version of the book *There's No Such Thing as a Hanukkah Bush, Sandy Goldstein* (see next page). Secular Jewish preteen Jason wishes he could celebrate Christmas and thinks "So what!" about Hanukkah. Then in a dream he meets the Maccabees, who show him all they went through to keep Judaism alive.

Pearl's Eight Days of Hanukkah, by Jane Breskin Zalben (Simon & Schuster, 1998)

Combining a story with activities for each night of Hanukkah—including recipes, songs, and a puppet show—this is a great collection to bring out the fun in the holiday for the whole family.

Rainbow Candles: A Hanukkah Counting Book, by Myra Shostak, illus. by Sally Springer (Kar-Ben Copies, 2001)

An adorable, colorful board book made especially for very young children, this gives kids practice in counting numbers up to nine and teaches the customs of Hanukkah. (Kar-Ben Copies also has other Jewish board books, including *The Colors of My Jewish Year, My Jewish Home,* and *Shalom Shabbat: A Book for Havdalah.*)

The Runaway Latkes, by Leslie Kimmelman, illus. by Paul Yalowitz (Albert Whitman, 2000)

This adorable take-off on the Gingerbread Man fable features a rabbi, cantor, police, and others in hot pursuit of some runaway latkes whose absence threatens the upcoming Hanukkah party. A recipe and background information on latkes accompany this silly tale.

There's No Such Thing as a Hanukkah Bush, Sandy Goldstein, by Susan Sussman, illus. by Charles Robinson (Albert Whitman, 1983)

Told from the perspective of a young secular Jewish girl who is always envious at Christmastime, this book is geared to preteens. It delivers a nice message about appreciating the traditions of others without having to make them our own.

▶ Tu B'Shvat

Listen to the Trees: Jews and the Earth, by Molly Cone, illus. by Roy Doty (UAHC Press, 1998)

A collection of environmental wisdom from Jewish tradition, delivered in the form of poems, stories, and fun illustrations. Good for kids ages nine and up.

The Never-Ending Greenness, by Neil Waldman (William Morrow, 1997)

A beautifully illustrated book, for ages six and up, about a boy who escapes wartime Europe and comes to Israel, then plants trees that sprout into entire orchards to revitalize the land.

A Prayer for the Earth: The Story of Naamah, Noah's Wife, by Sandy Eisenberg Sasso, illus. Bethanne Andersen (Jewish Lights Publishing, 1996)

This modern-day midrash involves Noah's wife, whom God put in charge of collecting two seeds from every plant in the world so that they too would survive the flood. Naamah's story conveys a beautiful message about preserving and caring for all living things.

A Seder for Tu B'Shevat, by Harlene Winnick Appelman and Jane Sherwin Shapiro, illus. by Chari R. McLean (Kar-Ben Copies, 1984)

This book not only provides all the information your family needs to have a Tu B'Shvat seder but also includes interesting stories, songs, nature facts, and activities to further celebrate the holiday.

Solomon and the Trees, by Matt Biers-Ariel, illus. by Esti Silverberg-Kiss (UAHC Press, 2001)

This story, loosely based on biblical tales, tells of King Solomon's dedication to the trees of Israel. It imparts an environmental message while suggesting a possible origin for Tu B'Shvat.

▶ Purim

Make Your Own Megillah, by Judyth Groner and Madeline Wikler, illus. by Katherine Janus Kahn (Kar-Ben Copies, 1998)

In addition to providing information on the history and traditions of Purim, as well as instructions on making crafts, recipes, and games, the book includes seven pages that tell the *Megillah* story and are designed to be colored, cut out, and pasted together to make a long scroll. This book is perfect for kids ages four and up but kids may require some help from adults on certain crafts and recipes.

Purim Play, by Roni Schotter, illus. by Marylin Hafner (Little, Brown, 1998)

This is a terrific book that tells the story of Purim in a very creative way—with the characters putting on a *Purim-shpiel* (play). Kids ages four and up will relate to and enjoy it, plus there's a warm message about friendship.

The Whole Megillah, by Shoshana Silberman, illus. by Katherine Janus Kahn (Kar-Ben Copies, 1990)

While not quite containing the whole text of the *Megillah*, this book features Hebrew excerpts from the Purim text as well as the English story for young kids. Plus it has songs, an entire Purim play script, and more ideas for adding fun to this already fun holiday.

▶ Passover

A Different Night: The Family Participation Haggadah, by Noam Zion and David Dishon (Shalom Hartman Institute, 1997)

Though it is constructed more like a textbook than a fun book, this Haggadah is packed with information to enrich a family's seder. At nearly two hundred large-size pages, it's not the book you want to hand out to your guests on Passover night, but it is a great tool for parents to prepare interesting and often humorous additions to the seder.

The Energizing Haggadah for Children, illus. by Janet Zwebner (Pitspopany Press, 1998)

A standard Haggadah, in both English and Hebrew, but full of colorful cartoons, seek-and-find games, and puzzles for young children.

A Family Haggadah, by Shoshana Silberman (Kar-Ben Copies, 1997)

This traditional Haggadah features the seder service on the right-hand page, while the left-hand page displays questions, commentaries, songs, activities, and games geared toward families with young children. A similar Haggadah by Kar-Ben Copies, *A Family Haggadah II*, is also valuable but geared toward teens and adults.

My Very Own Haggadah: A Seder Service for Young Children, by Judyth Groner and Madeline Wikler, illus. by Sally Springer (Kar-Ben Copies, 1999)

This coloring book takes young children through the Passover seder via easy-to-understand words and pictures.

Dayenu—Or How Uncle Murray Saved the Seder, by Rosalind Schilder, illus. by Katherine Janus Kahn (Kar-Ben Copies, 1988)

A sly, modern-day take on the *dayenu* idea, this book contains fun and lovable characters (especially Uncle Murray) and is great for younger kids.

Matzah Ball: A Passover Story, by Mindy Avra Portnoy, illus. by Katherine Janus Kahn (Kar-Ben Copies, 1994)

When Aaron goes to a Baltimore Orioles game during Passover, he's upset he can't enjoy all the stadium junk food like the rest of the kids. As it turns out, though, bringing matzah to the ballpark is the best thing that could've happened to him. Appropriate for kids ages four and up.

The Matzah Ball Fairy, by Carla Heymsfeld, illus. by Vlad Guzner (UAHC Press, 1996)

A truly delightful story that kids and parents alike will find hilarious. This is the charming tale of what happens to the Pinsky seder when Frieda (with the help of a tiny fairy) makes lighter-than-air matzah balls.

Miriam's Cup: A Passover Story, by Fran Manushkin, illus. Bob Dacey (Scholastic, 1998)

This beautifully illustrated book features a mother telling her daughter about Passover through the story of Moses' sister, the prophet Miriam. The idea of Miriam's Cup—a cup of water at the seder, similar to Elijah's cup of wine—is introduced as well (and lyrics to Debbie Friedman's song "Miriam's Song" are printed on back).

Only Nine Chairs: A Tall Tale for Passover, by Deborah Miller, illus. by Karen Ostrove (Kar-Ben Copies, 1982)

A fun and warmhearted story for all ages, written in rhymed verse, about a very familiar topic for families regardless of observance level: the overcrowded seder.

A Sesame Street Passover: Kippi and the Missing Matzah, by Louise Gikow, illus. Tom Brannon (Comet International, 1994)

Elmo's friend Kippi, who's visiting from Israel, invites the Sesame Street gang over for a seder, where he shares the foods and rituals of Passover with them all—that is, once they've solved the mystery of the missing matzah. Great for Sesame Street fans, the series also features a coloring and activity book as well as an audiocasette.

The Shalom Sesame Players Present: The Story of Passover, illus. by Peter Panas (Comet International, available through Kol-Ami)

A very enjoyable and well-made book for young kids (that parents will enjoy as well), featuring the Sesame Street characters, which traces the Passover story through a variety of activities.

▶ Shavuot

A Mountain of Blintzes, by Barbara Diamond Goldin, illus. by Anik McGrory (Harcourt, 2001)

Based on a folktale about Chelm, this charmingly illustrated story tells of a family's big Shavuot plan to cook up a pile of blintzes high enough to look like the mountain where Moses received the Ten Commandments. When other expenses take precedence, the entire family's cooperation is needed to round up the ingredients.

▶ Contacting Jewish Publishers Directly

- ▶ American Jewish Historical Society: 781-891-8110; ajhs@ ajhs.org; www.ajhs.org
- ▶ Jewish Lights Publishing: 800-962-4544; sales@jewishlights.com; www.jewishlights.com

- ► Jewish Publication Society: 800-355-1165; jpsmail@ presswarehouse.com; www.jewishpub.org
- ► Kar-Ben Copies: 800-4KARBEN; kar-ben@lernerbooks.com; www. karben.com
- ► Kol-Ami: 800-223-SISU; sisu@sisuent.com; www.sisuent. com
- ► Pitspopany Press: 800-232-2931; pitspop@netvision.net.il; www.pitspopany.com
- ► Union of American Hebrew Congregations (UAHC) Press: 888-489-UAHC; press@uahc.org; www.uahcpress.com

Make Your Own Books

Reading books with the entire family is a terrific activity that's fun, educational, and a great way of sharing experiences. But why not take it a step further and create your own book?

Depending on the age and interests of your children, homemade books can be a number of different things. They can tell the story of your family and ancestors, cover a topic of special interest to you and your kids, or re-write a story that you know from folklore. Or you and your kids can make up a story of your own.

How much you put into the book's design and construction is up to you: You can buy a pre-bound notebook and fill it with drawings, photos, and writing; or you can build your book with construction paper, then bind it using string, yarn, or a store-bought binder; or take it to a print shop and have it bound into a spiral book. You can collect all the material beforehand (write the text or story on a scrap paper first), or you can just make it up as you go.

Of course, the more planning that goes into the book, the better it will look in the end. But any book your family creates will no doubt become an extremely valuable document you'll want to hold on to for years and display prominently around the house. What's more, it's a wonderful way to teach your children about books and expose them to ways they can express themselves through writing and art.

Films & Videos
for Jewish Families

Family Fun Videos

It's not our intention to encourage your family to sit on the couch all day when there's plenty of fun activities to do in the house and out. But everyone needs a little change of pace sometimes, and these videos offer some of the best Jewish family entertainment around. It's possible to find some of these in Judaica stores or even regular video stores. Also, some Jewish community centers and libraries make them available to members, free of charge. But here are some other ways to order them: Kol-Ami (800-393-4264); www.jewishstore.com (888-597-8804) www.jewishvideo.com (877-JEWISHVIDEO); or Hataklit (800-HATAKLIT or www.shalom3000.com).

▶ Shabbat and Holidays

The Sabbath

This collection of four short films—featuring animation, clay characters, and live action—is an absolute delight. The joys, meanings, and importance of Shabbat are portrayed in funny ways that don't preach. The idea of Shabbat rest is presented in a very nice way.

Lights: The Miracle of Hanukkah

This terrific animated story, featuring the voices of Judd Hirsh and Leonard Nimoy, is simple enough for kids to enjoy but also sophisticated enough to fascinate adults. By symbolically equating magical Hanukkah lights with the light of Jewish spirit and learning, this video beautifully captures the essence of the Hanukkah story—if not the specifics—and also delivers an important message about everyone's right to be different.

Lovely Butterfly: Chanukah

This special Hanukkah episode of the Israeli children's program "Lovely Butterfly" features not only great animation but also puppets and people that play games and sing songs for the holiday. Though the overdubbing of English voices on top of the original Hebrew is somewhat distracting, overall the video is an enjoyable celebration of Hanukkah.

A Rugrats Passover

In this special episode of the extremely popular animated television series (and movies), the *Rugrats* kids learn about Passover from Grandpa Boris, who is trapped with them in the attic and missing the seder. While Boris tells the story of Moses and the Exodus from Egypt, three-year-old Angelica imagines herself as Pharaoh—and all the babies (including Tommy and Chuckie) as the Israelite slaves. When Tommy approaches her to "Let my babies go!" she finally meets her match. (The video also includes a bonus *Rugrats* episode, "Toys in the Attic.")

Shari's Passover Surprise

This is a delightful Passover celebration, with Shari Lewis, Lamb Chop, Charlie Horse, Hush Puppy, and some interesting special guests. Hush Puppy not only gets Dom DeLuise to cook the meal but also invites Robert Guillaume (a.k.a. "Benson") to the seder. As always, Lamb Chop and the other puppets are adorable. Plenty of musical numbers help tell the Passover story and explain the customs associated with this holiday. One highlight is a song performed by Guillaume, describing the story of the Ten Plagues. This show also emphasizes themes of diversity and the importance of inviting guests to our home on Passover.

Sing-Along at Bubbe's

This terrific video contains excerpts from two other tapes called *Chanuka at Bubbe's* and *Passover at Bubbe's*. The puppets in this series are Muppet-like characters, singing many original songs as well as traditional Hanukkah and Passover favorites in Hebrew and English. Songs explain various aspects of these two holidays and proclaim a general message to "be yourself."

▶ Israel

Jinja's Israeli Safari

In Tel Aviv's Safari Park, Jinja, the adorable Israeli lion cub, takes us on a visit with the park's unusual animals, including ostriches, giraffes, and rhinoceroses. Though Jinja's voiced-over British accent can be hard to understand at times, and the video is more enjoyable if one can understand the funny Hebrew animal songs that are interspersed, children are sure to be thrilled with simply hearing the music and seeing the terrific live-action animals.

Grandpa's Tree

This live-action short film, which follows an American musician on a quest to find the tree his grandfather planted years ago in Israel, is a great companion to Tu B'Shvat celebrations. Though somewhat corny and low on production values, it's a fun, music-filled story that covers the custom of the holiday as well as the institution of tree-planting in Israel.

▶ Songs and Stories

Bible Stories for Children

Israeli author Meir Shalev and illustrator Yossi Abulafia bring the classic Bible stories of Adam and Eve, Noah, and others to life with humor and color. A very entertaining and well-made video.

Enough Already

An animated musical retelling of the wonderful folktale about a family who doesn't realize how good they have it. Through humor and klezmer music, the video overcomes its simplistic animation and gives an important lesson about being thankful for what we have.

Fliegel's Flight

This "bird's-eye view of Jewish history" is narrated by a cartoon bird named Fliegel, but in general this is not a cartoon. It's more like a documentary, dealing with complex issues in Jewish history, including ancient and modern events, going all the way from Abraham up through Zionism and the Holocaust to the present day. Its themes are too complex for young children. But older kids (and even parents) will find it both interesting and educational.

The Shirim K'tanim Song Festival

Terrific for kids of all ages, this hour-long video features thirty-three of the best Hebrew children's songs. The adorable combination of animation, claymation, and live action is a lot of fun. There are songs about holidays, Bible stories, and everyday situations. With even the subtitles in Hebrew, the video is geared to families that know some Hebrew.

Shalom Sesame

This great series of videos (eleven in all) combines the popular American children's television show *Sesame Street* with Israel's version of it, *Rehov Sumsum.* Anyone familiar with *Sesame Street* will know what to expect: first-rate kids' programming that combines basic learning with humor that both kids and adults will appreciate. There's a mix of animation, muppets, and live action (featuring celebrities such as Sarah Jessica Parker, Joan Rivers, and Itzhak Perlman) with skits, songs, and educational shorts. The shows, approximately a half hour in length, can be bought individually or on longer videos that contain a bunch of episodes. The shows are:

- ▶ 1: *The Land of Israel*
- ▶ 2: *Tel Aviv*
- ▶ 3: *Kibbutz*
- ▶ 4: *The People of Israel*
- ▶ 5: *Jerusalem*
- ▶ 6: *Hanukkah*
- ▶ 7: *Sing Around the Seasons*
- ▶ 8: *Journey to Secret Places*
- ▶ 9: *Aleph-Bet Telethon*
- ▶ 10: *Passover*
- ▶ 11: *Kids Sing Israel*

Episodes 1–5, 6–8, and 9–11 are available grouped together or you can buy any of these eleven videos individually.

Alef, Bet, Blastoff!

This is an outstanding series of eight video episodes that introduces children to traditional Jewish values in meaningful ways. It's not a religious production. Rather, it focuses on values and concepts such as being different, helping others, freedom, forgiveness, and welcoming strangers.

The main characters are two puppets, David and Rachel, children who are led on exciting adventures through time by the fearless Mitzvah Mouse. Together they meet some of the most important people in Jewish history. It's magical and musical, and there's always a nice moral at the end of the story. It's recommended for kids ages three to ten.

Each video runs approximately thirty minutes. You can buy videos for $19.95 each, or the set of all eight for $107.95. The episodes are:

- 1: *You've Come to the Right Place*. Elliott Gould as Abraham.
- 2: *Fixing the World*. Ed Asner as Maimonides.
- 3: *Lights of Freedom*. Dom DeLuise as Pharoah.
- 4: *One Big Family*. Lauri Hendler as Golda Meir.
- 5: *A Hanukkah Mitzvah*. Don Diamont as Judah Maccabee.
- 6: *A Whale of a New Year*. Avery Schreiber as Jonah.
- 7: *A Light Unto the Nations*. Cathy Ladman as Emma Lazarus.
- 8: *The Whole Megillah*. Erin Simms as Queen Esther.

▶ Family Fun Films

Here we list some mainstream Hollywood (or, in some cases, Israeli) films that were once shown on television or the big screen and are now available on video. While they are all good films with Jewish backdrops and elements, tastes will vary as to how appropriate they are for your family—and at what age your children should watch these films (while none have objectionable sex or violence, opinions will differ about their adult situations and moral messages). As with any film, our advice is for parents to screen it first without the kids, then determine for themselves whether it is appropriate for their own children.

An American Tail (1986, directed by Don Bluth)

An animated classic about Fievel, a young Russian mouse who searches for his family while adapting to his new home in America. The whole family will love this very sophisticated and exciting cartoon about the immigrant (Jewish) experience. Three sequels—*Fievel Goes West*, *The Treasure of Manhattan Island*, and *The Mystery of the Night Monster*—have also been made.

The Apprenticeship of Duddy Kravitz (1974, directed by Ted Kotcheff)

A funny Canadian film based on Mordecai Richler's story, starring Richard Dreyfus in the title role as an ambitious kid from Montreal's Jewish ghetto in the 1940s.

Crossing Delancy (1988, directed by Joan Micklin Silver)

An amusing, warmhearted movie about the clash between tradition and modernity, set on the Lower East Side of New York. Good for older kids and adults.

Exodus (1960, directed by Otto Preminger)

An exciting and heroic film adaptation of Leon Uris' historical novel set during the Israeli struggle for independence, starring Paul Newman. A rousing film filled with Zionist passion.

Fiddler on the Roof (1971, directed by Norman Jewison)

The classic film adaptation of the stage musical based on Sholem Aleichem's old country tales of Tevye. A "must see" for every Jewish family.

The Frisco Kid (1979, directed by Robert Aldrich)

An offbeat comedy starring Gene Wilder and Harrison Ford about a Polish rabbi traveling through the Wild West and befriending a bank robber.

Kazablan (1974, directed by Menahem Golan)

An entertaining Israeli musical (in both Hebrew and English versions) about a tough guy who tries to save his neighborhood from being torn down. A fun and interesting slice of Israeli life at the time, with similarities to *West Side Story,* and a bunch of unforgettable songs.

Masada (1981, directed by Boris Sagal)

Originally a TV mini-series, this dramatic, inspiring, epic film depicts the struggle of a heroic Jewish desert outpost against the Romans.

The Outside Chance of Maximilian Glick (1988, directed by Allan A. Goldstein)

A meaningful family comedy about a young Jewish boy growing up in small-town Canada and the clash of cultures he encounters.

The Prince of Egypt (1998, directed by Brenda Chapman and Steve Hickner)

An animated retelling of the story of Moses and the Exodus from Egypt. Though it crams the story told in *The Ten Commandments,* a 3½-hour movie, into an hour and a half, its terrific animation and songs delight children.

Sallah Shabbati (1964, directed by Ephraim Kishon)

A light-hearted Israeli comedy starring Chaim Topol (who also plays Tevye in *Fiddler On the Roof*) as a recent Israeli immigrant who schemes ways to improve the situation for himself and his large family.

The Ten Commandments (1956, directed by Cecil B. DeMille)

A classic film that plays regularly on television, starring Charlton Heston as Moses, who grows up as Egyptian nobility only to reconnect with his Israelite roots and lead his people to freedom. This 3½-hour epic is a powerful, if somewhat sanitized and overacted depiction of the defining moment of the people of Israel.

Yentl (1983, directed by Barbra Streisand)

An award-winning musical with Streisand directing and starring, this story is an adaptation of Isaac Bashevis Singer's short story about a young Jewish woman who, in order to study Torah, must disguise herself as a boy. Though it is sappy at times, families will find both the story and the music entertaining and meaningful.

Making Your Own Jewish Family Videos

Movies are not only something Jewish families can enjoy watching together, they're also something families can actually make together. Producing home movies together gives children a sense that their family's story is important and worth recording. And of course, it's tons of fun.

These family videos will be precious documents that you'll watch together for years to come. The possibilities are endless, but here are just some of the ways you can put your family in the movies:

▶ *Record your family's history.* Create a simple and low-budget documentary by filming your kids, parents, grandparents, and great-grandparents as they talk about their lives and what it was like to grow up Jewish in a particular time period. Ask open-ended questions in order to bring back memories and to provoke complete and thought-provoking answers that will record forever how your relatives think and behave. Make several copies of the video to give as gifts to family members.

▶ *Film Jewish holiday observances.* Holidays are not only fun times to capture your family in action, they are times when you can record your family as it shares age-old customs. Families who do not operate mechanical devices on religious holidays can film observances that are more historically based, such as Purim, Hanukkah, and Yom Ha'Atzmaut.

▶ *Film trips, parties, and celebrations.* While weddings and bar mitzvahs are commonly recorded on video or in photographs, any type of *simchah* is a great opportunity to shoot a Jewish family video. Even ordinary family events can be fun to have on tape.

▶ *Direct your own Jewish epics.* Your Jewish films don't all have to be about your family. You can dress up and act out stories to create your own movies. Cast your family in Bible stories, folktales, or even stories that you make up yourself. Who knows, maybe the next Spielberg is living in your own house!

Internet & Software for Jewish Families

Jewish Fun Webguide

▶ Online Anytime!

Zig Zag World (www.zigzagworld.com/games/home.htm)

This site is full of great games that use Java technology to teach Hebrew while having fun. The main feature is called "Hebrew for Me," which includes nearly a dozen variations on a basic "click and drag" feature that Java enables. In the "Around the House" game, for instance, players click on the Hebrew words for various pieces of furniture found at home, then drag a picture of the corresponding piece of furniture onto a larger picture of an empty house, which they then decorate.

Other "Hebrew for Me" games center around holiday themes, such as dragging the objects found on a seder plate onto an empty plate, or dragging holiday symbols onto a Hebrew calendar. In a playful, interactive environment, families learn Hebrew words by visually connecting them to pictures.

In addition, Zig Zag's site includes other educational games, including "AlefBetGo!"—where you slide Hebrew letters into order in a race against the clock—and "Why Don't Zebras Play Chess?," a word search puzzle.

Jewish Funland
(www.bus.ualberta.ca/yreshef/funland/ funland.html)
Run by Dr. Nurit Reshef, a Jewish educator in Alberta, Canada, Jewish Funland features a whole bunch of Java games, each with Jewish concepts, Israeli history and geography, or learning Hebrew. While all the games are great educational tools, they're also very oriented toward keeping kids and parents entertained.

Jewish Funland games include an Israeli map puzzle that you have to slide into place (it's pretty tough!), two cute "Hebrew Hangman" games where you figure out Hebrew words commonly found in English (shofar, mezuzah) as well as Bible personalities, and a word match game where you connect pictures to their Hebrew and English names. There are also links to related sites devoted to Purim and Passover/Shavuot fun, a great Israel and Zionism game page, and a Bible challenge game page.

Your Page (www.yourpage.org)
The Family Fun section of this easy-to-use website features dozens of simple Java-based games that allow you to accumulate points as you go. There are also instructions on making a dozen crafts, including a water-glass chime "*mayim* piano" that you can play online or recreate at home. Ten mostly humorous stories feature pictures that pop up as you scan the words with your cursor. Add to that a set of online greeting cards you can send to family and friends, and Your Page is one you'll want to keep in your favorites list so you can return again and again.

Kid's Treehouse (www.tricityjcc.org/treehouse)
You don't have to be from Arizona to enjoy the cool kids site set up by the Tri-City Jewish Community Center in Tempe. Stories, music,

games, and crafts are only a click away. Particularly extensive is the arts and crafts section, which includes instructions on dozens of easy-to-do projects as well as coloring pages that you can complete online or print out for later.

The J Site (www.j.co.il)

A simple but well-done site created by a Brooklynite-turned-Israeli, the J Site features lyrics to Hebrew songs, coloring pages, an Israel geography quiz game (which ain't easy!), a Hebrew sign maker, and a concentration-style match game. As much as the activities themselves, the site's use of Flash technology makes it a lively and interactive visit.

Eileen's Favorite Camp Crafts and Other Fun Things! (www.chadiscrafts.com/fun/jewishcrafts.html)

Eileen knows her crafts, and this site combines all-purpose craft ideas and instructions with Jewish-related ones. The section titled "Jewish Crafts for Camps, Schools or Just for Fun at Home" provides some great projects, including clay mezuzahs and Jewish symbols made from beads.

Jewish Jugglers Home Page (www.juggling.org/~jews/)

Juggling goes back to biblical times—who knew?! This site, dedicated to Jewish jugglers, provides articles on the ancient Jewish history of jugglers (providing evidence from the Talmud) as well as information on great occasions for Jewish juggling and special tricks for Jewish jugglers.

▶ Holidays in Cyberspace

Torah Tots (www.torahtots.com)

This extensive site features loads of educational and religion-oriented information on holidays, the Hebrew alphabet, and the week's Torah portion—all geared toward kids. "Holiday Pages" tell about various holidays; "Coloring Pages" can be printed out and used for coloring (don't color on the computer screen!); and "Fun & Games" includes a word search, a word decoder puzzle, and "plopples"—nonsense sentences that, when read aloud, sound like sentences that actually mean something (for example, on Rosh Hashanah: "Weed hipped he yap pull sinned tea hun knee"). Silly, yes, but fun for everyone involved.

Aish HaTorah Holidays (www.aish.com/holidays)

While the holiday page on Aish HaTorah's extensive website contains links to valuable information on all the Jewish holidays, the Hanukkah, Purim, and Passover links take you to activities that are specifically fun for the entire family. The sections for these three holidays include coloring pages to print out as well as holiday-related stories. The Purim page also includes jokes in Real Audio (though you and your kids can be the judge whether these actually qualify as jokes!). And the Passover page features a bunch of arts-and-crafts projects as well as some pretty fun ideas for the seder.

Holidays on the Net (www.holidays.net)

You'll find lots of information on a wide variety of holidays at this site—Jewish holidays, secular holidays, and holidays of other religions. With each, you'll get the general background as well as articles on specific aspects of the holiday, plus activities, message boards, links to books, and other fun features. The page on the High Holy Days (Rosh Hashanah and Yom Kippur), for example, includes a Real Audio shofar that plays the sounds of the holidays at the click of a mouse (you must have a Real Audio player, which can be easily downloaded online).

Uncle Eli's Special-for-Kids Most Fun Ever Under-the-Table Passover Haggadah
(www.acs.ucalgary.ca/~elsegal/ Uncle_Eli/Eli.html)

This online version of the popular Passover book is not so much a usable Haggadah as a humorous commentary on all the sections of the Haggadah. Uncle Eli's funny rhymes read like a Dr. Seuss book for smart-aleck Jewish kids (and the parents who made them that way!).

Billy Bear's Playground (www.billybear4kids.com/holidays/fun.htm)
Billy Bear's Playground is a mostly secular site with a wide range of fun material for kids. In the holiday section, the site includes pages dedicated to Passover and Hanukkah activities. The Passover activities include a Chametz game, mazes, and a word search. The Hanukkah page has a fun Java-run dreidel game, instructions for making a real dreidel, printable Hanukkah stationery, and special utilities that kids and families can use on their own websites (Hanukkah clip art, wallpaper, and icons).

▶ Cool Sites for Kids and Teens (and Parents Too!)

BabagaNewz (www.babaganewz.com)
This colorful site is the online extension of *BabagaNews* magazine, a monthly publication geared toward young Jewish teens and distributed in classrooms. Plenty of activities are fun for middle-schoolers and their parents. In particular, the Games section features a Mad Libs–type word game called Baba-Meisas, plus word searches and crossword puzzles, all of which can be done online. There's also a cool virtual tour of Israel using Quicktime.

JVibe (www.jvibe.com)
This is a very hip Jewish site for teens that includes articles on popular culture, social action, politics, sports, and "real life," plus a chat area to let your opinions be known. Though clearly designed for teens—many of the articles are actually written by teens—parents will appreciate the site's sophistication and many of the articles as well.

JewishSports.com (www.jewishsports.com)
Also one of the more sophisticated sites. It offers information on a variety of Jewish sports topics, including in-depth articles on the latest exploits of prominent Jewish athletes. Plus, you can sign up to be on a JewishSports.com mailing list.

Jewhoo! (www.jewhoo.com)

A play on the popular Yahoo! search engine, Jewhoo is an endlessly fascinating and often surprising clearinghouse of information about celebrities who are (David Arquette, Jack Black) and who aren't (Ben Affleck) members of the Tribe.

Surfing the Hebrew-net: Hebrew Fonts on Your Computer

For those of us using English web browsers such as Netscape and Internet Explorer, surfing to a website that's written in Hebrew will more than likely turn up a bunch of gibberish that doesn't make sense in Hebrew or English. That's because our American browsers aren't equipped with Hebrew fonts that allow us to view Hebrew lettering on our computer screens.

The good news is that downloading Hebrew fonts onto your computer is extremely quick and easy. And once you download them, you'll open up a connection to an extensive network of Hebrew sites, many of them based in Israel, that provide a valuable link to the language and the land. If you know Hebrew, you'll be able to view up-to-the-minute news and entertainment from Israel; if you don't know Hebrew, it's a great way to help you learn.

HERE'S HOW TO DO IT:

1. Find a site that offers Hebrew fonts for download. Most of these sites will be Israeli sites, where Hebrew is used. Look for a button that says "Can't see Hebrew?" or "If you don't see Hebrew, click here." Many Hebrew sites will have this feature (though often it will be written in Hebrew). Sites with English instructions for downloading Hebrew fonts include
   - ▸ www.mct.co.il/hebrew.htm
   - ▸ www.aiweinberg.com/hebrew.html
   - ▸ www.huji.ac.il/unew/hebrew/hebrew.html
2. Determine which font to download, and click on the appropriate

link. You'll probably have to choose between Windows versions and also between Netscape and Internet Explorer.

3. Save the file onto your hard drive, and note the folder in which you save it. The file should be executable (have an ".exe" suffix).

4. Go into your File Manager (if using Windows, go to Start, then Explore, to call up "Exploring" window) and find the file you downloaded.

5. Click on the .exe file you downloaded. The program will then lead you through a few prompts as it unzips the file and installs it onto your computer. Simply follow along.

6. If you are still online, you will probably need to close your browser, then open it up again in order for the new Hebrew font to be usable. Otherwise, simply start up the browser and go surfing on the Hebrew-net.

Super Software

While there's hardly an unlimited selection, a fairly wide variety of software can be found for Jewish children and families—from more secular and entertainment-oriented to more religious and educational. The amount of fun your family has with each depends on your tastes and goals. The three main Jewish software manufacturers— JeMM, Davka, and T.E.S.—have websites (see end of chapter) that either allow you to order products directly or link to other sites where you can buy the software. In addition, www.jewishstore.com sells many of these products.

▶ Holidays

Davka's Jewish Holiday Fun House (Davka)

Featuring four basic holiday-related activities with simple, spoken directions (no reading required), this CD is good for children as young as age three, if not younger. Arrange the pieces of a puzzle to reveal a picture, pick out which picture doesn't belong, match the picture with the holiday song, and click on a picture to learn more about the holiday—these easy-to-follow games offer holiday learning as one of your child's earliest computer experiences. (Requires: Windows, 8 MB RAM, CD-ROM drive, sound card.)

Hanukkah Activity Center (Davka)

A collection of eight Hanukkah activities for the entire family, this CD includes a jukebox to play (and teach) holiday songs, a dreidel game, a trivia game, a coloring book, a "Nes-scape" web browser through Hanukkah history, and more. (Requires: Windows, 8 MB RAM, CD-ROM drive, sound card.)

The Interactive Haggadah (JeMM)

This program presents the Passover story through claymation figures from "The Animated Haggadah" video, with sections for songs, traditions, and games. (What else? A computerized *afikomen* hunt!) The various sections can be explored in any order, making the discovery process individual to the explorer, and in your choice of three languages: Hebrew, English, or Russian. It's a great learning tool for kids before the seder, and a great interactive addition to this, the most interactive of all Jewish holidays. (Requires: Windows or Macintosh, 8 MB RAM, double-speed CD-ROM drive, sound card.)

Purim Rock! (JeMM)

Another gem from JeMM's holiday software series, this one uses Claymation figures to mount a full-scale rock opera that tells the Purim tale, with songs in English or Hebrew. If you want a little more information, Scoop the spider fills in the plot details with humor and interactive bits. Plus there's a no-frills guide to the holiday's customs and history (more for parents than kids), as well as trivia and Purim songs to learn. (Requires: Windows or Macintosh, 16 MB RAM, double-speed CD-ROM drive, sound card, QuickTime 3.)

Torah Targets (T.E.S.)

Knowing about the holidays is more important than ever when the survival of Earth depends on it. That's the situation in this game, which requires players to blast off into space and destroy the invading Space Blobs. In order to get ammunition, though, players have to correctly answer questions about the holidays. You can play with one or two "captains" and customize both game and question difficulty. But at any level this game is a real challenge and a fun learning tool. (Requires: Windows, 8 MB RAM, CD-ROM drive.)

Who Stole Hanukkah?! The Great Interactive Mystery Game (JeMM)

If your family thinks dreidel is fun, wait 'til you get your hands on this Hanukkah game, a CD-ROM whodunit that's both educational and extremely entertaining. The object: to figure out who stole Professor Croak's priceless jar of oil. Along the way, there are games, songs, and a cast of colorful characters. There are tons of useful information on the history and observance of Hanukkah that will appeal to older kids, while the animation and funny animals keep younger children amused. And be ready to spend some time with this one—solving the mystery isn't easy! (Requires: Windows or Macintosh, 16 MB RAM, double-speed CD-ROM drive, sound card.)

▶ Fun and Jewish Learning

Davka Classic Game Pack (Davka)

This CD brings together three Davka educational games previously sold separately. Jewish IQ Basketball tests your abilities on the court—and in the field of Jewish learning. In either one-on-one competition against the computer or a three-point shoot-out, players who answer questions correctly in the areas of history and *mitzvot* (commandments) sink a basket. Mitzvah Mania challenges players to avoid obstacles and gather all the good deeds scattered on the screen while the clock is ticking. And Search for Your Israeli Cousin (also sold separately, see below) is a great way to teach older kids about Israel while having fun solving a mystery. (Requires: Windows, 16 MB RAM, CD-ROM drive, sound card.)

Mitzvah Man (T.E.S.)

Mitzvah Man—the Jewish version of Pac Man—feeds on knowledge. To keep him strong, players must answer questions dealing with Torah, ethics, and religious observances. There are levels for student and scholar. Because the game assumes a strictly Orthodox observance level in its questions, it's not designed for everyone. (Requires: Windows, floppy disk drive, sound card.)

Torah Tots Live! In Concert (T.E.S.)

This is the CD-ROM version of Torah Tots Live!, an Orthodox-oriented live stage show (as well as recording series) with life-size, cartoon-style characters—including Talmi D. Torah and Hardy Har Sinai—performing a full set of musical numbers such as "Lashon Hora" and "I've Got a Friend." The CD allows you to watch the show in its entirety or read the lyrics and sing along, karaoke-style. Plus there are coloring pages and a link accessing the Torah Tots website. (Requires: Windows, 32 MB RAM, sound card.)

Torah Tots: Parsha on Parade (T.E.S.)

The latest in an ever-expanding catalog of Torah Tots products, this series of software—still a work in progress—will eventually feature one CD-ROM for each of the five books of the Torah (as of now, *Bereishit, Sh'mot* and *Vayikra* are available, sold separately). Using the Torah Tots characters, the disc tells the story of each *parsha* (weekly Torah portion) in everyday language (though occasionally Hebrew terms are left unexplained). Each *parsha* also features games (decoding, word search, and a "Replace the Pickle" quiz), coloring pages (printable and on-the-screen), and a "Midrash Mavin" to give a little further information.

In addition to the *parsha* content, each CD-ROM includes a game show–style quiz on the entire book, an English translation of the biblical verses, and more puzzles in the "Teaching Materials" section. While the CDs feature the Torah Tots' usual Orthodox orientation—with Yiddish-style pronunciation and lifestyle assumptions that can be alienating to non-Orthodox Jews—the sheer amount of information provided will easily include something for everyone to learn and enjoy. (Requires: Windows or Macintosh, 16 MB RAM, sound card.)

Wisecrackers! (JeMM)

Designed for bar and bat mitzvah–age kids (the program even includes a Do-It-Yourself Bar/Bat Mitzvah Website Kit), *Wisecrackers!* is set up like a goofy game show, complete with a cheesy host and two players competing side by side. The object is to win all of the Jewish collectibles (including the world's only purple *etrog* and Jacob's wrestling shorts) by answering trivia questions. (Requires: Windows or Macintosh, 16 MB RAM, CD-ROM drive, sound card, QuickTime 4.)

▶ Hebrew Games

Alef-Bet Schoolhouse (Davka)

These three Hebrew language learning programs are sold separately or together in a set. Kids learn the basics of Hebrew with some fun mixed in. In addition to learning letters, numbers, vocabulary, and grammar exercises, the programs contain activities such as an *Alef-Bet* coloring book and a handful of games that make the learning enjoyable. (Requires: Windows, 8 MB RAM, CD-ROM drive, sound card.)

The Alef Bet Word Book (T.E.S.)

This program, a combination of word search and coloring book, provides a great way for young kids to learn basic Hebrew words. Though it is a bit one-dimensional, its attractive visual display will help users create mental pictures to enhance vocabulary, while playing a challenging game. (Requires: Windows or Macintosh, CD-ROM drive.)

Hebrew GAMETIME (Davka)

With three fast-paced games—Word Attack, Word Zapper, and Hebrew Hangman—this program offers more than one way to have fun while learning Hebrew. Each is full of neat sound effects, and with both a word editor and variable levels of difficulty, these games continue to challenge as players' vocabulary grows. Designed for ages eight and up. (Requires: Windows, 4 MB RAM, floppy disk drive, sound card recommended.)

Hebrew Wordquest (T.E.S.)

Featuring two games—a Tetris®-like game called Hebrew Wordmaster and a word search puzzle called Judaic Wordquest—this program offers a great way to build your Hebrew vocabulary and your comprehension of biblical terms while playing fun and challenging games. Because it requires a basic knowledge of Hebrew letters and reading, it is recommended for ages nine and up. (Requires: Windows, 4 MB RAM, floppy disk drive.)

▶ Israel and the Bible

Noah and the Rainbow (Davka)

Based on the Judaica Press children's storybook of the same name, this CD version uses state-of-the-art-animation, colorful graphics, and interesting sound effects to tell Noah's tale in rhyme. Full of humor and surprises, kids ages three and up will love experiencing this story as it unfolds on their computer screens. In addition to the story, the CD features a memory game, coloring book, and puzzle program. (Requires: Windows, 8 MB RAM, CD-ROM drive, sound card.)

Search for Your Israeli Cousin (Davka)

A clever way for older kids (ages ten and up) and adults to learn about Israel, this program takes you all over the Jewish state while you follow clues in search of your relatives. This race against the clock is not easy; you'll pick up tons of great information about Israeli cities along the way. With authentic Israeli music, funny characters, and beautiful photo-quality images, Israel is as close as your computer screen. (Requires: Windows, 8 MB RAM, CD ROM drive, sound card.)

Search for Your Israeli Cousin II—Global Quest (Davka)

This sequel is even tougher (also for ages ten and up), taking you beyond Israel to search the entire Jewish world—from New York to Poland and nineteen other locations—for your lost relatives. Your family will learn about the history of Jewish life in cities around the world while following the clues and tracking down family. (Requires: Windows, 8 MB RAM, CD ROM drive, sound card.)

▶ Jewish Software Makers

- ▶ Davka: 800-621-8227; www.davka.com
- ▶ JeMM: info@ejemm.com; www.ejemm.com
- ▶ T.E.S.: 800-925-6853; www.jewishsoftware.com

Fun on the Road

Jewish Museums for the Family

Where to Go throughout the U.S.

Fascinating Jewish museums exist all across the country, many of which have programs and exhibits specifically designed for kids and families. We encourage you to seek them out as you travel around.

We've picked out what we think are the best museums for families, including a popular one in Los Angeles especially for Jewish kids that opened branches in cities across the country. Plus we've included museums that offer fun and interesting programming for children on a permanent or regular basis. And finally, we've included a few just because they're Jewish museums off the beaten path.

▶ California

Zimmer Children's Museum

This is the world's very first Jewish museum designed specifically for kids. It's an exciting, hands-on type of place that's made for having fun, but it also teaches children—and the adults they bring along—

about Jewish history, values, holidays, and culture. The museum offers craft workshops, concerts, and holiday celebrations throughout the year. Some of the exhibits include:

- *The Mann Theatre:* Kids get on stage and use costumes, props, and various backdrops (Noah's Ark, Statue of Liberty) to perform, and they see themselves on a big TV screen.
- *The Western Wall:* At this small-scale replica, you can tuck your wishes between stones.
- *The Discovery Airplane:* It has real cockpit controls. Plus, you can strap in for its flight to Israel.
- *American Red Magen David for Israel:* This exhibit teaches children about saving lives and visiting the sick. They can get behind the wheel of a pretend ambulance and make get-well cards for patients in local hospitals.

The museum is located on the two lowest levels of the Los Angeles Jewish Federation community building. Coming up right through the middle of both levels is a two-story neon *"Tzedakah* pinball machine." This flashy, interactive centerpiece of the museum is a fun way for kids to learn about the different kinds of *tzedakah.* The pucks in the pinball machine are coins, clocks, and mirrors, representing ways we can give: money, time, and ourselves.

In case you can't make it to Los Angeles, the museum also has traveling exhibitions that visit cities all over America. Some of those cities built on the traveling exhibitions and started museums of their own, called My Jewish Discovery Place. None are as big as the L.A. version (which was originally called My Jewish Discovery Place), but they stick very close to the original model and feature many of the same fun exhibits. Hopefully you and your children will be able to visit one of these special museums.

VISITING INFORMATION ▶ Address: 6505 Wilshire Blvd., Suite 100, Los Angeles, CA 90048; Phone: 323-761-8989; e-mail: museum@mjdj.org; website: www.zimmermuseum.org. Hours: Tues.–Thurs. and Sun., 12:30 P.M. to 5 P.M. Admission: Adults, $5; children over age three, $3; children ages two and under, free. (Grandparents are free when accompanied by grandchildren.)

My Jewish Discovery Place

ATLANTA ▸ Sophie Hirsh Srochi Jewish Discovery Museum at the Marcus JCC of Atlanta: 5342 Tilly Mill Rd., Dunwoody, GA 30338. Phone: 770-395-2553; e-mail: myjewishdiscovery place@atlantajcc.org; website: www.atlantajcc.org.

FORT LAUDERDALE ▸ My Jewish Discovery Place at the Soref JCC: 6501 West Sunrise Blvd., Ft. Lauderdale, FL 33313. Phone: 954-792-6700; e-mail: info@sorefjcc.com; website: www. sorefjcc.com.

TORONTO ▸ Jewish Discovery Place at the Bathurst JCC, 4588 Bathurst St., Toronto, Ontario, Canada M2R1W6. Phone: 416-636-1880; e-mail: discovery@bjcc.ca; website: www.bjcc.ca.

Having a (Skir)ball in L.A.: Skirball Cultural Center

Situated in the beautiful Santa Monica mountains, the Skirball Cultural Center hosts family programs two Sundays a month. It's good to make reservations a few days in advance for these popular events.

The museum also has a Discovery Center for kids, featuring archaeology projects. There, children can make rubbings of ancient stone letters onto paper, build an ancient gate out of Legos®, and play interactive computer games.

Skirball's core exhibition is called "Visions and Values: Jewish Life from Antiquity to America." It's a multimedia tour through various representations of Jewish life and culture—from bandleader Benny Goodman playing jazz to an "immigrant mama" reciting kosher recipes—as well as traditional objects, photographs and artwork. A recent temporary exhibit focused on "Friz" Freleng, a pioneering *Looney Tunes* animator.

VISITING INFORMATION ▸ Address: 2701 North Sepulveda Blvd., Los Angeles, CA 90049. Phone: 310-440-4500; website: www.skirball.com. Hours: Tues.–Sat., Noon to 5 P.M.; Sun., 11 A.M. to 5 P.M. Closed Monday. Admission: Adults, $8; students and seniors, $6; free for children under age twelve. A kosher dairy restaurant is open during museum hours.

Magnes Museum

The Judah L. Magnes Museum in Berkeley and The Jewish Museum San Francisco recently merged, creating The Magnes Museum, which exhibits Jewish culture and art at both locations.

Located in an old mansion with a beautiful flower and sculpture garden perfect for picnic lunches, the Magnes Museum in Berkeley houses an impressively large collection of twelve thousand Jewish ceremonial objects, folk relics, and pieces of fine art. Each exhibit incorporates a workshop for kids, and docents (available on Wednesdays and Sundays) can also gear their tours for kids.

Every December 25 the museum hosts a "family day" program; other family events are scheduled throughout the year. Also, the museum holds an annual Jewish video competition and a poetry competition that includes a category for poets under age nineteen.

The Magnes San Francisco location houses Jewish art and artifacts from all over the world.

BERKELEY VISITING INFORMATION ▶ Address: 2911 Russell St., Berkeley, CA 94705. Phone: 510-549-6950; e-mail: pfpr@magnesmusuem. org; website: www.magnesmuseum.org. Hours: Sun.–Thurs., 10 A.M. to 4 P.M.; Admission: Free ($5 donation suggested).

SAN FRANCISCO VISITING INFORMATION ▶ Address: 121 Steuart St., San Francisco, CA 94105. Phone: 415-591-8800; e-mail: info@jmsf.org; website: www.jmsf.org. Call for museum hours and prices.

▶ New York

Camels and Caravans: The Jewish Museum

The Jewish Museum is located in a French Gothic château-style mansion on Manhattan's Upper East Side, directly across from Central Park. It is the largest Jewish museum in the Western Hemisphere is nearly a century old, and qualifies as a major American art museum.

They generally have one children's exhibition going at all times. For example, "Camels and Caravans: Daily Life in Ancient Israel," an interactive exhibit, is specially designed for kids ages four to ten.

Visitors are transported to a Jerusalem home and marketplace two thousand years ago. They explore life in ancient Israel through the eyes of Miriam and Simon, two fictional children living in Jerusalem in the first century C.E. Among other activities, kids dress up in period clothing, play instruments from the period, and participate in a weaving activity.

In addition, the Jewish Museum offers extensive family programming throughout the year, with a wide variety of events occurring most Sundays from September to May: a Shofar Parade in the fall, many holiday programs and performances in December, a children's film festival in January, and a Purim pageant in the spring. In the summer, the museum holds an intensive five-week arts program for high schoolers.

VISITING INFORMATION ▶ Address: 1109 5th Ave., New York, NY 10128. Phone: 212-423-3200; website: www.thejewishmuseum.org. Hours: Sun., 10:30 A.M. to 5:45 P.M.; Mon.–Wed., 11 A.M. to 5:45 P.M.; Thurs., 11 A.M. to P.M.; Fri. 11 A.M. to 3 P.M. Closed Saturday, major Jewish holidays, and some legal holidays. Admission: Adults, $8; students and seniors, $5.50; free for children under age twelve and museum members. A kosher café is open during museum hours.

SUMMER ARTS PROGRAM ▶ for high school students; five weeks; housing not provided. For more information: 212-423-3231.

Four Corners of the Earth: Yeshiva University Museum

Though perhaps not as well known as many other Jewish museums, the Yeshiva University Museum is probably the country's best Jewish university museum. The museum is located in the Center for Jewish History on West 16th Street, near Yeshiva University's Cardozo Law School.

Throughout the year, the museum hosts a great deal of children's programming and holiday events, including storytelling, musical performances, and craft workshops. In addition, many of the exhibits are hands-on—with no ropes protecting the displays—so kids are welcome to touch just about everything they see.

Museum tours are offered in Hebrew, Spanish, Russian, Yiddish, and other languages, as its brochure says: "Visitors as well as exhibitions come from the four corners of the earth."

VISITING INFORMATION ▶ Address: 15 West 16th St., New York, NY 10011. Phone: 212-294-8330. Hours: Sun., Tues., Wed., 11 A.M. to 5 P.M.; Thurs., 11 A.M. to 8 P.M. Admission: Adults, $6; seniors and children under age sixteen, $4; free for kids under age four.

▶ Chicago

A Matter of (Arti)fact: Spertus Museum

Among the many interesting attractions at Chicago's Spertus Museum, the one most likely to engage children is the ARTiFACT Center, which features a dig site for unearthing replicas of real archaeological treasures. Children in grades one through twelve are encouraged to take part, while preschoolers can explore a junior "dig" site, take a ride on a pretend camel, and dress up in costumes.

For kids of all ages, the museum has a workshop for creating a variety of crafts. In addition, programs for children and families are held regularly. Often tied to themes in Judaism or the Jewish holidays, they include puppet shows, magicians, and crafts.

VISITING INFORMATION ▶ Address: 618 South Michigan Ave., Chicago, IL 60605 (located close to public transportation). Phone: 312-322-1747; e-mail: museum@spertus.edu; website: www.spertus.edu. Hours: Sun.–Wed., 10 A.M. to 5 P.M.; Thurs., 10 A.M. to 8 P.M.; Fri., 10 A.M. to 3 P.M. Closed Saturday. Admission: Adults, $5; students and seniors, $3; $10 family rate. Fridays are free.

ARTiFACT CENTER ▶ Phone: 312-322-1747. Hours: Sun.–Thurs., 1 P.M. to 4:30 P.M. (Mornings reserved for groups and field trips.)

▶ Mid-Atlantic States

Remember the Children: U.S. Holocaust Memorial Museum

While the U.S. Holocaust Memorial Museum's regular exhibit is not recommended for children under age eleven, there is an exhibition called "Remember the Children: Daniel's Story" that is designed specifically for children age eight and older. It was carefully developed with the sensitivities of children in mind. The exhibit tells the story of a fictional child named Daniel, without the use of horrific images.

Through Daniel's diary entries, we follow him in his life before the Holocaust and then see how his life changes during the war years. The exhibit is completely hands-on. Though we never see Daniel himself, we can turn the pages of his diary, sit on his bed, touch his clothes, and look out his windows.

This exhibit can be scary for kids younger than age eight, because in the end we see that Daniel's parents couldn't protect him from disaster. It is by no means *fun*, but "Daniel's Story" can be an extremely valuable and memorable experience for child and parent alike.

VISITING INFORMATION ▶ Address: 100 Raoul Wallenberg Pl., SW, Washington, DC 20024-2150 (near the Smithsonian Metro stop; public transportation advised, as parking is limited). Phone: 202-488-0400; website: www.ushmm.org. Hours: Daily, 10 A.M. to 5:30 P.M. In spring and early summer, Tues. and Thurs., 10 A.M to 8 P.M. Closed Yom Kippur and Christmas. Admission: free. (The permanent exhibition requires a dated entry pass, which can be obtained on a "first come, first served" basis—except for members, who receive priority—beginning at 10 A.M. at the "pass desk." You can reserve passes in advance through tickets.com at 800-400-9373, for a $1.75 fee per pass plus a $1 handling charge per order.)

Philadelphia Freedom:
National Museum of American Jewish History

The National Museum of American Jewish History in Philadelphia offers storytelling programs throughout the year, tied to the themes in its permanent exhibit. It also has events connected to various Jewish and secular holidays. In particular, the annual Tu B'Shvat program involves puppet shows and other activities—including the handing out of saplings that you can take home to plant. On December 25, the museum hosts a family program called "Being Jewish at Christmas," a day of Jewish music, food, and family activities. And the museum's website features a fun page geared for kids.

The location of the museum—on Philadelphia's Independence Mall—is ideal for an institution that celebrates the freedoms of Jewish Americans. Its collection of more than ten thousand artifacts tells the story of three hundred years of Jewish life in America. Though the permanent exhibits are not specifically designed for children, docents can gear tours toward the ages of those in the group.

VISITING INFORMATION ▶ Address: 55 North 5th St., Independence Mall East, Philadelphia, PA 19106-2197. Phone: 215-923-3811; fax 215-923-0763; e-mail: nmajh@nmajh.org; website: www.nmajh.org. Hours: Sun., noon to 5 P.M.; Mon.–Thurs., 10 A.M. to 5 P.M.; Fri., 10 A.M. to 3 P.M. Closed Saturdays and major Jewish holidays. Admission: Adults, $4; students and seniors, $3; free for children under age six.

A Golden Place in Baltimore: Jewish Museum of Maryland

The Jewish Museum of Maryland, located in Baltimore's old downtown Jewish neighborhood, includes a museum and two historic synagogues.

A permanent installation specially geared for children ages five to nine is called "The Golden Land: A Jewish Family Learning Place." The interactive exhibit engages children's natural curiosity through seven learning stations. The first family learning center in a historic synagogue, it emphasizes local Jewish history and identity.

Throughout the year, the center hosts children's programs that are linked to the exhibits, as well as some related to Jewish culture, history, and holidays.

On the same grounds, the restored Lloyd Street Synagogue, built in 1845, is the oldest standing synagogue in Maryland; the B'nai Israel Synagogue dates back to 1876.

VISITING INFORMATION ▶ Address: 15 Lloyd St., Baltimore, MD 21202. Phone: 410-732-6400; e-mail: info@jewishmuseummd.org; website: www.jewishmuseummd.org. Hours: Tues.–Thurs. and Sun., noon to 4 P.M.; other times by appointment. Admission: Adults, $4; children, $2.

▶ The Southeast

Ol' Miss: The Museum of the Southern Jewish Experience

Located in Utica, Mississippi, the Museum of the Southern Jewish Experience was created to preserve the rich traditions of Jewish communities in the South, many of which are now inactive. Exhibits focus on the past and the present of Jews in the South.

The museum provides a free guidebook to Jewish historical sites along the Mississippi River, from Memphis to New Orleans, along Highway 61. It also arranges group tours of these sites, ranging from two to seven days.

The museum is housed on the grounds of Henry S. Jacobs camp, a Jewish sleepaway camp. It's a forty-minute drive southwest of Jackson, along rural rolling countryside.

VISITING INFORMATION ▶ 3863 Morrison Rd., Utica, MS 39175. Phone: 601-362-6357; e-mail: information@msje.org; website: www.msje. org. Hours: By appointment only.

Hands-On in Atlanta: William Breman Jewish Heritage Museum

The William Breman Jewish Heritage Museum in Atlanta is the largest Jewish museum in the Southeast. The museum, which explores regional Jewish heritage with a focus on the Atlanta Jewish experience, features a small Discovery Area for kids that offers self-guided hands-on activities. Special programs are offered the day after Thanksgiving and on Christmas day (except if Christmas falls on a Saturday).

VISITING INFORMATION ▶ 1440 Spring St. NW, Atlanta, GA 30309-2837. Phone: 404-873-1661; e-mail: www.wbjhm@jfga.org; website: www.atlantajewishmuseum.org. Hours: Mon.–Thurs., 10 A.M. to 5 P.M.; Fri., 10 A.M. to 3 P.M.; Sun. 1 P.M. to 5 P.M. Closed on major Jewish and secular holidays. Admission: Adults, $5; seniors and students, $3; free for children under age six.

▶ Southwest

Jewish Art in Tulsa: The Sherwin Miller Museum of Jewish Art

You might be surprised to find something like this in Tulsa, but the Sherwin Miller Museum of Jewish Art in fact contains the finest collection of Jewish art and artifacts in the Southwest. Its treasures span four thousand years, with a special emphasis on documents, photographs, and artifacts that reflect the Jewish influence in the Southwest region.

VISITING INFORMATION ▶ 1223 East 17th Pl., Tulsa, OK 74120. Phone: 918-294-1366; e-mail: jewishmuseum@webzone.net; website: www.jewishmuseum.net. Hours: By appointment only; Mon.–Fri., 9 A.M. to 5 P.M. Closed Saturday, Sunday, and Jewish and federal holidays. Admission: free.

Sylvia Plotkin Judaica Museum in Arizona

This collection of art and artifacts is housed at Temple Beth Israel in Scottsdale. They have a replica of a section of the Western Wall where you can place your own personal prayers between the stones. You'll also find a biblical botanical garden with flax, papyrus, fig, date, and olive.

VISITING INFORMATION ▶ 10460 N. 56th St., Scottsdale, AZ 85253. Phone: 480-951-0323; e-mail: museum@templebethisrael.org; website: www.sylviaplotkinjudaicamuseum.org. For more information, contact the museum.

Jewish Historical Sites

Learning History on the Road

Historical sites can be a tough sell for small kids. It's hard to convey the significance of a two hundred-year-old building to someone who's too young to remember life before the Internet. But what children lack in perspective they make up for in imagination. Touring historical sites offers kids the challenge of placing themselves back in time to conjecture how life might have been in some long ago age. Discovering the differences between Jewish life of the past and their lives today will only enhance their identity and stretch their minds. And besides, what kid doesn't like to play a little make-believe?

While the relative newness of Jewish life in the United States does not lend itself to a wide variety of historical sites, some of the oldest and most significant locales also offer fine possibilities for family fun and discovery. The following offers a tour through some of the best.

▶ Ellis Island and the Statue of Liberty

For most Jewish families in America, this is where it all began. Between 1892 and 1954, millions of immigrants—including Jews arriving from Europe—took their first steps in this country at Ellis Island, just a few hundred yards from the country's greatest monument to freedom and opportunity, the Statue of Liberty. Though no longer in operation as an immigrant processing center, Ellis Island remains a great symbol of Jewish America's birthplace.

Statue of Liberty

Take a ride on a ferryboat in the New York Harbor and imagine you are arriving in the New World and gazing up at Lady Liberty for the first time. On Liberty Island, enjoy the view of Manhattan with a picnic lunch on the lawn. At the base of the statue, read along with your family the words of Jewish American poet Emma Lazarus: "Give me your tired, your poor / Your huddled masses yearning to breathe free" (a great example of the shared values that are both Jewish and American). Take a hike up the statue's towering staircases to see if you and your kids can reach the crown.

Ellis Island

Then get back on the boat and head to Ellis Island, a perfect opportunity to tell (or retell) your children the story of your family's arrival in America. If your ancestors arrived at Ellis Island (and chances are they did), the island affords numerous ways to seek out and rediscover your immigrant forefathers and mothers. The Ellis Island Immigration Museum provides an overview of the entire immigrant experience, from arrival to assimilation, through photos, artifacts, computers, and interactive media. Within the museum, be sure to check out the film and theater presentations as well as the Children's Visitor Center, specially designed to present the immigrant experience in ways kids will find approachable and enjoyable.

As you stand inside Ellis Island's Great Hall, you can imagine immigrants enduring long lines for processing. After your tour of the building and museum, venture out to the American Immigrant Wall of Honor, which contains the names of over five hundred thousand immigrants. Can you locate your ancestors on the seemingly never-ending wall of names?

Ellis Island's American Family Immigration History Center provides families with an even closer glimpse into their past. Computer records enable anyone who can trace his or her roots to the port of New York to obtain data on immigrant ancestors. For a nominal fee, descendants can obtain a copy of the passenger log of the original ship on which their family members arrived as well as a picture of that ship. The history center is a terrific tool for empowering kids to discover their family heritage.

VISITING INFORMATION ▶ Located in New York Harbor, both Ellis Island and Liberty Island are accessible by boat from Battery Park in New York City and from Liberty State Park in New Jersey. Call Circle Line for a boat schedule and prices: 212-269-5755. Or for more information, contact the National Park Service: 212-363-3200; website: www.nps.gov/stli.

Historic Synagogues:
▶ Newport, Charleston, and New York City

The two oldest synagogues still in existence in the United States also happen to be located (not coincidentally) in beautiful, historic cities full of colonial charm and fascinating historical sites of interest to the entire family. Plus, both are in close proximity to beach and vacation destinations. What better way to combine family fun with Jewish enrichment than with a visit to the cities of Newport, Rhode Island, and Charleston, South Carolina?

Another historic synagogue is located in New York City. As the result of a massive restoration project, visitors can now enjoy this site as well.

Touro Synagogue: Newport, Rhode Island

Touro Synagogue, in Newport, Rhode Island, was dedicated in December 1763, making it America's oldest synagogue. The synagogue was constructed at an angle with the street so that the Ark could face directly east toward Jerusalem. Though there was a period of time when the synagogue was not in use, today it is home to an active Orthodox congregation, Jeshuat Israel, which has services on Friday evenings, Saturday mornings, and all Jewish holidays. The synagogue was founded by Sephardic Jews, and congregants today observe the traditional Sephardic-style customs.

Touro Synagogue stands in the city's downtown historic district, a short walk to the busy Newport boat pier, popular shops, and other fascinating tourist sites. And it's just minutes away from the gorgeous New England coastline.

VISITING INFORMATION ► 85 Touro St., Newport, RI 02840. Phone: 401-847-4794; website: www.tourosynagogue.org. Tours are given Sunday through Friday except on Jewish holidays (dress code: no jeans, shorts, or sleeveless tops; and women are asked to wear skirts or dresses).

Kahal Kadosh Beth Elohim: Charleston, South Carolina

Newport's southern colonial cousin is Charleston, South Carolina. Like Newport, Charleston was home to one of the earliest Jewish communities in America and continues to thrive as a vibrant modern city that has preserved its historic character.

Established in 1749, Charleston's Congregation Kahal Kadosh Beth Elohim is currently the second oldest synagogue in the country (after Touro) but has the distinction of being the oldest synagogue *in continuous use*. In 1841, it became the first Reform congregation in the U.S. The synagogue building is located in the downtown historic district. Services are held on Friday at 8 P.M., Saturday at 11 A.M., and on Jewish holidays.

Also located in downtown Charleston are two more Jewish historical sites: the Coming Street cemetery, which is the oldest Jewish burial ground in the South; and the Salvador Memorial, which stands in memory of Francis Salvador, the first Jew elected to a legislative body in America and also the first Jew to die in the American Revolution. Both of these Jewish historical sites are located a short walk, horse-and-buggy carriage ride, or bike ride (rentals are available near-by) to Charleston's famous open-air market. It's also close to the waterfront, where boats can be boarded for tours of beautiful Charleston Harbor and Fort Sumter, the site of the Civil War's opening battle. The synagogue also has a nice gift shop, with a variety of Judaica items.

VISITING INFORMATION ▶ 90 Hasell St., Charleston, SC 29401 (office: 86 Hasell St., Charleston, SC 29401). Phone: 843-723-1090; website: www.kkbe.org. Parking is available on the street and directly across the street at the Charleston Place parking garage. If you visit for worship services, an usher will stamp your parking garage ticket; or you can save your service program and present it to the garage attendant for complementary parking. Tours of the synagogue are available during gift shop hours, which are Mon.–Fri., 10 A.M. to noon.

Eldridge Street Synagogue: New York City

When it was built in 1886, the Eldridge Street Synagogue was called K'hal Adath Jeshurun. Founded in the 1850s, it was home to the first Eastern European Orthodox Jewish congregation in the United States.

For fifty years, the congregation flourished. Then, during the Great Depression, membership began to dwindle. By the mid-1950s the synagogue's once-beautiful main sanctuary had deteriorated so badly that it had to be abandoned. The sanctuary remained empty for nearly thirty years, and religious services were moved downstairs into the *Bet Hamidrash* (where Orthodox services are still conducted today).

In the 1980s, The Eldridge Street Project, Inc., a nonprofit cultural organization, began raising funds to restore the sanctuary and build a heritage center at the site. Work began in 1989. And while the project is still ongoing, the Eldridge Street synagogue has been open for tours since 1991. A variety of cultural and educational programs are offered throughout the year for families and school groups.

VISITING INFORMATION ▸ 12 Eldridge St., New York, NY 10002. Phone: 212-978-8800; e-mail: contact@eldridgestreet.org; website: www. eldridgestreet.org. Tours: Sun., 11 A.M. and 4 P.M.; Tues. and Thurs. 11:30 A.M. and 2:30 P.M., or by appointment. Admission: Adults, $4; students and seniors, $2.50.

▶ Other Unique Historical Sites

One-of-a-Kind House: The Gomez Mill House

In 1714, Luis Moses Gomez, a Sephardic Jew who was searching for a life of freedom in the New World, built a house for use as a trading post in Marlboro, New York, about seventy miles north of New York City. This Hudson River valley house has remained in use for nearly three hundred years. The oldest Jewish residence in North America, it is today an important center for historical preservation and Jewish activity.

In addition to tours of the historic residence, the Gomez Mill House hosts a number of fun and enriching programs for kids throughout the year. Because the house was converted for use as a paper mill earlier this century, visitors can participate in creating handmade paper. Special events are held for holidays throughout the year. Activities include workshops to teach children how to make a shofar or decorate a sukkah, and parties for Purim and Hanukkah.

One particularly popular program for young people is the Archaeological Dig for Children. After learning the proper use of the tools—the brushes, shovels, and sifters—children dig in a yard peppered with buried colonial artifacts. Afterward, the treasures are examined, and their functions explained. Then the staff buys back the artifacts from the children (with lollipops as the payment), so that the "relics" can be reburied.

VISITING INFORMATION ▸ 11 Mill House Rd., Marlboro, NY 12542. Phone: 914-236-3126; e-mail: gomezmillhouse@juno.com; website: www.gomez.org. Hours: after Passover through the end of October, open Weds.–Sun., 10 A.M. to 4:30 P.M. (The last tour begins at 2:30

P.M.) Tours can sometimes be arranged in the off-season, depending on availability of volunteers; call first.

The Hebrew Confederate Cemetery

Since Richmond, Virginia, was an important early American center for Jewish life, it's no surprise that many nineteenth-century Richmond Jews served in the Confederate Army during the Civil War. To commemorate the Jewish soldiers who died in the South's losing cause, in 1866 the Hebrew Ladies Memorial Association of Richmond erected a plot adjacent to the city's Shockoe Hill Cemetery. The Hebrew Confederate Cemetery remains today the only Jewish military cemetery in the world outside the State of Israel.

VISITING INFORMATION ▶ Shockoe Hill Cemetery is located at Hospital St. and 2nd St. in Richmond. Website: www.jewish-history.com/shockoe.htm

▶ Jewish History Biking and Walking Tours

Jews and Blues Alley: Bike Tour of the Jewish South

Want a vacation that's fun for whole family, that's healthy and outdoor-oriented—and that combines Jewish discovery with adventure travel? Try Historical Cycling International's "Jews and Blues Alley" bike tour of the South.

In both spring and fall, cycling tour director Rob Paperno (with the help of the Museum of the Southern Jewish Experience) takes groups on a leisurely paced ride along the historic Natchez Trace, past forest, swamps, and white-columned antebellum mansions and plantations. Along the way, you'll see famous Civil War battlefields and small towns full of southern hospitality and local color. You'll also visit Temple Gemiluth Chassed, Mississippi's oldest surviving synagogue, and the Anshe Chesed cemetery, located adjacent to Vicksburg's Civil War battleground. After discovering the region's beautiful scenery and rich Jewish heritage, you'll take a hydrojet boat cruise on the Mississippi River.

Though the riding pace is designed to account for cyclists of all skill levels, and the tours are thoroughly "kid friendly," children under age thirteen may find the constant pedaling a bit much to handle on their own. But families are enthusiastically welcomed, and Rob is open to adapting the itinerary to suit the needs of the group. A van travels along with the cyclists to transport supplies and bags as well as to carry anyone too tired to pedal. For those who don't ride on Shabbat, the van will also make sure you catch up with the rest of the cyclists at the end of the day.

The one-week tours include bikes, accommodations, meals, and all sightseeing costs. Though kosher meals cannot be provided, vegetarian food is available. Costs vary, depending on the type of room and meals you want. Since the tour group's size is generally eight to twelve people, a few families can book a tour together.

CONTACT INFORMATION▶Historical Cycling International. Phone: 1-877-PEDAL-18 (toll-free); e-mail: cycling@gte.net; website: www.historical-cycling.com. "Jews and Blues Alley" tours usually occur in April and October. Overseas tours are available as well.

BostonWalks' Jewish Friendship Trail Programs

When you visit Boston, be sure to take your kids to see the harbor where New England colonists perpetrated the Boston Tea Party, and go for a walk through the Boston Common. But even with all this great historical scenery surrounding you, don't forget to take the opportunity to also see the wealth of the city's Jewish heritage. That's what the BostonWalks' Jewish Friendship Trail Programs are all about.

Run by native Bostonian Michael Ross, a lawyer for a living and a Jewish tour guide for fun, four different walking tours allow you to choose the area of town you'd like to explore, with each featuring the synagogues, sites, and stories of Jewish Boston.

Some tours can be done on bicycle rather than on foot. And tours of Boston's other ethnic neighborhoods are available as well.

CONTACT INFORMATION▶50 Grove St., Belmont, MA 02478. Phone: 617-489-5020; e-mail: rossocp@gis.net; website: members.tripod. com/~BostonWalks. Dates and times for some tours are scheduled in advance, or can be arranged to meet the needs and interests of a group. Prices range from $10.75 to $17.50 per person, depending on the tour and the number of people in the group.

Radical Walking Tours of New York

For a very different kind of Jewish history walking tour, just leave it those crazy New Yorkers. Bruce Kayton, who used to teach a class at Manhattan's The New School on the history of the city's Jewish progressives, leads interested sightseers on a series of "radical walking tours of New York." One in particular—Radical Jews of the Lower East Side—revisits the places where famous and infamous Jews from Emma Goldman to the Rosenbergs lived and worked.

Starting at the original building that housed the popular Yiddish newspaper the *Jewish Daily Forward*, the tour takes you through the neighborhoods once inhabited by many of our grandparents and great-grandparents, from the old garment industry sweatshops to the site of the Women's Anti–High Price League to the former Communist Party headquarters and much more. All the while, Kayton entertains and informs you with jokes, stories, and a whole lot of facts about Jewish—particularly left-wing Jewish—roots in the area.

More for teens and adults than for young kids (though special kid-oriented tours can be arranged)—and probably not for the conservative-minded—this tour takes an irreverent trip back to a time when Jews struggled to make a better life for themselves and for Americans as a whole. Mixed in with the fun and fascination, there's a powerful message on the value of activism.

CONTACT INFORMATION▶Phone: 718-492-0069; e-mail: radtours@ he.net; website: he.net/~radtours. Tours generally begin at 1 P.M. on Sundays and last about three hours; call for dates. The price is $10 per person; no reservations required.

Kids' Jerusalem Adventures

Though we've limited our overview of fun Jewish historical sites to those that can be reached without leaving the country, it seems appropriate to mention at least one of the possibilities for family excitement in Israel. Sure, Israel is itself one big Jewish historical site, and there are countless ways to enjoy the Land with your family. But one tour company in particular caters itself to the interests and needs of English-speaking tourists with children.

Kids' Jerusalem Adventures will arrange an entire tour for you and your family, with a special emphasis on fun. Depending on what your family wants to do, tours can include a trip to the Jerusalem Biblical Zoo, a jeep trip through the desert, mule and camel rides, exploring caves and tunnels, swimming and hiking in nature reserves, and visits to Masada and the Dead Sea. David Schoenfeld, a Californian now settled in Israel, will lead you and your family on a trip through Israel that's sure to be fun for your kids as well as for the kid in you.

Kids' Jerusalem Adventures will handle all the details of your trip to Israel: hotel, transportation, and activities. If you are planning to celebrate your child's bar or bat mitzvah in Israel, KJA will even make all those arrangements as well.

CONTACT INFORMATION ▶ Phone/fax: 011-972-2-536-3449; e-mail: kids@tourisrael.co.il; website: www.tourisrael.co.il.

Jewish Family Camps, Getaways & Festivals

Away-from-Home Fun for the Entire Family

If you've never been to camp with your whole family, what are you waiting for? Going to a Jewish family camp is a great way to get away from it all, bond as a family, meet new people, enjoy a memorable Shabbat, and connect with the environment. There are campfire cookouts, sing-alongs, arts and crafts, Israeli dancing, and a lot of fun outdoor sports and activities.

Many children's summer camps offer family programs for a weekend or a whole week. Here are some we've picked out.

▶ Treats and Retreats: Jewish Family Camps

New Jersey YMHA–YWHA Camps

The New Jersey YMHA–YWHA offers family camp programs ranging from two nights to seven nights, with kosher meals and all programs included. Prices range from $150 to $490 for adults and $125 to $420 for kids. There are lots of Jewish activities, plus jetskiing, swimming, arts and crafts, and more!

The camp is in Milford, Pennsylvania, 1½ hours northwest of New York City. Each family gets its own cabin, with a porch, screened windows, and an indoor bathroom with showers. Bed linens are provided. You can choose from four camping options:

- ▶ *Family Camp Weekend:* This program is offered three times a summer.
- ▶ *Single Parent Family Camp:* This program is offered twice a summer. Parents with children under five can bring a babysitter for free. Staff is available in the evening to keep an eye on the kids.
- ▶ *Multi-generations Family Camping:* This weekend is geared for grandparents and their grandchildren, and focuses on getting to know each other without that middle generation there. Participants are housed in small motel-like rooms, rather than the more rustic cabins with bunks used for other camps.
- ▶ *Back to Nature Family Camping:* This program is led by Dr. Gabe Goldman from the Jewish Nature Center.

FOR MORE INFORMATION ▶ New Jersey YMHA-YWHA Camps, 21 Plymouth St., Fairfield, NJ 07004. Phone: 973-575-3333 x127; e-mail: carrie@njycamps.org; website: www.njycamps.org/families.

Camp Newman

Located in the California wine country, off a winding road in the rolling hills of Santa Rosa, Camp Newman offers a family camp program once a year on Labor Day weekend. The focus is on Jewish family education in a Reform setting, and families at all levels of Jewish education are encouraged to take part. The family camp weekend has a different theme each year, such as "Talking to Your Children about God." Parents and children explore topics together and also as separate groups. Adults take part in a scholars-in-residence program, while the children have age-appropriate programming.

Besides the Jewish learning that takes place at camp, there's lots of singing, dancing, games, arts and crafts, sports, and sometimes even overnight camping trips in the woods.

The food is kosher-style. Usually each family has its own cabin (with bunks) and bathroom. There's optional daycare included for children ages four and under. Costs vary, and there are discounts for Union of American Hebrew Congregation members. There's no charge for children under age two.

FOR MORE INFORMATION ▸ In winter: 703 Market St., Suite 1300, San Francisco, CA 94103-2193. Phone: 415-392-7080. In summer: 4088 Porter Creek Rd., Santa Rosa, CA 95404; Phone: 707-571-7657; e-mail: info@campnewmanswig.com; website: www.campnewmanswig.org.

Camp Ramah

Ramah (www.ramah.org) has one of the largest and best-known Jewish kids' summer camp programs in North America. It has locations in New England, the Poconos, the Berkshires, the South, California, Wisconsin, and Canada. It's affiliated with the Conservative movement. The food is kosher, Shabbat is observed, and worship services are held daily. There's also singing, dancing, arts and crafts, sports, swimming, boating, hiking, and more.

Most Ramah camps offer family programs where you can experience all that Ramah has to offer, as a part of a dynamic Jewish community. Here's the lowdown on three of them:

RAMAH IN THE POCONOS. Camp Ramah in the Poconos offers a program every summer specifically for Jewish families with deaf or hard-of-hearing members. The week-long program is called "Kesher Family Camp." It's $215 for adults, $120 for children. Scholarships are available.

They have also offered a one-week family camp program, designed for families with kids ages five to twelve who have not previously attended Ramah.

Families stay in the camp guesthouse, and babysitting is provided in the evenings. Linens and towels are provided as well.

For more information: In winter: 261 Old York Rd., Suite 734, Jenkintown, PA 19046. Phone: 215-885-8556. In summer: HCR60 Box

4000, Lake Como, PA 18437. Phone: 570-798-2504; website: www. ramahpoconos.org.

RAMAH IN WISCONSIN. Camp Ramah in Wisconsin offers a five-day family camp program in the summer that's geared toward families with children ages five to fourteen. Families stay in hotel-like rooms with private bathrooms, and linens are provided. Cost: $550 per couple; $275 per single adult; $100–$150 per child (five and over).

For more information: In winter: 65 East Wacker Pl. #820, Chicago, IL 60601. Phone: 312-606-9316. In summer: 6150 East Buckatabon Rd., Conover, WI 54519. Phone: 715-479-4400; website: www.jtsa. edu/ramah/wisconsin.

RAMAH DAROM (RAMAH SOUTH). Ramah Darom has a four-night family camp program in August, in the Chattahoochee National Forest. There is plenty of family time, but there are also separate activities for parents and children. You can choose between two types of accommodations: a cabin with bunks and a shared bathroom, or the retreat center where each family has its own private bathroom, two queen beds, and linens included.

For more information: Family Camp Director, 6075 Roswell Rd. NE, Suite 410, Atlanta, GA 30328. Phone: 404-531-0801; website: www. ramahdarom.com.

Maurice B. Shwayder Camp

Schwayder Camp is one of the oldest Reform Jewish summer camps in the United States. It is 10,200 feet up in the Rocky Mountains, one hour west of Denver on the slopes of Mount Evans, in Idaho Springs, Colorado. Every Labor Day weekend, the camp offers a three-day family camp program. The Shabbat experience includes a traditional meal, singing, services, and Israeli dancing. There's hiking, climbing, horseback riding, and more. The food is kosher-style, with vegetarian options available. One or two families share a cabin; each has heat and its own bathroom, but it's rustic.

FOR MORE INFORMATION ▶ In winter: Congregation Emanuel, 51 Grape St., Denver, CO 80220. Phone: 303-388-4013. In summer: 9118 State

Highway, #103, Idaho Springs, CO 80452. Phone: 303-567-2722; e-mail: info@shwayder.com; website: www.schwayder.com.

Camp Tawonga

Camp Tawonga is just outside Yosemite National Park on the beautiful Tuolumne River. The accommodations are rustic—two or three families share single-room cabins, and there's a short walk to the bathrooms and showers. Kids under age seven bunk with their parents, while older kids stay together, with camp staff members. You can bring your own tent if you prefer to really rough it. There are activities for the whole family, as well as times when kids are with camp staff. Food is kosher-style, with vegetarian and vegan options available. Costs vary, depending on program. Seven different Jewish family camp options are offered:

- ▶ Memorial Day Weekend
- ▶ Fall Family Camp
- ▶ Single-Parent Family Camp
- ▶ Spirituality Weekend
- ▶ Grief and Growing: A Healing Weekend for Bereaved Families
- ▶ Keshet Camp: For Jewish Lesbian and Gay Families
- ▶ Mosaic: A Multi-Racial Family Camp

FOR MORE INFORMATION ▶ 131 Steuart St., Suite 460, San Francisco, CA 94105. Phone: 415-543-2267 (415-KID-CAMP); e-mail: info@ tawonga.org; website: www.tawonga.org.

▶ Other Jewish Family Getaways

Bed and Breakfast: Admiral Weaver Inn

This kosher bed and breakfast is blocks away from the historic Touro synagogue in the scenic town of Newport, Rhode Island. The neo-Italianate villa (circa 1863) has five standard rooms and one two-bedroom suite just right for families. Choose from a variety of full dairy breakfasts, cooked to order and served in a cozy dining room or outside on a deck. Prices vary depending on room and time of year.

FOR MORE INFORMATION ▸ 28 Weaver Ave., Newport, RI 02840. Phone: 401-849-0051; e-mail: innkeeper@kosherbedandbreakfast.com; website: www.kosherbedandbreakfast.com.

Elat Chayyim: A Jewish Spiritual Retreat Center

Elat Chayyim is located in the Catskill Mountains, two hours north of New York City. All of its programs focus on Jewish spirituality and mysticism, incorporating forms of prayer, meditation, yoga, and the arts. There is a full children's program designed to complement the adult program, though parents and kids do not attend the sessions together. There is also free time each day for families to hike together or take part in a variety of other activities. Elat Chayyim welcomes participants from all branches of Judaism. Its programs cost an average of $100 a day for adults and about half that for children. Retreats range in length from a weekend to a few weeks.

FOR MORE INFORMATION ▸ 99 Mill Hook Rd., Accord, NY 12404. Phone: 800-398-2630; e-mail: info@elatchayyim.org; website: www. elatchayyim.org.

Endangered Spirit: A Jewish Outdoor Adventure Program

The goal of this program is to get you out of the city and into nature. Their trips provide adventure travel, and an opportunity for Jews of all backgrounds and all ages to experience the connection between Judaism and the environment. Program director Aaron Katler calls it a "re-Jew-venating" experience and says they'll take you to some of the most exhilarating locations in the world. All of their programs observe traditional laws of Shabbat and *kashrut*.

FOR MORE INFORMATION ▸ P.O. Box 13316, Chicago, IL 60613. Phone: 888-202-2930; e-mail: info@endangeredspirit.com; website: www. endangeredspirit.com.

Golden Acres Farm

It's a working farm and dude ranch, but guests don't exactly "rough it" at this kosher resort in the heart of the Catskill Mountains. Package deals include hotel room, kosher food, and a variety of farm activities like cow-milking, horseback riding, baby animal feeding, hayrides, and more. Plus there are pools, Jacuzzis®, a sauna, and miniature golf.

Families can enjoy the day together, or kids can take part in nursery and camp programs. Golden Acres is open from mid-June through Labor Day.

FOR MORE INFORMATION ▶ County Route #14, Gilboa, NY 12076. Phone: 800-252-7787; website: www.goldenacres.com.

Havurah Retreats

A *havurah* is a fellowship—a group of Jewish people coming together, whether to celebrate holidays and Shabbat, to pray or study, or to just have fun! The National Havurah Committee helps *havurah* groups get started around the country and assists them in developing programming.

The organization has retreats that are great for the whole family, including one national gathering in August and three regional retreats in winter (West Coast, New England, and upstate New York or Toronto). For people who are a member of a *havurah,* the idea is to come away with ideas that will help you make your group stronger. For those who are not a member of a *havurah,* the goal is that you'll be inspired to join an existing one or develop a new one of your own.

FOR MORE INFORMATION ▶ Phone: 215-248-1335; e-mail: office@havurah.org; website: www.havurah.org.

Inward Bound: Father-Son Vacations

Orthodox Rabbi Manis Friedman leads these Jewish camping and fishing trips in the U.S. and Canada. Most of the fathers and sons who go on these trips are from the Twin Cities. It's a religious Jewish experience, but the program is also dedicated to teaching and sharing the joys of camping and fishing in the great outdoors.

FOR MORE INFORMATION ▶ 1517 McCarthy Rd., Eagan, MN 55121. Phone: 651-686-4455; e-mail: ib@ib.org; website: www.ib.org.

▶ Jewish "Song and Dance" Camps and Festivals

KlezKamp: Yiddish Folk Arts Program

KlezKamp is a weeklong program celebrating Yiddish culture, held every December in the New York/New Jersey area. The event features workshops focusing on Klezmer music, Yiddish language, dance, history, folklore, crafts, food, theater, and more.

Throughout the week, children take part in the KlezKids program, where they are divided into age groups for their own special workshops. Young musicians can play klezmer music with the "Oomchicks" or the Klezmer Youth Orchestra.

Kosher and vegetarian meals are available. Double occupancy costs for the week: adults, $715; teens, $620; kids ages two to five, $315; kids ages six to eleven, $360; kids under age two, free. Babysitting is available in the evenings for an extra fee.

FOR MORE INFORMATION ▶ Living Traditions, 45 E. 33rd St.—Level B, New York, NY 10016. Phone: 212-532-8202; e-mail: klezkamp@aol.com; website: www.livingtraditions.org.

Dance Washington and Gilron

These two Israeli folk dance events are held in the mid-Atlantic region. Dance Washington is held on Memorial Day weekend, at Penn State College at Berks Campus, in Reading, Pennsylvania; Gilron is held during one weekend of winter break, at the Sheraton Hotel in Atlantic City. Both of these programs offer a weekend of fun and dance for all ages and skill levels. There are dance parties at night and workshops all day long. Or if that's too much dancing for some family members, there are also other activities. Three meals a day are included (kosher and vegetarian meals are available), including a festive Shabbat dinner. Prices vary depending on accommodations. There are discounts for early registration and for non-dancing members of the family.

FOR MORE INFORMATION ▶ Capital Dance, 5 Grason Ct., Rockville, MD 20850. Phone: 301-762-8978; e-mail: Shmuel@capitaldance.com; website: www.capitaldance.com.

The Israel Folkdance Festival of Boston

This festival, held every March, offers a great opportunity to see an enthusiastic display of Israeli dance. Folk dancers from around the country come to take part and, after the show, the audience is invited to join the dancers at a huge dance party. The whole event is sponsored by M.I.T.'s Hillel, where the first festival was held in 1977. Organizers and performers all work on a volunteer basis to put the festival together.

FOR MORE INFORMATION ▶ P.O. Box 397226, Cambridge, MA 02139-7226. Phone: (MIT Hillel) 617-253-2982; e-mail: ISRFDFestBos@hotmail.com; website: www.israelidance.com/bostonfestival.

New York: The Israel Folk Dance Festival

This festival has been in existence for more than fifty years. It's a one-day celebration, held every spring in New York City. There's an arts fair with craft activities for the whole family, as well as participatory Israeli dancing, singing, and, of course, food. After the fair, there's a performance by over 250  adult and youth dancers and singers. These performers represent youth groups, day schools, university organizations, and community centers from across the United States, Canada, and Israel. The event is run by the Israeli Dance Institute, a nonprofit educational organization.

FOR MORE INFORMATION ▶ Israeli Dance Institute, Inc., JCRC, 70 West 36th St., Suite 700, New York, NY 10018. Phone: 212-983-4806 x143/144; e-mail: idi_nirkoda@juno.com; website: www.israelidanceinstitute.org.

▶ Jewish Film Festivals

In many cities around the country, you'll find Jewish film festivals offered through community centers or museums. In other places, a Jewish Film Festival is an organization unto itself that runs its own annual event.

Here's a listing of some of the best-known Jewish film festivals in America. Check with individual festivals about whether they're featuring "family-friendly" flicks.

Boston Jewish Film Festival

Held in November. For information: phone: 617-244-9899; website: bjff.cyways.com.

New York Jewish Film Festival

Presented each January by the Jewish Museum and the Film Society of Lincoln Center. For information: phone: 212-423-3229 or 212-875-5600; website: www.filmlinc.com.

San Francisco Jewish Film Festival

Held from late July to early August, with events in San Francisco, Berkeley, Redwood City, and San Rafael. Whole festival passes or individual tickets are available. For information: phone: 415-621-0556; website: www.sfjff.org.

Toronto Jewish Film Festival

Held in late April or early May, at the Bloor Cinema. For information: phone: 416-324-9121; website: www.tjff.com.

Washington Jewish Film Festival

Held in December at the D.C. Jewish Community Center. For information: phone: 202-777-3248; website: www.wjff.org.

A Guide to the Funnest Kosher Restaurants in the U.S.

Good Eats and People to Meet

Anyone who's ever dared to entertain the notion that Jewish food isn't as fun as can be has obviously never chowed down a kosher hot dog at a major league baseball game or scarfed up a falafel on the Las Vegas strip!

But besides being kosher and fun, these restaurants offer travelers a sense of community—a place where everybody may not "know your name" but where, in a quick game of Jewish geography, you're sure to find someone who knows your father-in-law's best friend's nephew.

In most major cities you'll have a variety of decent kosher or Jewish-oriented restaurants from which to choose. We're interested here in those that really stand out as great places to take the whole family. They offer more than the typical fare of knishes and matzah balls; or they're located in particularly fun places; or they're just in places where you wouldn't expect to find them. They all offer Jewish cuisine with a twist (and we're not just talking about their challah!).

From twenty-five states, all over the U.S., here is our list of the best places to nosh during your family's travels. (Call ahead if you have questions about the level of *kashrut*.) Bon appétit, or as the Israelis say, *be-tei'avon!*

 ## Arizona

Segal's Kosher Foods
4848 North Seventh St., Phoenix. Phone: 602-285-1515.

Located in Phoenix's North Central neighborhood, this kid-friendly restaurant serves up lunch Monday through Friday, and dinner a few nights a week. They have deli, Italian, and American food; ribs are their specialty. Be sure to check out their butcher, who carries a huge assortment of knives in a special holster around his waist! The restaurant also has a display of Texas longhorns on the wall.

 ## California

ANAHEIM

The Plaza Inn
Main St., Disneyland, Anaheim. Phone: 714-781-4565.

The Blue Bayou
New Orleans Square, Disneyland, Anaheim. Phone: 714-781-7290.

These are two places to get kosher meals inside Disneyland. Both have packaged frozen meals, like the kind you'd get on an airplane. The food itself is not very kid-friendly. But hey, it's at Disneyland.

LOS ANGELES

Chick-N-Chow
12422 Burbank Blvd., North Hollywood. Phone: 818-763-4600.

This restaurant has a variety of Chinese and American selections, but it is best known for its finger-lickin' fried chicken. They offer kids' meals that come with a toy, and they do take-out, too.

Jeff's Gourmet Kosher Sausage Factory
8930 West Pico Blvd., Los Angeles. Phone: 310-858-8590.

This claims to be the only kosher sausage factory on the West Coast. They make eighteen different kinds of sausages (like any good kosher sausage factory would!), hot dogs, corned beef, pastrami, roast turkey, different kinds of jerky, and more. There's both indoor and outdoor seating. Order at the counter, where you'll also get free samples of the featured sausage of the day.

Milky Way
9108 West Pico Blvd., Los Angeles. Phone: 310-859-0004.

A restaurant in the heart of L.A.'s Jewish neighborhood, this classy kosher dairy establishment is owned and operated by Steven Spielberg's mom, Leah Adler, who is often at the restaurant chatting with customers. And like any Jewish mother, Mrs. Adler is always happy to hear friendly praise of her son.

Nagila Meating Place
9407 West Pico Blvd., Los Angeles. Phone: 310-788-0119.

Also in the West Pico area, this restaurant is a great place to take the whole family for some Israeli and Middle Eastern fast food! They have falafel, *shwarma,* and shish-kabobs as well as burgers and chicken nuggets for kids. They even have a mechanical horse and fire truck outside for your kids to ride before dinner!

Pizza Delight
435 N. Fairfax Ave., Los Angeles. Phone: 323-655-7800.

This kosher pizza restaurant has an extensive selection of Italian and Mexican foods. Health conscious customers can order a pizza with a multi-grain crust. This restaurant does deliver.

SAN DIEGO

Sheila's Café and Bakery
4577 Clairemont Dr., San Diego. Phone: 858-270-0251.

Along with the zoo, Sea World, and the Wild Animal Park, while in

San Diego you'll want to make a stop at this restaurant, where Sheila serves up yummy food and treats you like family. The menu includes various meat and vegetarian options. And there is a kids' menu where all items are $5.

SAN FRANCISCO

Sabra Grill
419 Grant Ave., San Francisco. Phone: 415-982-3656.

This kosher Israeli restaurant in the Chinatown area is open for breakfast, lunch, and dinner. Their menu has a lot of variety, including lots from the grill, cold cuts, salads, fish, and a kids' menu. For breakfast they have omelets. This restaurant is very good, but it's not stroller or wheelchair accessible. You have to go up a big flight of stairs to get in.

▶ Colorado

East Side Kosher Deli
499 South Elm St., Denver. Phone: 303-322-9862.

Centrally located in Denver, this restaurant is also a deli, grocery, and butcher shop, so it'll meet all your kosher food needs. They have a wide selection of choices for you, plus a special kids' menu. You can eat your meal here or call ahead for take-out, and they deliver to the ski areas.

Jeff's Diner
731 Quebec St., Denver. Phone: 303-333-4637.

This busy kosher diner offers burgers, hot dogs, salads, and steaks. They also have special kids' portions. There's a TV overhead, and the crowd here is usually watching sports.

▶ Connecticut

Claire's Corner Copia
1000 Chapel St., New Haven. Phone: 203-562-3888.

Try saying the name of this all-natural kosher vegetarian restaurant five times fast. Tongue-twisted? Well now it's time to let it unravel on the wide variety of selections offered at this dairy/pareve establishment. In the mood for Italian? Mexican? Middle Eastern? It's all here, just off the beautiful and historic Yale campus. In addition to the wide variety of food, the clientele is quite varied too. You'll find everyone from artists to rabbis to students dining here. It's a friendly environment, with outdoor seating.

 Florida

BOCA RATON

Falafel Armon
22767 State Road #7, Boca Raton. Phone: 561-477-0633.

Even if your kids aren't big on falafel, there's something for everyone at this Boca restaurant. A special kids' menu offers chicken nuggets, hot dogs, and spaghetti. There's a wide selection of Israeli meat and vegetarian dishes, or visit the salad bar for some all-you-can-eat veggies! And if you meet this restaurant's Israeli proprietor, try out some all-you-can-speak Hebrew!

MIAMI

Kosher Ranch
740 41st St., Miami Beach. Phone: 305-8-KOSHER.

You deserve a break today—and your kids will thank you for it! Next time you're in Miami Beach, treat them to some thoroughly American, thoroughly kosher, fast food cuisine, with everything from flame-grilled burgers to steaks to chicken wings. This spacious restaurant has a "ranch" atmosphere, and cowboy pictures are hanging everywhere.

Shemtov's Pizza
514 41st St., Miami Beach. Phone: 305-538-2123.

Locals say this place has the best pizza in town! They also have pasta, fish, calzones, and more.

ORLANDO

Disney World

Orlando. Phone: 407-WDW-DINE; website: www.disneyworld.com.

Kosher food is available at any Walt Disney World restaurant if ordered at least twenty-four hours in advance. The meals are frozen and pre-packaged. You'll pay about $10 for breakfast and $25 for a lunch or dinner entree, and kids' meals are $10. Kosher meals are also available with dinner shows for the regular dinner show prices (about $50 for adults and $25 for children). Choose from a variety of entrees, soups, and desserts. A credit card is required to hold the reservation. The full price will be charged for no-shows.

The Lower East Side

8548 Palm Pkwy., Orlando. Phone: 800-747-0013; website: www.kosherorlando.com.

There are many reasons to visit this close-to-Disney-World restaurant. They have a wide variety of international food and a kids' menu. And they're more than just a restaurant. They also have a mini-synagogue, and they offer package deals with three local hotels (the Radisson, the Marriott, and the Hawthorn Suites) for hotel accommodations and kosher meals. That can include box lunches to take to Disney during the day. They're also open during Passover.

TAMPA

Jerusalem Café and Deli

1140 Main St. #3, Dunedin. Phone: 727-736-8438.

With falafel, hummus, and a wide variety of salads, this eat-in or take-out café offers a slice of Israel just outside of Tampa. Deli meats and schnitzel are also available for eat-in or take-out. And since the restaurant is located inside a kosher food store, many other packaged items can be taken to go as well.

▶ Georgia

Wall Street Pizza
2470 Briarcliff Rd., Atlanta. Phone: 404-633-2111.

This place makes great pizzas with a wide variety of vegetarian toppings, including soy-based fake pepperoni, sausage, and Canadian bacon. They also serve fish, pasta, falafel, salads, and calzones.

Café Ofi
Marcus Jewish Community Center, 5342 Tilly Mill Rd., Dunwoody. Phone: 770-395-2663.

Located inside a beautiful, newly renovated JCC (where there is a small children's museum, see p. 187), this is food-court dining. With separate meat and dairy kitchens, you can order a variety of kid-friendly selections, including burgers and chicken nuggets. Eat inside and watch swimmers doing laps in the indoor pool, or outside on the deck if weather permits.

▶ Illinois

Ken's Diner
3353 West Dempster St., Skokie. Phone: 847-679-2850.

Some say this is the most fun kosher restaurant in the United States! An authentic '50s-style diner in the Chicago suburb of Skokie, this restaurant is complete with colorful period decor, juke boxes, pinball machines, and thirty-six toy and gum machines. On the menu you'll find kosher hot dogs, hamburgers, fries, and even pareve ice cream sodas.

Tel Aviv Kosher Pizza and Dairy
6349 N. California Ave., Chicago. Phone: 773-764-3776.

With a choice of pizza, falafel, or burritos, what kid's going to turn away from this kosher joint? There are many other choices as well, and delivery is available, too.

Iowa

The Nosh

800 First St., West Des Moines. Phone: 515-255-4047.

The only kosher restaurant for miles and miles around, this is a great place to stop for a deli sandwich or a cup of soup. They even bake their own bagels! Call ahead and they can cook up some specialty items. There are a few tables where you can sit and eat, or you can take your food to go. And there's a kosher market, too.

 Kentucky

Café J

Jewish Community Center of Louisville, 3600 Dutchmans Ln., Louisville. Phone: 502-459-0660.

In this JCC restaurant, there's everything from grilled chicken to tuna salad to hot dogs. In the summer they have an outdoor snack bar at the pool. And (as is the rule in most JCCs across the country), if you're a member of a JCC in your hometown, you can swim here for free.

▶ **Louisiana**

Creole Kosher Kitchen

115 Chartres St., New Orleans. Phone: 504-529-4120.

This place offers kosher Creole cuisine right in the heart of New Orleans' French Quarter, just off Canal Street. There's an excellent kosher jambalaya, plus there's Persian food, deli, and vegetarian dishes. The restaurant doesn't have a special kids' menu, but you can order kids' portions.

▶ **Maine**

Perry's Sidewalk Café

Corner of Commercial and Moulton Sts., Portland. Phone: 207-77-KOSHR.

This sidewalk café-pushcart is located right in Portland's Old Port District on the historic waterfront. Perry Mogul is there April through October, weather permitting (call first to make sure the place is open).

The hot dogs are fantastic! It's not under rabbinical supervision, since it's open on Saturday, but the food is all strictly kosher. Perry even has a washing station and *bentshers* (booklets with the Grace after Meals) on his pushcart.

▶ Maryland

Ben Yehuda Café and Pizzeria

1370-B Lamberton Dr., Silver Spring. Phone: 301-681-8900.

Located in the Kemp Mill neighborhood, this is a hot spot for local Jewish families, especially during the summer months. You'll find pizza, pasta, salads, sandwiches, and ice cream on the menu. There's some outdoor seating.

Kosher Bite

6309 Reisterstown Rd., Baltimore. Phone: 410-358-6349.

This place has fast food—burgers, hot dogs, chicken, *shwarma,* the works—with portions available that are specially designed for the smaller (kosher) bite of kids. If you order at the counter, you can be in and out of there in no time at all.

Oriole Park: Kosher Food Stand

Oriole Park at Camden Yards, 333 West Camden St., Baltimore (main concourse, in front of gate F, opposite section 78, in the left field area). Contact: Project Ezra, 410-764-7902.

"Take me out to the ball game, take me out with the crowd / Buy me some hot dogs and knishes…." What? It's true, Camden Yards is home to major league baseball's very first kosher food stand.

Ravens Stadium: Kosher Food Stand

PSINet Stadium, 1101 Russell St., Baltimore (main concourse, in section 123). Contact: Project Ezra, 410-764-7902.

Across the parking lot from the Orioles' stadium, the Ravens football arena has an even larger selection of kosher snacks, with all the typical ballpark snacks plus deli sandwiches, chicken nuggets, and more. This was the first kosher stand in an NFL stadium.

▶ Massachusetts

Milk Street Café
Two locations in Boston: 50 Milk St. Phone: 617-542-FOOD; and in the park at Post Office Square. Phone: 617-350-PARK.

At both locations, the food is terrific and the atmosphere is equally impressive. Although Milk Street is strictly kosher, the majority of the clientele is non-Jewish. Customers come because the food is good. You'll find salads, sandwiches, wraps, soups, and more. The park location is perfect for a picnic on a nice summer day.

Rami's Falafel
324 Harvard St., Brookline. Phone: 617-738-3577.

The owner says people come from all over to eat this delicious food. Falafel, *shwarma*, kabob, *bourekas*, and more—all made from scratch. There's lots that kids will enjoy, and a very casual, family atmosphere. You can eat in or take out.

Zaatar's Oven
242 Harvard St., Brookline. Phone: 617-731-6836.

With lots of Middle Eastern and Mediterranean choices, this hot spot specializes in flatbreads and breads stuffed with vegetables, called *sanbusaks*. It's a pretty restaurant with cool decor. There's a young clientele, and many of the regulars are local families.

▶ Michigan

Taste of Class
25254 Greenfield Rd., Oak Park. Phone: 248-967-6020.

Eating here is like being at grandma's house for dinner; this family-style kosher restaurant has a real *heimish* feel. Their all-you-can-eat buffet takes on different themes (Italian, Mexican, Chinese, Polish). Plus they have lots of Middle Eastern and American selections on the regular menu. There's a children's menu, and coloring books and crayons keep kids busy at the table. Chuck, the owner, says they have the best french fries in the state of Michigan.

▶ Nevada

Haifa Restaurant
855 East Twain, Las Vegas. Phone: 702-791-1956.

Located just four lights away from the Las Vegas strip, this restaurant serves up all kinds of Israeli dishes (falafel, kabobs, Israeli salads) plus some deli foods. They also have hot dogs and chicken nuggets for the picky eaters in your group.

▶ New Jersey

Maxim Restaurant
404 East State Highway 70, Cherry Hill. Phone: 856-428-5045.

Whether you're traveling on vacation or driving to see relatives, this kosher Middle Eastern pit stop, convenient to I-295 and the New Jersey Turnpike, is just the thing to refuel the family.

▶ New York

NEW YORK CITY

2nd Avenue Delicatessen
156 2nd Ave., New York. Phone: 212-677-0606.

This is the quintessential New York kosher deli. The sandwiches are piled high with scrumptious deli meat, and they have all the traditional Ashkenazic food, including matzah ball soup and gefilte fish. Plus there's stuff that's sure to gross out your kiddies, like *ptcha*, which are jellied calves' feet! When this deli opened in 1954, its funky East Village locale was a center for Yiddish culture. In front of the restaurant, stars on the sidewalk pay tribute to prominent Yiddish Theatre personalities. Inside, photographs of famous people who've eaten here line the walls. The restaurant is open on Saturday, but it is strictly kosher.

Eden Wok
127 West 72nd St., New York. Phone: 212-787-8700.

This restaurant has both Chinese and Japanese food as well as a sushi bar. Plus they have the first kosher hibachi in New York. Up to ten people sit around the table with a cook in the middle, who makes the food right in front of you with flames and flare.

H&H Bagels
2239 Broadway (80th St.), New York. Phone: 212-595-8000.

This is what you've always dreamed a New York bagel would be like! You haven't had a bagel until you've sunk your teeth into a hot, fresh, kosher, gargantuan H&H bagel. H&H is take-out only.

Kosher Deluxe
10 West 46th St. (between 5th and 6th Aves.), New York. Phone: 212-869-6699.

You can't go sightseeing in Manhattan without visiting Rockefeller Center, Radio City Music Hall, and other midtown spectacles. Once all that walking and gazing up at the skyscrapers has got you and your family famished, stop in to this conveniently located kosher fast food joint. They have burgers, fries, falafel, and more!

Moshe's Falafel
Southeast corner of 46th St. and 6th Ave, New York.

Check out this mobile kosher food spot, right in the heart of midtown Manhattan! It's a falafel stand, set up in a trailer-on-wheels, close to Grand Central Station and Times Square. Moshe makes a particularly Israeli-style falafel that may just be the best in the city!

Shea Stadium: Kosher Food Carts
123-01 Roosevelt Ave., Flushing. Phone: 718-672-4032

If rooting for the Mets puts you in the mood for a kosher hot dog, you're in luck! There are two kosher food carts at Shea Stadium. One is located on the field level, in the rightfield food court area. The other is on the mezzanine level, in section 6. They sell hot dogs, knishes, cookies, pretzels, and drinks.

Yankee Stadium: Kosher Food Carts
161st St. and River Ave., Bronx. Phone: 718-293-4300.

The venerable home of the Bronx Bombers boasts a kosher food cart. It's on the main level, in section 10. At large events (like the World Series) they bring a second cart with kosher food onto the tier level, also in section 10. Both carts sell hotdogs, knishes, and drinks.

SYRACUSE

Pickles Kosher Deli
4467 East Genesee St., Syracuse. Phone: 315-445-1294.

Many say this is the best deli in New York state outside of Manhattan. Pickles serves up scrumptious sandwiches, homemade matzah ball soup, and other traditional kosher "deli-cacies." It's been in business for twenty years because people come back again and again to this great family restaurant.

▶ North Carolina

The Kosher Mart and Delicatessen, Inc.
3840 East Independence Blvd., Charlotte. Phone: 800-849-8288.

If you're craving kosher deli meat in North Carolina, this is the place to get it! They're mostly a grocery, but also have a few tables if you want to stay and eat your sandwiches there. Then you can take some extras for the road!

▶ Ohio

Abba's Restaurant
13937 Cedar Rd., South Euclid. Phone: 216-321-5660.

This restaurant is in Cleveland's Jewish South Euclid neighborhood. Locals say the food is terrific, particularly the pita that they bake at the restaurant! They also have steaks, *shwarma*, kabobs, beef and veal ribs, deli, falafel, and salads, plus a children's menu with chicken fingers, hot dogs, mini-burgers, and bow-tie pasta.

Chocolate Emporium
14439 Cedar Rd., Cleveland. Phone: 216-382-0140; website: www.choclat.com.

If you're anywhere in Ohio—no, make that anywhere in the Midwest—just try and convince your kids that it's a good idea to skip this place! It's a kosher ice cream parlor and chocolate shop, offering treats made with both dairy and pareve ingredients. Perfect for dessert, or a sweet treat any time! One specialty: They make chocolate bowls, which can be filled with chocolate-covered popcorn, pretzels, or strawberries. They also ship by UPS all over the U.S.

▶ Pennsylvania

Singapore Vegetarian
1006 Race St., Philadelphia. Phone: 215-922-3288.

Located in Philadelphia's Chinatown district, this kosher vegetarian restaurant offers a mix of all sorts of southeast Asian cuisine: Chinese, Malaysian, and others. With a cook and staff who are all Asian, the food is very authentic.

Time Out Falafel Kingdom
9846 Bustleton Ave., Philadelphia. Phone: 215-969-7545.

If you're in Philly and craving a kosher Philly steak, this is the place to go! It comes on a big hoagie roll with all the fixin's (except cheese). They also have great Middle Eastern and Israeli food, deli, salads, and lots more, plus daily specials and a kids' menu. Israeli music plays at dinnertime, and there are pictures of Israel on the walls.

Platters Restaurant
2020 Murray Ave., Pittsburgh. Phone: 412-422-3370.

This outstanding restaurant serves up scrumptious deli. They also have great dishes from the grill, and Chinese food on the menu. They cater fantastic deli platters for carry-out or delivery. And with a special children's menu, they cater to the younger members of your family. Tell Pinky we said hi!

Central PA's Kosher Mart
Hershey Park, Hersey. Phone: 717-392-5111.

This may be the only food stand at any amusement park in the country where they're cooking up kosher food (as opposed to pre-packaged meals). It won't be hard having fun in and around this place, during a visit to Hershey Park. Stop in and say hello to Sally, the stand's friendly proprietor, who will set you up with knishes, hot dogs, chicken, falafel, latkes, and more! Just be sure to let your food digest before jumping on the roller coasters. Sally's stand opens when the park does, in May, and stays open through the summer.

▶ Rhode Island

Davis's Delicatessen
721 Hope St., Providence. Phone:401-331-4239.

Located in Providence's Jewish section on the east side of town, this deli is just a five-minute drive from downtown. It's a deli, and it's take-out only. They don't make sandwiches here, but you can buy the deli meat and rolls and make them yourself. They also have dairy on the other side of the store, with bagels, lox, and other stuff.

▶ South Carolina

Jerusalem Restaurant
1007 Withers Dr., Myrtle Beach. Phone: 843-946-6650.

Right in the middle of town, this restaurant is close to the beach and all the fun kid attractions that Myrtle Beach has to offer. They specialize in Israeli food, but also have deli sandwiches, salads, a kids' menu, and they bake all their own desserts.

▶ Texas

Delicious Foods
7460 Callaghan Rd., San Antonio. Phone: 210-366-1844.

Remember the Alamo, especially when you're visiting San Antonio. And while you're in the Lone Star State, also remember this place—

a kosher deli that makes great sandwiches and side dishes. They bake their own bread, bagels, and challah. They also have a mini-grocery store, and they make deliveries to area hotels.

JCC Kosher Kid's Café
7900 Northhaven Rd., Dallas. Phone: 214-739-2737.

This is just a small snack shop with limited hours, located in the Dallas JCC. What makes it special is that it's run entirely by kids. They cook the food, take orders, and run the cash register. It's open Sunday afternoons and serves things like hamburgers, hot dogs, and sandwiches.

King David Grill and Deli
5925 South Breaswood, Houston. Phone: 713-729-5741.

With a large outdoor patio, yummy homemade desserts, and fresh baked pita bread, this is a restaurant you and your children are sure to all give a thumbs up. Their specialty is Middle Eastern cuisine, but they have items on the menu from all over the world.

▶ Virginia

The Kosher Place
738 West 22nd St., Norfolk. Phone: 757-623-1770.

Twenty minutes from the Virginia Beach oceanfront and less than an hour from Busch Gardens in Williamsburg, this restaurant is a nice find. It is located in the artsy historic area of Ghent, where there are nice craft shops, antiques, and pretty homes—a great area to walk around with the kids. They serve deli sandwiches, burgers, hot dogs, and more.

▶ Washington

Bamboo Gardens
364 Roy St., Seattle. Phone: 206-282-6616.

Interested in trying kosher sweet-and-sour pork? This kosher vegetarian Chinese restaurant offers meatless versions of that dish and many others. It's right in the heart of Seattle, across from the opera house and near the famous Seattle Center. There are 120 items on the menu, so you can take your family and order a bunch of different things to share!

AFTERWORD

OK, then. If you've been following along, by now you've picked up some new ways to celebrate the holidays. You've worked together to help others, created artsy crafts and crafty arts, mastered great new games, and made a mess of the kitchen making tasty foods. You sang and danced along to cool music, flipped through the pages of classic books and stories, given your "thumbs up" to terrific films and videos, and surfed your way through the Internet and software programs. You've also wandered through museums and explored historical sites, set up your tent at family camps and swung through adventure programs, partied at cultural festivals, and noshed at kosher restaurants across the United States.

What's no doubt clear at this point: There's no end to the possibilities for Jewish family fun.

Now it's up to you to take it from here! Adapt these activities to suit your family's interests and tastes, and mix in your own custom-made ideas as well. It's not hard to figure out what's fun for the whole *mishpachah*; after all, there's still a little "kid" left in all of us.

And when you're looking out for it, there's Jewish family fun around every corner.

Finally, let us know about your experiences with Jewish family fun! Which of these activities worked well for you, and which not so well? How were you able to adapt them to make the activities even better? E-mail your comments to us at JewishFamilyFun@aol.com.

APPENDIX OF PRAYERS

There are Hebrew prayers *(brakhot)* for every occasion—when you're sitting in a sukkah, washing your hands, even seeing a rainbow. Below is a list of prayers mentioned specifically in this book—some we included because they are not found in most prayer books; others we included because they're so common, we thought it would be nice to have a handy list of them right here. For others not listed below, check in any standard prayer book or ask a rabbi, cantor, or Jewish educator.

Shabbat Candlelighting

בָּרוּךְ אַתָּה יְיָ
אֱלֹהֵינוּ מֶלֶךְ הָעוֹלָם,
אֲשֶׁר קִדְּשָׁנוּ בְּמִצְוֹתָיו
וְצִוָּנוּ לְהַדְלִיק נֵר
שֶׁל שַׁבָּת.

Barukh attah Adonai
Eloheinu melekh ha-olam,
asher kidshanu bemitzvotav
vetzivanu lehadlik ner
shel Shabbat.

Praised are You, Adonai, our God, Ruler of the universe, whose *mitzvot* add holiness to our lives and who gave us the mitzvah to kindle the Shabbat lights.

Family Blessings

For the Sons

יְשִׂמְךָ אֱלֹהִים
כְּאֶפְרַיִם וְכִמְנַשֶּׁה.

*Yesimkha Elohim
keEfrayim vekhiMenasheh.*

(May) God make you like Ephraim and Menasseh.

For the Daughters

יְשִׂמֵךְ אֱלֹהִים
כְּשָׂרָה רִבְקָה רָחֵל וְלֵאָה.

*Yesimekh Elohim
keSarah Rivkah Rakhel veLeah.*

(May) God make you like Sarah, Rebecca, Rachel, and Leah.

For All Children

יְבָרֶכְךָ יְיָ
וְיִשְׁמְרֶךָ.
יָאֵר יְיָ פָּנָיו אֵלֶיךָ
וִיחֻנֶּךָּ.
יִשָּׂא יְיָ פָּנָיו אֵלֶיךָ
וְיָשֵׂם לְךָ שָׁלוֹם.

*Yevarekhekha Adonai
veyishmerekha.
Ya'er Adonai panav elekha
vikhuneka.
Yisa Adonai panav elekha
veyasem lekha shalom.*

(May) God bless you and watch over you. (May) God cause the Divine face to shine upon you and be gracious to you. (May) God lift up the Divine face toward you and give you peace.

Blessing on Wine

בָּרוּךְ אַתָּה יְיָ
אֱלֹהֵינוּ מֶלֶךְ הָעוֹלָם,
בּוֹרֵא פְּרִי הַגָּפֶן.

*Barukh attah Adonai
Eloheinu melekh ha-olam,
boreh peri hagafen.*

Praised are You, Adonai, our God, Ruler of the universe, Creator of the fruit of the vine.

Blessing for Handwashing

בָּרוּךְ אַתָּה יְיָ *Barukh attah Adonai*
אֱלֹהֵינוּ מֶלֶךְ הָעוֹלָם, *Eloheinu melekh ha-olam,*
אֲשֶׁר קִדְּשָׁנוּ בְּמִצְוֹתָיו *asher kidshanu, bemitzvotav*
וְצִוָּנוּ עַל נְטִילַת יָדָיִם. *vetzivanu al netilat yadayim.*

Praised are You, Adonai, our God, Ruler of the universe,
whose *mitzvot* add holiness to our lives and who gave us the
mitvah of the washing of hands.

Blessing on Bread

בָּרוּךְ אַתָּה יְיָ *Barukh attah Adonai*
אֱלֹהֵינוּ מֶלֶךְ הָעוֹלָם, *Eloheinu melekh ha-olam*
הַמּוֹצִיא לֶחֶם מִן הָאָרֶץ. *hamotzi lekhem min ha-aretz.*

Praised are You, Adonai, our God, Ruler of the universe,
who brings forth bread from the earth.

Shehekheyanu

בָּרוּךְ אַתָּה יְיָ *Barukh atah Adonai*
אֱלֹהֵינוּ מֶלֶךְ הָעוֹלָם, *Eloheinu melekh ha-olam*
שֶׁהֶחֱיָנוּ וְקִיְּמָנוּ *shehekheyanu vekiyemanu*
וְהִגִּיעָנוּ *vehigiyanu*
לַזְּמַן הַזֶּה. *laz'man hazeh.*

Praised are You, Adonai, our God, Ruler of the universe,
who has given us life and sustained us
and enabled us to reach this occasion.

Blessing on Fruit from a Tree

בָּרוּךְ אַתָּה יְיָ
אֱלֹהֵינוּ מֶלֶךְ הָעוֹלָם,
בּוֹרֵא פְּרִי הָעֵץ.

Barukh attah Adonai
Eloheinu melekh ha-olam,
boreh peri ha-etz.

Praised are You, Adonai, our God, Ruler of the universe,
Creator of the fruit of the tree.

Blessing on Food from the Ground

בָּרוּךְ אַתָּה יְיָ
אֱלֹהֵינוּ מֶלֶךְ הָעוֹלָם,
בּוֹרֵא פְּרִי הָאֲדָמָה.

Barukh attah Adonai
Eloheinu melekh ha-olam,
boreh peri ha-adamah.

Praised are You, Adonai, our God, Ruler of the universe,
Creator of the fruit of the ground.

Blessing on Food (Other Than Bread) from Wheat, Barley, Rye, Oats, or Spelt

בָּרוּךְ אַתָּה יְיָ
אֱלֹהֵינוּ מֶלֶךְ הָעוֹלָם,
בּוֹרֵא מִינֵי מְזוֹנוֹת.

Barukh attah Adonai
Eloheinu melekh ha-olam,
boreh minei mezonot.

Praised are You, Adonai, our God, Ruler of the universe,
Creator of various kinds of nourishment.

Blessing on Other Food and Drink

בָּרוּךְ אַתָּה יְיָ
אֱלֹהֵינוּ מֶלֶךְ הָעוֹלָם,
שֶׁהַכֹּל נִהְיֶה בִּדְבָרוֹ.

Barukh attah Adonai
Eloheinu melekh ha-olam,
shehakol nihyeh bidvaro.

Praised are You, Adonai, our God, Ruler of the universe,
at whose word all things come into being.

Blessing over the *Lulav*

בָּרוּךְ אַתָּה יְיָ
אֱלֹהֵינוּ מֶלֶךְ הָעוֹלָם,
אֲשֶׁר קִדְּשָׁנוּ בְּמִצְוֹתָיו
וְצִוָּנוּ עַל נְטִילַת לוּלָב.

Barukh attah Adonai
Eloheinu melekh ha-olam,
asher kidshanu bemitzvotav
vetzivanu al netilat lulav.

Praised are You, Adonai, our God, Ruler of the universe,
whose mitzvot add holiness to our lives
and who gave us the mitzvah to take up the *lulav*.

Blessing for Counting the *Omer*

בָּרוּךְ אַתָּה יְיָ
אֱלֹהֵינוּ מֶלֶךְ הָעוֹלָם,
אֲשֶׁר קִדְּשָׁנוּ בְּמִצְוֹתָיו
וְצִוָּנוּ עַל סְפִירַת הָעֹמֶר.

Barukh attah Adonai
Eloheinu melekh ha-olam,
asher kidshanu bemitzvotav
vetzivanu al sfirat ha-omer.

Praised are You, Adonai, our God, Ruler of the universe,
whose mitzvot add holiness to our lives
and who gave us the mitzvah of counting the *omer*.

Blessing for Putting on the *Tallit*

בָּרוּךְ אַתָּה יְיָ
אֱלֹהֵינוּ מֶלֶךְ הָעוֹלָם,
אֲשֶׁר קִדְּשָׁנוּ בְּמִצְוֹתָיו
וְצִוָּנוּ לְהִתְעַטֵּף בַּצִּיצִת.

Barukh attah Adonai
Eloheinu melekh ha-olam,
asher kidshanu bemitzvotav
vetzivanu lehit'atef batzitzit.

Praised are You, Adonai, our God, Ruler of the universe,
whose mitzvot add holiness to our lives
and who gave us the mitzah of wrapping ourselves in *tzitzit.*

The Sephardic/Persian Rosh Hashanah Seder
Blessing for Sweet Year/Apples and Honey

יְהִי רָצוֹן מִלְפָנֶיךָ,
יְיָ אֱלֹהֵינוּ וֵאלֹהֵי אֲבוֹתֵינוּ,
שֶׁתִּתְחַדֵּשׁ (שֶׁתְּחַדֵּשׁ) עָלֵינוּ
שָׁנָה טוֹבָה וּמְתוּקָה.
מֵרֵאשִׁית הַשָּׁנָה
וְעַד אַחֲרִית הַשָּׁנָה.

Yehi ratzon milfanekha
Adonai Eloheinu Velohei avoteinu,
shetit'khadesh (shetekhadesh) aleinu
shanah tovah umetukah,
mereshit hashanah
ve-ad akharit hashanah.

May it be Your will, Adonai, our God and God of our ancestors,
to renew this year for us with sweetness and happiness,
from the beginning of the year to the end of the year.

Prayer with the Leek

יְהִי רָצוֹן מִלְּפָנֶיךָ,
יְיָ אֱלֹהֵינוּ וֵאלֹהֵי אֲבוֹתֵינוּ,
שֶׁיִּכָּרְתוּ אוֹיְבֶיךָ וְשׂוֹנְאֶיךָ
וְכָל מְבַקְשֵׁי רָעָתֵינוּ.
תָּרוֹם יָדְךָ עַל צָרֶיךָ
וְכָל אוֹיְבֶיךָ יִכָּרֵתוּ.

Yehi ratzon milfanekha,
Adonai, Eloheinu Velohei avoteinu,
sheyikartu oivekha veson'ekha
vekhol mevakshei ra'atenu.
Tarom yadkha al tzarekha
vekhol oivekha yikaretu.

°May it be Your will, Adonai, our God and God of our ancestors, that all evil in the world be cut off. Rise up against evil and put an end to it.

° interpretation

Prayer with the Beet

יְהִי רָצוֹן מִלְּפָנֶיךָ,
יְיָ אֱלֹהֵינוּ וֵאלֹהֵי אֲבוֹתֵינוּ,
שֶׁיִּסְתַּלְּקוּ אוֹיְבֶיךָ וְשׂוֹנְאֶיךָ
וְכָל מְבַקְשֵׁי רָעָתֵנוּ:
סוּרוּ מִמֶּנִּי כָּל פֹּעֲלֵי אָוֶן
כִּי שָׁמַע יְיָ קוֹל בִּכְיִי:
סוּרוּ סוּרוּ צְאוּ
מִשָּׁם טָמֵא אַל תִּגָּעוּ
צְאוּ מִתּוֹכָהּ
הִבָּרוּ נֹשְׂאֵי כְלֵי יְיָ.

Yehi ratzon milfanekha,
Adonai Eloheinu Velohei avoteinu,
sheyistalku oivekha veson'ekha
vekhol mevakshei ra'atenu.
Suru mimmeni kol po'alei aven
ki shama Adonai kol bikhyi.
Suru suru tze'u
misham tameh al tiga'u
tze'u mitokhah
hibaru nos'ei khlei Adonai.

°May it be Your will, Adonai, our God and God of our ancestors, that all evil in the world be wiped out. Remove all evil, because You, God, have heard the sound of my crying. Distance yourselves from evil and that which is unpure. Cleanse yourselves, those who are followers of God.

° interpretation

Prayer with the Dates

יְהִי רָצוֹן מִלְפָנֶיךָ,
יְיָ אֱלֹהֵינוּ וֵאלֹהֵי אֲבוֹתֵינוּ,
שֶׁיִּתַּמּוּ אוֹיְבֶיךָ וְשׂוֹנְאֶיךָ
וְכָל מְבַקְשֵׁי רָעָתֵנוּ:
יִתַּמּוּ חַטָּאִים מִן הָאָרֶץ
וּרְשָׁעִים עוֹד אֵינָם
בָּרְכִי נַפְשִׁי אֶת יְיָ הַלְלוּיָהּ:
וּבְחַסְדְּךָ תַּצְמִית אוֹיְבַי
וְהַאֲבַדְתָּ כָּל צוֹרְרֵי נַפְשִׁי
כִּי אֲנִי עַבְדֶּךָ.

Yehi ratzon milfanekha,
Adonai Eloheinu Velohei avoteinu,
sheyitamu oivekha veson'ekhah
vekhol mevakshei ra'atenu.
Yitammu khatta'im min ha-aretz
ursha'im od einam
barkhi nafshi et Adonai halleluyah.
Uvkhasdekha tatzmit oivai
veha'avadeta kol tzorerei nafshi
ki ani avdekha.

°May it be Your will, Adonai, our God and God of our ancestors, that all evil cease to exist. All evil should be wiped out from the earth. Bless the Lord, oh my soul, halleluyah. And with Your righteousness erase all evil, because I am Your servant.

° interpretation

Prayer with the Squash

יְהִי רָצוֹן מִלְפָנֶיךָ,
יְיָ אֱלֹהֵינוּ וֵאלֹהֵי אֲבוֹתֵינוּ,
שֶׁתִּקְרַע רוֹעַ גְּזַר דִּינֵנוּ
וְיִקָּרְאוּ לְפָנֶיךָ זְכִיּוֹתֵינוּ.

Yehi ratzon milfanekha,
Adonai Eloheinu Velohei avoteinu,
shetikra ro'a gezar dinenu
veyikar'u lefanekha zakhiyoteinu.

May it be Your will, Adonai, our God and God of our ancestors,
to tear up the evil decree against us,
and let our good deeds present themselves to You.

Prayer with the Beans

יְהִי רָצוֹן מִלְפָנֶיךָ,
יְיָ אֱלֹהֵינוּ וֵאלֹהֵי אֲבוֹתֵינוּ,
שֶׁיִּרְבּוּ זְכִיּוֹתֵינוּ
(וּתְלַבְּבֵנוּ).

Yehi ratzon milfanekha,
Adonai Eloheinu Velohei avoteinu,
sheyirbu zakhiyoteinu
(Persian tradition: *utlabevenu*).

May it be Your will, Adonai, our God and God of our ancestors,
that our merits (*Persian tradition:* and our inspirations) will multiply.

Prayer with the Pomegranate

יְהִי רָצוֹן מִלְפָנֶיךָ,
יְיָ אֱלֹהֵינוּ וֵאלֹהֵי אֲבוֹתֵינוּ,
(שֶׁיִּרְבּוּ
זְכִיּוֹתֵינוּ)
(שֶׁנִּהְיֶה
מְלֵאִים מִצְוֹת)
כָּרִמּוֹן.

Yehi ratzon milfanekha,
Adonai Eloheinu Velohei avoteinu,
(Sephardic tradition: *sheyirbu*
zakhiyoteinu)
(Persian tradition: *shenihyeh*
mele'im mitzvot)
karimon.

May it be Your will, Adonai, our God and God of our ancestors,
that (*Sephardic tradition:* our merits will multiply) (*Persian tradition:*
we should be full of good deeds) like the seeds of the pomegranate.

Prayer with the Fish

יְהִי רָצוֹן מִלְפָנֶיךָ,
יְיָ אֱלֹהֵינוּ וֵאלֹהֵי אֲבוֹתֵינוּ,
שֶׁנִּפְרֶה וְנִרְבֶּה כַּדָּגִים
וְתַשְׁגַּח עָלָן בְּעֵינָא פְּקִיחָא.

Yehi ratzon milfanekha,
Adonai Eloheinu Velohei avoteinu,
shenifreh venirbeh kadagim
vetishgakh alan be-aina pekikha.

May it be Your will, Adonai, our God and God of our ancestors,
that we should be fruitful and multiply like fish,
and You should watch over us with open eyes.

Prayer with the Lung

יְהִי רָצוֹן מִלְפָנֶיךָ,
יְיָ אֱלֹהֵינוּ וֵאלֹהֵי אֲבוֹתֵינוּ,
שֶׁיִּהְיוּ עֲוֹנוֹתֵינוּ קַלִּים
כְּרֵיאָה.

Yehi ratzon milfanekha,
Adonai Eloheinu Velohei avoteinu,
sheyihyu avonotenu kalim
kere'ah.

May it be Your will, Adonai, our God and God of our ancestors,
that our wrongdoings will be light like the lung.

Prayer with Something
from the Head of an Animal

יְהִי רָצוֹן מִלְפָנֶיךָ,
יְיָ אֱלֹהֵינוּ וֵאלֹהֵי אֲבוֹתֵינוּ,
שֶׁנִּהְיֶה לְרֹאשׁ וְלֹא לְזָנָב
וְתִזְכּוֹר לָנוּ אֵילוֹ שֶׁל יִצְחָק
(אָבִינוּ עָלָיו
הַשָּׁלוֹם בֶּן אַבְרָהָם אָבִינוּ
עָלָיו הַשָּׁלוֹם).

Yehi ratzon milfanekha,
Adonai Eloheinu Velohei avoteinu,
shenihyeh lerosh velo lezanav.
Vetizkor lanu eilo shel Yitzkhak
(Persian tradition: *avinu alav*
hashalom ben Avraham avinu
alav hashalom).

May it be Your will, Adonai, our God and God of our ancestors,
that we should be like the head not like the tail.
And for our benefit, remember the story of Isaac
(*Persian tradition:* our forefather, may peace be with him,
son of Abraham our forefather, may peace be with him).

APPENDIX OF STENCILS

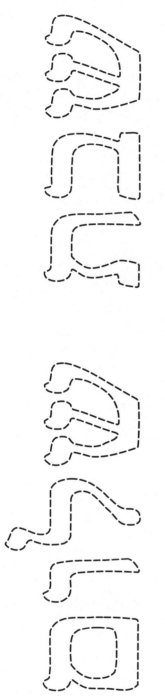

(Shabbat Shalom)

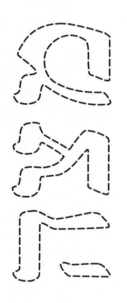

(Matzah)

(Chag Sameach)

(Shanah Tovah)

INDEX
By Activity

By Location

Our Family's Ideas

Our Family's Ideas

Our Family's Ideas

Our Family's Ideas

About JEWISH LIGHTS Publishing

People of all faiths and backgrounds yearn for books that attract, engage, educate, and spiritually inspire.

Our principal goal is to stimulate thought and help all people learn about who the Jewish People are, where they come from, and what the future can be made to hold. While people of our diverse Jewish heritage are the primary audience, our books speak to people in the Christian world as well and will broaden their understanding of Judaism and the roots of their own faith.

We bring to you authors who are at the forefront of spiritual thought and experience. While each has something different to say, they all say it in a voice that you can hear.

Our books are designed to welcome you and then to engage, stimulate, and inspire. We judge our success not only by whether or not our books are beautiful and commercially successful, but by whether or not they make a difference in your life.

We at Jewish Lights take great care to produce beautiful books that present meaningful spiritual content in a form that reflects the art of making high quality books. Therefore, we want to acknowledge those who contributed to the production of this book.

Stuart M. Matlins, Publisher

PRODUCTION
Tim Holtz, Martha McKinney & Bridgett Taylor

EDITORIAL
Amanda Dupuis, Polly Short Mahoney,
Lauren Seidman & Emily Wichland

COVER DESIGN
Tim Holtz

TYPESETTING
Chelsea Cloeter, Tucson, Arizona

COVER / TEXT PRINTING & BINDING
Versa Press, East Peoria, Illinois

The Way Into... Series

A major multi-volume series to be completed over the next several years, **The Way Into... provides an accessible and usable "guided tour" of the Jewish faith, its people, its history and beliefs—in total, an introduction to Judaism for adults that will enable them to understand and interact with sacred texts.** Each volume is written by a major modern scholar and teacher, and is organized around an important concept of Judaism.

The Way Into... will enable all readers to achieve a real sense of Jewish cultural literacy through guided study. Available volumes:

The Way Into Torah
by *Dr. Norman J. Cohen*

What is "Torah"? What are the different approaches to studying Torah? What are the different levels of understanding Torah? For whom is study intended? Explores the origins and development of Torah, why it should be studied and how to do it. An easy-to-use, easy-to-understand introduction to an ancient subject.
6 x 9, 176 pp, HC, ISBN 1-58023-028-8 **$21.95**

The Way Into Jewish Prayer
by *Dr. Lawrence A. Hoffman*

Opens the door to 3,000 years of the Jewish way to God by making available all you need to feel at home in Jewish worship. Provides basic definitions of the terms you need to know as well as thoughtful analysis of the depth that lies beneath Jewish prayer.
6 x 9, 224 pp, HC, ISBN 1-58023-027-X **$21.95**

The Way Into Encountering God in Judaism
by *Dr. Neil Gillman*

Explains how Jews have encountered God throughout history—and today—by exploring the many metaphors for God in Jewish tradition. Explores the Jewish tradition's passionate but also conflicting ways of relating to God as Creator, relational partner, and a force in history and nature.
6 x 9, 240 pp, HC, ISBN 1-58023-025-3 **$21.95**

The Way Into Jewish Mystical Tradition
by *Rabbi Lawrence Kushner*

Explains the principles of Jewish mystical thinking, their religious and spiritual significance, and how they relate to our lives. A book that allows us to experience and understand the Jewish mystical approach to our place in the world.
6 x 9, 224 pp, HC, ISBN 1-58023-029-6 **$21.95**

Or phone, fax, mail or e-mail to: **JEWISH LIGHTS Publishing**
Sunset Farm Offices, Route 4 • P.O. Box 237 • Woodstock, Vermont 05091
Tel: (802) 457-4000 • Fax: (802) 457-4004 • www.jewishlights.com
Credit card orders: (800) 962-4544 (9AM–5PM ET Monday–Friday)
Generous discounts on quantity orders. SATISFACTION GUARANTEED. Prices subject to change.

Spirituality

My People's Prayer Book: *Traditional Prayers, Modern Commentaries*
Ed. by *Dr. Lawrence A. Hoffman*

Provides a diverse and exciting commentary to the traditional liturgy, helping modern men and women find new wisdom in Jewish prayer, and bring liturgy into their lives. Each book includes Hebrew text, modern translation, and commentaries *from all perspectives* of the Jewish world.

Vol. 1—*The Sh'ma and Its Blessings,* 7 x 10, 168 pp, HC, ISBN 1-879045-79-6 **$23.95**
Vol. 2—*The Amidah,* 7 x 10, 240 pp, HC, ISBN 1-879045-80-X **$23.95**
Vol. 3—*P'sukei D'zimrah* (Morning Psalms), 7 x 10, 240 pp, HC, ISBN 1-879045-81-8 **$24.95**
Vol. 4—*Seder K'riat Hatorah* (The Torah Service), 7 x 10, 264 pp, HC, ISBN 1-879045-82-6 **$23.95**
Vol. 5—*Birkhot Hashachar* (Morning Blessings), 7 x 10, 240 pp, HC, ISBN 1-879045-83-4 **$24.95**

 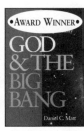   

Becoming a Congregation of Learners
Learning as a Key to Revitalizing Congregational Life by Isa Aron, Ph.D.;
Foreword by Rabbi Lawrence A. Hoffman, Co-Developer, Synagogue 2000
6 x 9, 304 pp, Quality PB, ISBN 1-58023-089-X **$19.95**

Self, Struggle & Change
Family Conflict Stories in Genesis and Their Healing Insights for Our Lives
by Dr. Norman J. Cohen   6 x 9, 224 pp, Quality PB, ISBN 1-879045-66-4 **$16.95**

Voices from Genesis: *Guiding Us through the Stages of Life*
by Dr. Norman J. Cohen   6 x 9, 192 pp, Quality PB, ISBN 1-58023-118-7 **$16.95**

Ancient Secrets: *Using the Stories of the Bible to Improve Our Everyday Lives*
by Rabbi Levi Meier, Ph.D.   5½ x 8½, 288 pp, Quality PB, ISBN 1-58023-064-4 **$16.95**

The Business Bible: *10 New Commandments for Bringing Spirituality &*
Ethical Values into the Workplace
by Rabbi Wayne Dosick   5½ x 8½, 208 pp, Quality PB, ISBN 1-58023-101-2 **$14.95**

Being God's Partner: *How to Find the Hidden Link Between Spirituality and Your Work*
by Rabbi Jeffrey K. Salkin; Intro. by Norman Lear   **AWARD WINNER!**
6 x 9, 192 pp, Quality PB, ISBN 1-879045-65-6 **$16.95**; HC, ISBN 1-879045-37-0 **$19.95**

God & the Big Bang
Discovering Harmony Between Science & Spirituality **AWARD WINNER!**
by Daniel C. Matt   6 x 9, 224 pp, Quality PB, ISBN 1-879045-89-3 **$16.95**

Soul Judaism: *Dancing with God into a New Era*
by Rabbi Wayne Dosick   5½ x 8½, 304 pp, Quality PB, ISBN 1-58023-053-9 **$16.95**

Finding Joy: *A Practical Spiritual Guide to Happiness* **AWARD WINNER!**
by Rabbi Dannel I. Schwartz with Mark Hass
6 x 9, 192 pp, Quality PB, ISBN 1-58023-009-1 **$14.95**; HC, ISBN 1-879045-53-2 **$19.95**

Spirituality/Jewish Meditation

Aleph-Bet Yoga
Embodying the Hebrew Letters for Physical and Spiritual Well-Being
by *Steven A. Rapp*

Foreword by *Tamar Frankiel* and *Judy Greenfeld*; Preface by *Hart Lazer*

Blends aspects of hatha yoga and the shapes of the Hebrew letters. Connects yoga practice with Jewish spiritual life. Easy-to-follow instructions, b/w photos.
7 x 10, 128 pp, Quality PB, ISBN 1-58023-162-4 **$16.95**

Discovering Jewish Meditation
Instruction & Guidance for Learning an Ancient Spiritual Practice
by *Nan Fink Gefen*

Gives readers of any level of understanding the tools to learn the practice of Jewish meditation on their own. 6 x 9, 208 pp, Quality PB, ISBN 1-58023-067-9 **$16.95**

One God Clapping: *The Spiritual Path of a Zen Rabbi* AWARD WINNER!
by *Alan Lew* with *Sherril Jaffe*

A fascinating personal story of a Jewish meditation expert's roundabout spiritual journey from Zen Buddhist practitioner to rabbi. 5½ x 8½, 336 pp, Quality PB, ISBN 1-58023-115-2 **$16.95**

 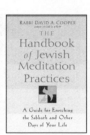 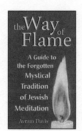 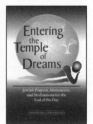 

The Handbook of Jewish Meditation Practices
A Guide for Enriching the Sabbath and Other Days of Your Life
by *Rabbi David A. Cooper*

Jewish practices and traditions, easy-to-use meditation exercises, and contemplative study of Jewish sacred texts. 6 x 9, 208 pp, Quality PB, ISBN 1-58023-102-0 **$16.95**

Stepping Stones to Jewish Spiritual Living: *Walking the Path Morning, Noon, and Night*
by Rabbi James L. Mirel & Karen Bonnell Werth
6 x 9, 240 pp, Quality PB, ISBN 1-58023-074-1 **$16.95**; HC, ISBN 1-58023-003-2 **$21.95**

Meditation from the Heart of Judaism: *Today's Teachers Share Their Practices,*
Techniques, and Faith Ed. by Avram Davis
6 x 9, 256 pp, Quality PB, ISBN 1-58023-049-0 **$16.95**; HC, ISBN 1-879045-77-X **$21.95**

The Way of Flame: *A Guide to the Forgotten Mystical Tradition of Jewish Meditation*
by Avram Davis 4½ x 8, 176 pp, Quality PB, ISBN 1-58023-060-1 **$15.95**

Minding the Temple of the Soul: *Balancing Body, Mind, and Spirit through Traditional*
Jewish Prayer, Movement, and Meditation by Tamar Frankiel and Judy Greenfeld
7 x 10, 184 pp, Quality PB, Illus., ISBN 1-879045-64-8 **$16.95**

Entering the Temple of Dreams: *Jewish Prayers, Movements, and Meditations for*
the End of the Day by Tamar Frankiel and Judy Greenfeld
7 x 10, 192 pp, Illus., Quality PB, ISBN 1-58023-079-2 **$16.95**

Theology/Philosophy

Love and Terror in the God Encounter: *The Theological Legacy of Rabbi Joseph B. Soloveitchik*
by *Dr. David Hartman*

Renowned scholar David Hartman explores the sometimes surprising intersection of Soloveitchik's rootedness in halakhic tradition with his genuine responsiveness to modern Western theology. An engaging look at one of the most important Jewish thinkers of the twentieth century.
6 x 9, 240 pp, HC, ISBN 1-58023-112-8 **$25.00**

These Are the Words: *A Vocabulary of Jewish Spiritual Life*
by *Arthur Green*

What are the most essential ideas, concepts and terms that an educated person needs to know about Judaism? From *Adonai* (My Lord) to *zekhut* (merit), this enlightening and entertaining journey through Judaism teaches us the 149 core Hebrew words that constitute the basic vocabulary of Jewish spiritual life. 6 x 9, 304 pp, Quality PB, ISBN 1-58023-107-1 **$18.95**

Broken Tablets: *Restoring the Ten Commandments and Ourselves*
Ed. by *Rabbi Rachel S. Mikva*; Intro. by *Rabbi Lawrence Kushner* AWARD WINNER!

Twelve outstanding spiritual leaders each share profound and personal thoughts about these biblical commands and why they have such a special hold on us.
6 x 9, 192 pp, Quality PB, ISBN 1-58023-158-6 **$16.95**; HC, ISBN 1-58023-066-0 **$21.95**

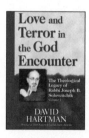  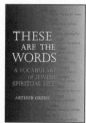 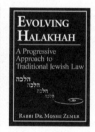 

A Heart of Many Rooms: *Celebrating the Many Voices within Judaism* AWARD WINNER!
by Dr. David Hartman 6 x 9, 352 pp, Quality PB, ISBN 1-58023-156-X **$19.95**;
HC, ISBN 1-58023-048-2 **$24.95**

A Living Covenant: *The Innovative Spirit in Traditional Judaism* AWARD WINNER!
by Dr. David Hartman 6 x 9, 368 pp, Quality PB, ISBN 1-58023-011-3 **$18.95**

Evolving Halakhah: *A Progressive Approach to Traditional Jewish Law*
by Rabbi Dr. Moshe Zemer 6 x 9, 480 pp, HC, ISBN 1-58023-002-4 **$40.00**

The Death of Death: *Resurrection and Immortality in Jewish Thought* AWARD WINNER!
by Dr. Neil Gillman 6 x 9, 336 pp, Quality PB, ISBN 1-58023-081-4 **$18.95**

The Last Trial: *On the Legends and Lore of the Command to Abraham to Offer Isaac as a Sacrifice* by Shalom Spiegel 6 x 9, 208 pp, Quality PB, ISBN 1-879045-29-X **$17.95**

Tormented Master: *The Life and Spiritual Quest of Rabbi Nahman of Bratslav*
by Dr. Arthur Green 6 x 9, 416 pp, Quality PB, ISBN 1-879045-11-7 **$18.95**

The Earth Is the Lord's: *The Inner World of the Jew in Eastern Europe*
by Abraham Joshua Heschel 5½ x 8, 128 pp, Quality PB, ISBN 1-879045-42-7 **$14.95**

A Passion for Truth: *Despair and Hope in Hasidism* by Abraham Joshua Heschel
5½ x 8, 352 pp, Quality PB, ISBN 1-879045-41-9 **$18.95**

Your Word Is Fire: *The Hasidic Masters on Contemplative Prayer* Ed. by Dr. Arthur Green and Dr. Barry W. Holtz 6 x 9, 160 pp, Quality PB, ISBN 1-879045-25-7 **$15.95**

Life Cycle/Grief

Against the Dying of the Light
A Parent's Story of Love, Loss and Hope
by *Leonard Fein*

The sudden death of a child. A personal tragedy beyond description. Rage and despair deeper than sorrow. What can come from it? Raw wisdom and defiant hope. In this unusual exploration of heartbreak and healing, Fein chronicles the sudden death of his 30-year-old daughter and reveals what the progression of grief can teach each one of us.

5½ x 8½, 176 pp, HC, ISBN 1-58023-110-1 **$19.95**

Mourning & Mitzvah, 2nd Ed.: *A Guided Journal for Walking the Mourner's Path through Grief to Healing* with Over 60 Guided Exercises
by *Anne Brener, L.C.S.W.*

For those who mourn a death, for those who would help them, for those who face a loss of any kind, Brener teaches us the power and strength available to us in the fully experienced mourning process. Revised and expanded. 7½ x 9, 304 pp, Quality PB, ISBN 1-58023-113-6 **$19.95**

Grief in Our Seasons: *A Mourner's Kaddish Companion*
by *Rabbi Kerry M. Olitzky*

A wise and inspiring selection of sacred Jewish writings and a simple, powerful ancient ritual for mourners to read each day, to help hold the memory of their loved ones in their hearts. Offers a comforting, step-by-step daily link to saying Kaddish.

4½ x 6½, 448 pp, Quality PB, ISBN 1-879045-55-9 **$15.95**

Tears of Sorrow, Seeds of Hope
A Jewish Spiritual Companion for Infertility and Pregnancy Loss
by Rabbi Nina Beth Cardin   6 x 9, 192 pp, HC, ISBN 1-58023-017-2 **$19.95**

A Time to Mourn, A Time to Comfort
A Guide to Jewish Bereavement and Comfort
by Dr. Ron Wolfson   7 x 9, 336 pp, Quality PB, ISBN 1-879045-96-6 **$18.95**

When a Grandparent Dies
A Kid's Own Remembering Workbook for Dealing with Shiva and the Year Beyond
by Nechama Liss-Levinson, Ph.D.
8 x 10, 48 pp, HC, Illus., 2-color text, ISBN 1-879045-44-3 **$15.95**   For ages 7–13

Healing/Wellness/Recovery

Jewish Paths toward Healing and Wholeness
A Personal Guide to Dealing with Suffering
by *Rabbi Kerry M. Olitzky*; Foreword by *Debbie Friedman*

Why me? Why do we suffer? How can we heal? Grounded in personal experience with illness and Jewish spiritual traditions, this book provides healing rituals, psalms and prayers that help readers initiate a dialogue with God, to guide them along the complicated path of healing and wholeness. 6 x 9, 192 pp, Quality PB, ISBN 1-58023-068-7 **$15.95**

Healing of Soul, Healing of Body
Spiritual Leaders Unfold the Strength & Solace in Psalms
Ed. by *Rabbi Simkha Y. Weintraub, CSW,* for The National Center for Jewish Healing

For those who are facing illness and those who care for them. Inspiring commentaries on ten psalms for healing by eminent spiritual leaders reflecting all Jewish movements make the power of the psalms accessible to all.
6 x 9, 128 pp, Quality PB, Illus., 2-color text, ISBN 1-879045-31-1 **$14.95**

Jewish Pastoral Care
A Practical Handbook from Traditional and Contemporary Sources
Ed. by *Rabbi Dayle A. Friedman*

Gives today's Jewish pastoral counselors practical guidelines based in the Jewish tradition.
6 x 9, 464 pp, HC, ISBN 1-58023-078-4 **$35.00**

Twelve Jewish Steps to Recovery: *A Personal Guide to Turning from Alcoholism & Other Addictions . . . Drugs, Food, Gambling, Sex . . .* by Rabbi Kerry M. Olitzky & Stuart A. Copans, M.D. Preface by Abraham J. Twerski, M.D.; "Getting Help" by JACS Foundation 6 x 9, 144 pp, Quality PB, ISBN 1-879045-09-5 **$13.95**

One Hundred Blessings Every Day: *Daily Twelve Step Recovery Affirmations, Exercises for Personal Growth & Renewal Reflecting Seasons of the Jewish Year* by Rabbi Kerry M. Olitzky 4½ x 6½, 432 pp, Quality PB, ISBN 1-879045-30-3 **$14.95**

Recovery from Codependence: *A Jewish Twelve Steps Guide to Healing Your Soul* by Rabbi Kerry M. Olitzky 6 x 9, 160 pp, Quality PB, ISBN 1-879045-32-X **$13.95**

Renewed Each Day: *Daily Twelve Step Recovery Meditations Based on the Bible* by Rabbi Kerry M. Olitzky & Aaron Z. *Vol. I: Genesis & Exodus; Vol. II: Leviticus, Numbers and Deuteronomy*
Vol. I: 6 x 9, 224 pp, Quality PB, ISBN 1-879045-12-5 **$14.95**
Vol. II: 6 x 9, 280 pp, Quality PB, ISBN 1-879045-13-3 **$14.95**

Spirituality—The Kushner Series
Books by Lawrence Kushner

The Way Into Jewish Mystical Tradition

Explains the principles of Jewish mystical thinking, their religious and spiritual significance, and how they relate to our lives. A book that allows us to experience and understand the Jewish mystical approach to our place in the world.

6 x 9, 224 pp, HC, ISBN 1-58023-029-6 **$21.95**

Jewish Spirituality: *A Brief Introduction for Christians*

Addresses Christian's questions, revealing the essence of Judaism in a way that people whose own tradition traces its roots to Judaism can understand and appreciate.

5½ x 8½, 112 pp, Quality PB, ISBN 1-58023-150-0 **$12.95**

Eyes Remade for Wonder: *The Way of Jewish Mysticism and Sacred Living*
A Lawrence Kushner Reader Intro. by *Thomas Moore*

Whether you are new to Kushner or a devoted fan, you'll find inspiration here. With samplings from each of Kushner's works, and a generous amount of new material, this book is to be read and reread, each time discovering deeper layers of meaning in our lives.

6 x 9, 240 pp, Quality PB, ISBN 1-58023-042-3 **$16.95**; HC, ISBN 1-58023-014-8 **$23.95**

   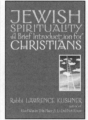 

Invisible Lines of Connection: *Sacred Stories of the Ordinary* AWARD WINNER!
5½ x 8½, 160 pp, Quality PB, ISBN 1-879045-98-2 **$15.95**

Honey from the Rock: *An Introduction to Jewish Mysticism* SPECIAL ANNIVERSARY EDITION
6 x 9, 176 pp, Quality PB, ISBN 1-58023-073-3 **$15.95**

The Book of Letters: *A Mystical Hebrew Alphabet* AWARD WINNER!
Popular HC Edition, 6 x 9, 80 pp, 2-color text, ISBN 1-879045-00-1 **$24.95**; *Deluxe Gift Edition,* 9 x 12, 80 pp, HC, 4-color text, ornamentation, slipcase, ISBN 1-879045-01-X **$79.95**; *Collector's Limited Edition,* 9 x 12, 80 pp, HC, gold-embossed pages, hand-assembled slipcase. With silkscreened print. Limited to 500 signed and numbered copies, ISBN 1-879045-04-4 **$349.00**

The Book of Words: *Talking Spiritual Life, Living Spiritual Talk* AWARD WINNER!
6 x 9, 160 pp, Quality PB, 2-color text, ISBN 1-58023-020-2 **$16.95**; HC, ISBN 1-879045-35-4 **$21.95**

God Was in This Place & I, i Did Not Know: *Finding Self, Spirituality and Ultimate Meaning*
6 x 9, 192 pp, Quality PB, ISBN 1-879045-33-8 **$16.95**

The River of Light: *Jewish Mystical Awareness* SPECIAL ANNIVERSARY EDITION
6 x 9, 192 pp, Quality PB, ISBN 1-58023-096-2 **$16.95**

Because Nothing Looks Like God
by Lawrence and Karen Kushner; Full-color illus. by Dawn W. Majewski
11 x 8½, 32 pp, HC, Full-color illus., ISBN 1-58023-092-X **$16.95** For ages 4 & up

Spirituality & More

The Jewish Lights Spirituality Handbook
A Guide to Understanding, Exploring & Living a Spiritual Life
Ed. by *Stuart M. Matlins, Editor-in-Chief, Jewish Lights Publishing*

Rich, creative material from over fifty spiritual leaders on every aspect of Jewish spirituality today: prayer, meditation, mysticism, study, rituals, special days, the everyday, and more. 6 x 9, 456 pp, Quality PB, ISBN 1-58023-093-8 **$18.95**; HC, ISBN 1-58023-100-4 **$24.95**

The Story of the Jews: *A 4,000-Year Adventure*
Written and illustrated by *Stan Mack*

Through witty cartoons and accurate narrative, illustrates the major characters and events that have shaped the Jewish people and culture. For all ages. 6 x 9, 304 pp, Quality PB, ISBN 1-58023-155-1 **$16.95**

Cast in God's Image
Discover Your Personality Type Using the Enneagram and Kabbalah
by *Rabbi Howard A. Addison*

With more than twenty hands-on spiritual exercises, will help you understand your own personality type and those of the people around you—enriching your relationships, your work...your life. 7 x 9, 176 pp, Quality PB, ISBN 1-58023-124-1 **$16.95**

The Enneagram and Kabbalah: *Reading Your Soul*
by Rabbi Howard A. Addison 6 x 9, 176 pp, Quality PB, ISBN 1-58023-001-6 **$15.95**

Mystery Midrash: *An Anthology of Jewish Mystery & Detective Fiction* AWARD WINNER!
Ed. by Lawrence W. Raphael 6 x 9, 304 pp, Quality PB, ISBN 1-58023-055-5 **$16.95**

Criminal Kabbalah: *An Intriguing Anthology of Jewish Mystery & Detective Fiction*
Ed. by Lawrence W. Raphael; Foreword by Laurie R. King
6 x 9, 256 pp, Quality PB, ISBN 1-58023-109-8 **$16.95**

Six Jewish Spiritual Paths: *A Rationalist Looks at Spirituality*
by Rabbi Rifat Sonsino 6 x 9, 208 pp, HC, ISBN 1-58023-095-4 **$21.95**

Sacred Intentions: *Daily Inspiration to Strengthen the Spirit, Based on Jewish Wisdom*
by Rabbi Kerry M. Olitzky & Rabbi Lori Forman
4½ x 6½, 448 pp, Quality PB, ISBN 1-58023-061-X **$15.95**

Restful Reflections: *Nighttime Inspiration to Calm the Soul, Based on Jewish Wisdom*
by Rabbi Kerry M. Olitzky & Rabbi Lori Forman
4½ x 6½, 448 pp, Quality PB, ISBN 1-58023-091-1 **$15.95**

Embracing the Covenant: *Converts to Judaism Talk About Why & How* Ed. by Rabbi Allan Berkowitz & Patti Moskovitz 6 x 9, 192 pp, Quality PB, ISBN 1-879045-50-8 **$16.95**

Wandering Stars: *An Anthology of Jewish Fantasy & Science Fiction* Ed. by Jack Dann; Intro. by Isaac Asimov 6 x 9, 272 pp, Quality PB, ISBN 1-58023-005-9 **$16.95**

Israel—A Spiritual Travel Guide: *A Companion for the Modern Jewish Pilgrim* AWARD WINNER!
by Rabbi Lawrence A. Hoffman 4¾ x 10, 256 pp, Quality PB, ISBN 1-879045-56-7 **$18.95**

Life Cycle & Holidays

How to Be a Perfect Stranger, 2nd Ed. In 2 Volumes
A Guide to Etiquette in Other People's Religious Ceremonies
Ed. by *Stuart M. Matlins* & *Arthur J. Magida*   AWARD WINNER!

What will happen? What do I do? What do I wear? What do I say? What are their basic beliefs? Should I bring a gift? Explains the rituals and celebrations of North America's major religions/denominations, helping an interested guest to feel comfortable. *Not* presented from the perspective of any particular faith. SKYLIGHT PATHS Books
Vol. 1: *North America's Largest Faiths,* 6 x 9, 432 pp, Quality PB, ISBN 1-893361-01-2 **$19.95**
Vol. 2: *Other Faiths in North America,* 6 x 9, 416 pp, Quality PB, ISBN 1-893361-02-0 **$19.95**

The Book of Jewish Sacred Practices
CLAL's Guide to Everyday & Holiday Rituals & Blessings
Ed. by *Rabbi Irwin Kula* & *Vanessa L. Ochs, Ph.D.*

A meditation, blessing, profound Jewish teaching, and ritual for more than one hundred everyday events and holidays. 6 x 9, 368 pp, Quality PB, ISBN 1-58023-152-7 **$18.95**

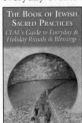    

Celebrating Your New Jewish Daughter: *Creating Jewish Ways to Welcome Baby Girls into the Covenant—New and Traditional Ceremonies*
by Debra Nussbaum Cohen; Foreword by Rabbi Sandy Eisenberg Sasso
6 x 9, 272 pp, Quality PB, ISBN 1-58023-090-3 **$18.95**

The New Jewish Baby Book AWARD WINNER!
Names, Ceremonies & Customs—A Guide for Today's Families
by Anita Diamant 6 x 9, 336 pp, Quality PB, ISBN 1-879045-28-1 **$18.95**

Parenting As a Spiritual Journey
Deepening Ordinary & Extraordinary Events into Sacred Occasions
by Rabbi Nancy Fuchs-Kreimer 6 x 9, 224 pp, Quality PB, ISBN 1-58023-016-4 **$16.95**

Putting God on the Guest List, 2nd Ed. AWARD WINNER!
How to Reclaim the Spiritual Meaning of Your Child's Bar or Bat Mitzvah
by Rabbi Jeffrey K. Salkin 6 x 9, 224 pp, Quality PB, ISBN 1-879045-59-1 **$16.95**

The Bar/Bat Mitzvah Memory Book: *An Album for Treasuring the Spiritual Celebration* by Rabbi Jeffrey K. Salkin and Nina Salkin
8 x 10, 48 pp, Deluxe HC, 2-color text, ribbon marker, ISBN 1-58023-111-X **$19.95**

For Kids—Putting God on Your Guest List
How to Claim the Spiritual Meaning of Your Bar or Bat Mitzvah
by Rabbi Jeffrey K. Salkin 6 x 9, 144 pp, Quality PB, ISBN 1-58023-015-6 **$14.95**

Bar/Bat Mitzvah Basics, 2nd Ed.: *A Practical Family Guide to Coming of Age Together*
Ed. by Cantor Helen Leneman 6 x 9, 240 pp, Quality PB, ISBN 1-58023-151-9 **$18.95**

Hanukkah, 2nd Ed.: *The Family Guide to Spiritual Celebration*—The Art of Jewish Living
by Dr. Ron Wolfson 7 x 9, 240 pp, Quality PB, Illus., ISBN 1-58023-122-5 **$18.95**

Shabbat, 2nd Ed.: *Preparing for and Celebrating the Sabbath*—The Art of Jewish Living
by Dr. Ron Wolfson 7 x 9, 320 pp, Quality PB, Illus., ISBN 1-58023-164-0 **$19.95**

The Passover Seder—The Art of Jewish Living
by Dr. Ron Wolfson 7 x 9, 352 pp, Quality PB, Illus., ISBN 1-879045-93-1 **$16.95**

Women's Spirituality

The Women's Torah Commentary: *New Insights from Women Rabbis on the 54 Weekly Torah Portions* Ed. by *Rabbi Elyse Goldstein*

For the first time, women rabbis provide a commentary on the entire Five Books of Moses. More than twenty-five years after the first woman was ordained a rabbi in America, these inspiring teachers bring their rich perspectives to bear on the biblical text. In a week-by-week format; a perfect gift for others, or for yourself. 6 x 9, 496 pp, HC, ISBN 1-58023-076-8 **$34.95**

Moonbeams: *A Hadassah Rosh Hodesh Guide*
Ed. by *Carol Diament, Ph.D.*

This hands-on "idea book" focuses on *Rosh Hodesh*, the festival of the new moon, as a source of spiritual growth for Jewish women. A complete sourcebook that will initiate or rejuvenate women's study groups, it is also perfect for women preparing for *bat mitzvah*, or for anyone interested in learning more about *Rosh Hodesh* observance and what it has to offer. 8½ x 11, 240 pp, Quality PB, ISBN 1-58023-099-7 **$20.00**

 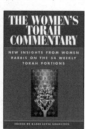   

Lifecycles In Two Volumes **AWARD WINNERS!**
V. 1: *Jewish Women on Life Passages & Personal Milestones*
Ed. and with Intros. by Rabbi Debra Orenstein
V. 2: *Jewish Women on Biblical Themes in Contemporary Life*
Ed. and with Intros. by Rabbi Debra Orenstein and Rabbi Jane Rachel Litman
V. 1: 6 x 9, 480 pp, Quality PB, ISBN 1-58023-018-0 **$19.95**
V. 2: 6 x 9, 464 pp, Quality PB, ISBN 1-58023-019-9 **$19.95**

ReVisions: *Seeing Torah through a Feminist Lens* **AWARD WINNER!**
by Rabbi Elyse Goldstein 5½ x 8½, 224 pp, Quality PB, ISBN 1-58023-117-9 **$16.95**;
208 pp, HC, ISBN 1-58023-047-4 **$19.95**

The Year Mom Got Religion: *One Woman's Midlife Journey into Judaism*
by Lee Meyerhoff Hendler 6 x 9, 208 pp, Quality PB, ISBN 1-58023-070-9 **$15.95**

Ecology

Torah of the Earth: *Exploring 4,000 Years of Ecology in Jewish Thought*
In 2 Volumes Ed. by *Rabbi Arthur Waskow*

An invaluable key to understanding the intersection of ecology and Judaism. Leading scholars provide a guided tour of Jewish ecological thought.
Vol. 1: *Biblical Israel & Rabbinic Judaism*, 6 x 9, 272 pp, Quality PB, ISBN 1-58023-086-5 **$19.95**
Vol. 2: *Zionism & Eco-Judaism*, 6 x 9, 336 pp, Quality PB, ISBN 1-58023-087-3 **$19.95**

Ecology & the Jewish Spirit: *Where Nature & the Sacred Meet* Ed. and with Intros.
by Ellen Bernstein 6 x 9, 288 pp, Quality PB, ISBN 1-58023-082-2 **$16.95**

The Jewish Gardening Cookbook: *Growing Plants & Cooking for Holidays & Festivals*
by Michael Brown 6 x 9, 224 pp, Illus., Quality PB, ISBN 1-58023-116-0 **$16.95**;
HC, ISBN 1-58023-004-0 **$21.95**

Children's Spirituality

Cain & Abel AWARD WINNER!
Finding the Fruits of Peace
by *Sandy Eisenberg Sasso*
Full-color illus. by *Joani Keller Rothenberg*

For ages 5 & up

A sensitive recasting of the ancient tale shows we have the power to deal with anger in positive ways. Provides questions for kids and adults to explore together. "Editor's Choice"—American Library Association's *Booklist*

9 x 12, 32 pp, HC, Full-color illus., ISBN 1-58023-123-3 **$16.95**

For Heaven's Sake AWARD WINNER!

For ages 4 & up

by *Sandy Eisenberg Sasso*; Full-color illus. by *Kathryn Kunz Finney*
Everyone talked about heaven, but no one would say what heaven was or how to find it. So Isaiah decides to find out. 9 x 12, 32 pp, HC, Full-color illus., ISBN 1-58023-054-7 **$16.95**

God Said Amen AWARD WINNER!

For ages 4 & up

by *Sandy Eisenberg Sasso*; Full-color illus. by *Avi Katz*
Inspiring tale of two kingdoms: one overflowing with water but without oil to light its lamps; the other blessed with oil but no water to grow its gardens. The kingdoms' rulers ask God for help but are too stubborn to ask each other. Shows that we need only reach out to each other to find God's answer to our prayers. 9 x 12, 32 pp, HC, Full-color illus., ISBN 1-58023-080-6 **$16.95**

God in Between AWARD WINNER!

For ages 4 & up

by *Sandy Eisenberg Sasso*; Full-color illus. by *Sally Sweetland*
If you wanted to find God, where would you look? This magical, mythical tale teaches that God can be found where we are: within all of us and the relationships between us.
9 x 12, 32 pp, HC, Full-color illus., ISBN 1-879045-86-9 **$16.95**

Noah's Wife: *The Story of Naamah*

For ages 4 & up

by *Sandy Eisenberg Sasso*; Full-color illus. by *Bethanne Andersen* AWARD WINNER!
Opens religious imaginations to new ideas about the story of the Flood. When God tells Noah to bring the animals onto the ark, God also calls on Naamah, Noah's wife, to save each plant on Earth. 9 x 12, 32 pp, HC, Full-color illus., ISBN 1-879045-60-5 **$16.95**

But God Remembered AWARD WINNER!
Stories of Women from Creation to the Promised Land

For ages 8 & up

by *Sandy Eisenberg Sasso*; Full-color illus. by *Bethanne Andersen*
Vibrantly brings to life four stories of courageous and strong women from ancient tradition; all teach important values through their actions and faith.
9 x 12, 32 pp, HC, Full-color illus., ISBN 1-879045-43-5 **$16.95**

Children's Spirituality

In Our Image
God's First Creatures AWARD WINNER!

For ages 4 & up

by *Nancy Sohn Swartz*
Full-color illus. by *Melanie Hall*

A playful new twist on the Creation story—from the perspective of the animals. Celebrates the interconnectedness of nature and the harmony of all living things. "The vibrantly colored illustrations nearly leap off the page in this delightful interpretation." —*School Library Journal*
9 x 12, 32 pp, HC, Full-color illus., ISBN 1-879045-99-0 **$16.95**

God's Paintbrush AWARD WINNER!

For ages 4 & up

by *Sandy Eisenberg Sasso*; Full-color illus. by *Annette Compton*

Invites children of all faiths and backgrounds to encounter God openly in their own lives. Wonderfully interactive; provides questions adult and child can explore together at the end of each episode. 11 x 8½, 32 pp, HC, Full-color illus., ISBN 1-879045-22-2 **$16.95**

Also available: A Teacher's Guide: **A Guide for Jewish & Christian Educators and Parents**
8½ x 11, 32 pp, PB, ISBN 1-879045-57-5 **$8.95**

God's Paintbrush Celebration Kit 9½ x 12, HC, Includes 5 sessions/40 full-color Activity Sheets and Teacher Folder with complete instructions, ISBN 1-58023-050-4 **$21.95**

In God's Name AWARD WINNER!

For ages 4 & up

by *Sandy Eisenberg Sasso*; Full-color illus. by *Phoebe Stone*

Like an ancient myth in its poetic text and vibrant illustrations, this award-winning modern fable about the search for God's name celebrates the diversity and, at the same time, the unity of all people. 9 x 12, 32 pp, HC, Full-color illus., ISBN 1-879045-26-5 **$16.95**

What Is God's Name? (A Board Book)

For ages 0–4

An abridged board book version of award-winning *In God's Name.*
5 x 5, 24 pp, Board, Full-color illus., ISBN 1-893361-10-1 **$7.95** A SKYLIGHT PATHS Book

The 11th Commandment: *Wisdom from Our Children*

For all ages

by *The Children of America* AWARD WINNER!

"If there were an Eleventh Commandment, what would it be?" Children of many religious denominations across America answer this question—in their own drawings and words. "A rare book of spiritual celebration for all people, of all ages, for all time."—*Bookviews*
8 x 10, 48 pp, HC, Full-color illus., ISBN 1-879045-46-X **$16.95**

Children's Spirituality

Because Nothing Looks Like God

by *Lawrence and Karen Kushner*
Full-color illus. by *Dawn W. Majewski*

For ages 4 & up

MULTICULTURAL, NONDENOMINATIONAL, NONSECTARIAN

What is God like? The first collaborative work by husband-and-wife team Lawrence and Karen Kushner introduces children to the possibilities of spiritual life. Real-life examples of happiness and sadness—from goodnight stories, to the hope and fear felt the first time at bat, to the closing moments of life—invite us to explore, together with our children, the questions we all have about God, no matter what our age.

11 x 8½, 32 pp, HC, Full-color illus., ISBN 1-58023-092-X **$16.95**

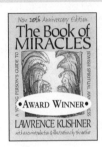

Where Is God?
What Does God Look Like?
How Does God Make Things Happen? (Board Books)

For ages 0–4

by *Lawrence and Karen Kushner*; Full-color illus. by *Dawn W. Majewski*

Gently invites children to become aware of God's presence all around them. Three board books abridged from *Because Nothing Looks Like God* by Lawrence and Karen Kushner.
Each 5 x 5, 24 pp, Board, Full-color illus. **$7.95** SKYLIGHT PATHS Books

Sharing Blessings
Children's Stories for Exploring the Spirit of the Jewish Holidays

For ages 6 & up

by *Rahel Musleah* and *Rabbi Michael Klayman*; Full-color illus.

What is the spiritual message of each of the Jewish holidays? How do we teach it to our children? Through stories about one family's life, *Sharing Blessings* explores ways to get into the *spirit* of thirteen different holidays.
8½ x 11, 64 pp, HC, Full-color illus., ISBN 1-879045-71-0 **$18.95**

The Book of Miracles AWARD WINNER!
A Young Person's Guide to Jewish Spiritual Awareness

For ages 9 & up

by *Lawrence Kushner*

Introduces kids to a way of everyday spiritual thinking to last a lifetime. Kushner, whose award-winning books have brought spirituality to life for countless adults, now shows young people how to use Judaism as a foundation on which to build their lives.
6 x 9, 96 pp, HC, 2-color illus., ISBN 1-879045-78-8 **$16.95**

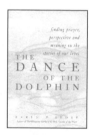 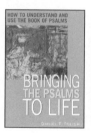